WRESTLING WITH THE ELEPHANT

WRESTLING WITH THE ELEPHANT

The Inside Story of the Canada-US Trade Wars

GORDON RITCHIE

Macfarlane Walter & Ross
Toronto

Macfarlane Walter & Ross
37A Hazelton Avenue
Toronto, Canada M5R 2E3

CANADIAN CATALOGUING IN PUBLICATION DATA

Ritchie, Gordon
Wrestling with the elephant: the inside story of the Canada-US trade wars

Includes index.
ISBN 1-55199-015-6

1. Canada. Treaties, etc. 1992 Oct. 7.   2. Free trade – Canada.
3. Free trade – United States. 4. Canada – Commerce – United States.
5. United States – Commerce – Canada. I. Title.

HF1766.R58 1997   382'.971073   C97-931918-8

Printed and bound in Canada

Book design and typesetting by James Ireland Design Inc.

Macfarlane Walter & Ross gratefully acknowledges the support of the Canada Council for the Arts and the Ontario Arts Council for its publishing program.

Contents

PREFACE

When the Canada-US Free Trade Agreement was reached in Washington on the first Sunday in October 1987, I promised myself that I would one day write a book about this historic event as seen through the eyes of one of the chief participants. Over the following months and years, there were many invitations, some much more serious than others, to write the story of the negotiations. For a number of reasons, I was not prepared to take up the challenge until now.

The fall of 1997 marks the passage of ten full years since the original agreement was reached in Washington. That has given ample time for others to write their own accounts. It has given me the opportunity to look back on those days with some detachment while the events are still fresh in my mind and clear in my notes. I can only hope the results give a glimpse into how great affairs of state really operate in a world populated by passionate and imperfect human beings.

I have not attempted to provide the definitive chronology of the free trade negotiations. That job has already been ably done by my former colleagues Michael Hart, Bill Dymond, and Colin Roberts in their book, *Decision at Midnight*. These three foreign service officers were seconded to the Trade Negotiations Office early in the process, and while none was in the top management of the negotiating team, they have pieced together a generally accurate and complete account of the negotiations themselves. I strongly recommend it to the serious student of Canadian trade policy.

This book is instead very much a personal memoir of my experiences before the FTA, the negotiations themselves, and the aftermath. It does not pretend to be the authoritative version of the truth – whatever that is. Others will have different impressions and recollections. This is strictly my own account of what I saw and felt and believed as I took part in Canada's redefinition of our trade relationship with the United States over the past thirty years and more.

Free trade with the United States is an issue that has preoccupied Canadians for a century and a half, from the pre-Confederation reciprocity treaty negotiated by Lord Elgin; through the great election on the issue that toppled Sir Wilfrid Laurier early in this century; to the free trade deal negotiated in the late 1940s only to be rejected by Mackenzie King; culminating in the Canada-US Free Trade Agreement (FTA) signed by President Reagan and Prime Minister Mulroney on January 2, 1988; and carrying on with the North American Free Trade Agreement (NAFTA) in 1994 and the Canada-Chile Free Trade Agreement in 1997. With royal commissions, Senate committee reports, and studies by the Economic Council of Canada, this is arguably the most examined, most debated, and possibly least understood issue of Canadian public policy. Through all the controversy, we have somehow managed to establish the greatest trading relationship that has ever existed between any two countries, with trade in both directions totalling nearly $400 billion per annum.

The heart of this account is the negotiation of the Free Trade Agreement itself. In 1986, I became Canadian ambassador for trade negotiations and deputy chief trade negotiator of the Canada-US FTA. I was centrally involved in the negotiations and was the senior official responsible for the agreement's implementation in Canadian law. I have tried to give the reader an accurate sense of how things actually happened behind the closed doors of the negotiating room, the cabinet chamber, or the in-camera meetings of the first ministers.

My personal involvement in these issues began years earlier with my father, whose career as one of Canada's outstanding diplomats was centred on our relationship with the United States. He served as our ambassador to Washington before returning to Ottawa as the undersecretary of state for external affairs.

I joined the government service in Centennial Year, 1967, and remained a public official for more than twenty years. During that period, the government of Canada went through dizzying changes. I was promoted rapidly up the ranks of an expanding system at a time of remarkable government activism. The job titles changed as I progressed from working as a policy analyst to heading a division, then an office, then a branch, and finally a great department of government. Virtually my entire career was devoted to Canadian economic development through the use of various tools – trade negotiations, financial assistance programs, industrial strategies, and government budgets. The underlying challenge throughout was the successful management of our relationship with the economic superpower to the south.

Once the agreement was in place, in the fall of 1988, my career moved to the private sector, where I counselled companies and industries on making free trade work for them and using the agreement to fight American protectionism for Canadian advantage. I saw the transformation of Canadian industry from the perspective of a director of some of Canada's leading corporations. I was also called upon to advise governments – Canadian, provincial, and foreign – on free trade and its implications as well as the next step in the process, the NAFTA.

This book draws on many of these experiences to provide a personal context for an historic development. In so doing, I hope it may deepen the reader's insight into these great national issues.

ACKNOWLEDGMENTS

Without the support of my wife, Margaret, and the understanding of our children, Jillian and Martin, this book would never have been started. Without the example and advice of my father, Ed Ritchie, and my mother, Gwen, two of Canada's outstanding diplomats, there would have been no story to tell. Without the leadership and encouragement of two of Canada's top trade warriors, Jake Warren and Simon Reisman, I would never have had the opportunity to take part in these events. Finally, without the gentle but incisive handling of my publisher, Jan Walter, and my agent, Linda McKnight, the project would never have been completed.

1

BIG FOOTSTEPS

In the lobby newsstand of a hotel in Halifax, two months after the Free Trade Agreement was reached, I came across an audiotape that promised to "Teach you everything you need to know about negotiating in just three minutes." I must be a very slow learner. I am still fascinated by the negotiating process after more than forty years – the last ten years as a business consultant, the previous twenty as a public servant, and the first decade as a teenager observing my father in action.

My father, A. Edgar (Ed) Ritchie, is recognized as one of Canada's great public servants of the postwar era. He may have been unable to teach me to be diplomatic, but I was profoundly influenced by him and his experience. Through him, I saw firsthand the satisfactions and the frustrations of the life of a senior Canadian official. No one is more surprised than I that I followed even a short distance in his footsteps.

Our case was exceptional. It is, I am told, the only instance in which a deputy minister's son became a deputy minister himself. Indeed, my father left the DM ranks less than two weeks before I was first promoted to that level (although he was in the very top grade while I was the new boy to the class). It is also one of the very few cases where father and son served as Canadian ambassadors (although, again, he was in the most senior posts while I was merely a trade negotiator).

In yet another sense, our careers were linked: we both devoted the bulk of our energies to working out a relationship with the United States that would serve Canada's best interests – although we did not always see eye to eye on what those interests were. While he could not have been more cordial personally to his American counterparts, he was wary of Canada drawing too close to the friendly giant, and suffocating in America's embrace. My style was more confrontational, even abrasive, but, perhaps naively, I was more confident of Canada's ability to stand up for its interests, even in a closer relationship.

My father was born to a poor family in the rural backwater of Andover, New Brunswick, nestled on the upper reaches of the Saint John River, a few miles from the American border. He attended a typical one-room school-house but demonstrated such exceptional qualities that he won a scholarship to attend Mount Allison University, at Sackville in the far southeast corner of the province. At Mount A, while holding down two jobs to help pay his way, he finished at the top of his class, with outstanding grades that have not been matched to this day. His performance earned him a Rhodes Scholarship to Oxford in 1938 – and entry to another world. The son of a self-taught country veterinarian read PPE (philosophy, politics, and economics) at that temple of wisdom. He also took the opportunity with a couple of classmates to tour the continent by motorbike just ahead of the storm clouds of war.

On graduation with his B.A. from Oxford in 1940 (having declined to pay the five guineas required to receive his M.A.), he joined the war effort. Recruited by the British, he was assigned to New York to work with the British Purchasing Commission and then to the Ministry of Economic Warfare mission attached to the British embassy in Washington. My mother, Gwen Perdue, the daughter of a senior officer with the Canadian Department of Immigration, also worked at the British embassy as the head of secretarial services.

It must have been a bizarre atmosphere for these young Canadians in Washington at the beginning of the 1940s. Canada was at war, standing beside the valiant British under the inspired leadership of Winston Churchill, enduring the onslaught of the German-led Axis. For over two years, America stood on the sidelines, declining to bloody its hands in the fray. President Franklin Roosevelt played a crafty political game. The administrative apparatus of official Washington provided increasing support and assistance to the beleaguered British and Canadians. But Roosevelt moved very cautiously, sensitive to the isolationist mood of the American heartland.

This situation continued until Pearl Harbor forced the Americans to take a stand in December 1941. My parents joined the crowd watching through the fence railings as the staff at the Japanese embassy in Washington burned their official papers on the front lawn behind heavy security. Horror at the reports of Japanese attacks on the outposts of the British Empire was mixed with relief that the Americans were finally joining the battle on the side of the Allies.

This calamity may have spurred my parents to action. They were married a few days later, on my father's birthday, December 20, 1941. I was born just over two years later in a Washington hospital. As the son of Canadian parents, I was a Canadian citizen from birth – although in those days we were all still technically "British subjects." I later learned that I also enjoyed the right to become an American citizen by virtue of being born on American soil. It is an option I have never seriously considered.

After the war, Dad was recruited into Canada's External Affairs Department by Lester B. (Mike) Pearson and Norman Robertson, two of the great mandarins of the postwar period. He did a brief stint with the Canadian embassy in Washington before he was offered a position by the fledgling United Nations – with the impressive title of special assistant to the assistant secretary general for the Economic Affairs Department. His job took him to Geneva for the founding conference of the General Agreement on Tariffs and Trade (GATT), the organization that was to govern international trade for half a century. He served as special assistant to the first head of the GATT, Sir Eric Wyndham White. (Another young Canadian, Simon Reisman, was a junior member of the Canadian delegation at those initial talks in Geneva.)

My parents took me along. I have little recollection of Geneva itself but I well remember our subsequent holiday in Zermatt, a resort in the Swiss Alps. I can still recall breathtaking Alpine views, the little train working its way up and through the mountain, a subterranean river gushing forth in a spectacular waterfall, a skating palace of ice, and a ride on a sleigh pulled by Huskies.

My mother and I had crossed the Atlantic on an old cargo ship, a banana boat with limited space for passengers. The voyage was an ordeal and my mother was determined not to repeat it. The return trip was complicated, as the sea and air transportation system had yet to return to normalcy after the war. Finally, we took passage on the *Bermuda Sky Queen* on October 12, 1947.

This extraordinary old plane began life as one of the fabled Boeing Pan Am Clippers that represented the height of luxury travel before the war. The *Sky Queen* was a "flying boat" capable of taking off and landing in waves up to two or three feet high. It was more than a hundred feet long with a wingspread of half as much again. It had seen better days before it was bought by three American ex-flyboys who saw it as their passport to riches.

The plane was loaded with sixty-two passengers and crew in the estuary at Foynes, Ireland, before lumbering off across the Atlantic. The plan, apparently, was to land in the Hudson River. It was just as well this harebrained scheme was never put to the test since the port of New York, America's busiest, was completely clogged with ships.

In any event, these intrepid flyers had failed to allow for the demands on fuel as the heavily overloaded plane flew straight into the teeth of a North Atlantic gale. We first knew something was badly wrong when the sun rose on the same side of the plane as it had set on the night before. We were finally told that the engineer had determined that we were unable to make land. Since we had "passed the point of no return," in the aviator's jargon, we would be turning back to splash down in mid-Atlantic. I was too young to understand fully what was happening, but I could almost taste the fear aboard the doomed aircraft.

Near the midpoint of the North Atlantic, more than 750 miles from Newfoundland and nearly 1,000 from Ireland, the US Coast Guard maintained a weather station which, in those days before seeing-eye satellites, was a Coast Guard ship, the USS *Bibb*. There was, however, a small problem: the waves were now cresting below us at heights of up to fifty feet. As the fuel ran dry, the pilot had no choice but to bring the plane down in the midst of the storm. On his first attempt, he pulled up just before impact and, with the mighty engines straining, swooped back into the air. On the second try, we bounced off the first huge wave and then smashed into the next.

The Coast Guard came rushing over to rescue us and promptly crushed the nose of the plane. The *Bibb* beat a hasty retreat and for the next few hours contented itself with releasing pitiful quantities of oil in a futile attempt to calm the troubled waters. Meanwhile, the *Sky Queen* was foundering in the mountainous seas. The screams subsided, to be replaced by the sounds of passengers retching.

Finally some merchant seamen, deadheading home on the plane, took matters into their own hands. They flung themselves overboard in a rubber raft and were promptly swept away. At that point, a rescue mission was launched from the cutter. The first step was to recover the merchant seamen, who reported that conditions on the plane were deteriorating rapidly. A full-scale rescue was then begun.

My mother went ahead with a nine-year-old boy belonging to another family whose hands were already full with the rest of the brood. My father and I followed some time later. It was a terrifying experience, even for a three-year-old who did not fully appreciate the dangers. We had to jump from the door of the plane to hit the cold black water, some ten feet below, near a rubber raft. The sailors pulled us aboard and, when the raft was full, made their way to a motorboat to which we were transferred, not an easy operation in those frightful conditions. I vividly remember looking up at the *Sky Queen* across the mountainous black waves from the bottom of the life raft. My main concern was for my teddy bear, which had been left in the plane.

The final step involved somehow getting the passengers onto the ship itself – this in Force Nine waves tossing the little motor launch like a cork beside the mother ship, which was itself rising and falling in the storm. The side of the ship was rigged with netting and covered with a swarm of sailors, each clinging with one hand. The other hand was used to catch the passengers as they leapt – or, as in my case, were thrown – across the yawning gulf to safety. I am told that I was unconscious when they hauled me aboard. The sailors cut off my life jacket and I quickly revived.

Most of the passengers were brought to safety before nightfall shut down the rescue operation. The crew and a handful of male passengers remained aboard the sinking plane, with no expectation of survival. Amazingly, the heavily waterlogged craft remained barely afloat through the night and the last survivors were brought across the next morning. Even then, the *Queen* refused to surrender to the sea until fire from the cutter's cannon sank her below the waves.

We received a hero's welcome in the *Bibb*'s home port of Boston. As we steamed in, with a broom inverted at the masthead to herald a clean sweep, the place went wild. Fireboats sprayed their water cannons into the air. Every ship's horn in the harbour tooted and honked. The air force performed a flypast. On landing, we learned that we had indeed been headline news for the past few days and were now celebrities.

The *New York Times* seized on my mother's account of the incident as the definitive version for the record. For my part, I was interviewed on radio for the first time, although my performance was memorable mainly for the sound effect I was able to achieve by giving the microphone a loud raspberry, undoubtedly blowing the tubes in radio sets around the country.

For my father, this was all in the line of duty. He took me on the next plane back home to New Brunswick. My mother, meanwhile, took the train up to Ottawa, where my sister had been left in the care of her maternal grandparents. Mum understandably refused to fly again for more than a decade.

❧ ❧ ❧

Following the GATT meetings in Geneva and then Havana, Dad re-entered the Canadian foreign service. His initial assignment was to London, where Norman Robertson represented Canada as high commissioner. Then it was back to Ottawa for a few years in the economics division of the Department of External Affairs.

By my early teens, I was beginning to develop a keen interest in the public affairs that were my father's bread and butter. He took me with him to the gallery of the House of Commons to see the Louis St. Laurent government fall under the weight of its own arrogance in the infamous Pipeline Debate. The towering figure of postwar development, the legendary C. D. Howe, was no respecter of the meddlesome traditions of parliamentary democracy. He resolved to ram through legislation providing guarantees to American energy interests to build a pipeline from Alberta to eastern Canada. He won the battle but condemned his Liberal Party to defeat in the subsequent electoral wars. It was high drama.

In 1957, Dad was posted to Washington as the number two in the Canadian embassy, again under Norman Robertson. Although traditionalists back home still clung to the British connection, Washington had replaced London as the crucial link in Canadian diplomacy. While the rest of the family took the train, my father and I drove down to the American capital in our old Hillman Minx, a tiny black sedan made in Britain. I did not enjoy the trip. The motion bothered me and the sunlight gave me a headache. When we arrived at the Shoreham Hotel in Washington, I was eager to stretch my legs, only to find that they had turned to rubber.

When the hotel doctor was called in three days later, he took one long look at me and called an ambulance. I was rushed to the Washington Children's Hospital, which offered a level of care significantly above anything available back in Ottawa. It was just as well. I slipped into delirium that night and emerged three weeks later to find myself almost completely paralyzed. My parents had been braced to expect the worst. On three successive evenings they were warned that it was unlikely that I would live through the night. Fortunately, the paralysis stopped its progress just before it crippled my lungs. From the experience of friends and neighbours struck down with polio, we knew that this was only the beginning.

The recovery was hard for a previously active thirteen-year-old. It was four months before I could even attempt to walk. My mulishness was an asset. It never occurred to me that I would not recover, and the sooner the better. At the earliest opportunity – long before the usual practice – I had badgered my way into a rigorous regimen of physical therapy. This involved being lowered on a sling into a whirlpool tank to attempt to stimulate some use of my limbs. It was torment. My skin was painful even to the touch.

Later, I would will one of my legs to move and be convinced I had succeeded, only to be disproved with the evidence of my eyes as the offending limb lay immobile on the bed. One day I decided that the problem was that I was lying down – I would do much better if I could only stand. My doctor tried to dissuade me but finally decided to teach me a lesson the hard way. Using my hands, I swung my legs over the side of the bed and launched myself into space. I have never felt more excruciating pain. Lacking any support from the muscles, my legs were like sacks of bones as I went crunching to the floor. That shut me up for a while.

Through all of this, my parents were attempting to get established in a demanding new assignment. My mother spent hours at my bedside, reading to me, as I could not even hold a book. My father did his best, coming in after a gruelling day's work to sit beside my bed – and invariably fall fast asleep.

Eventually I started to recover. I was unbelievably fortunate. The hotel doctor, Fred Burke, was a superb diagnostician without whose prompt action I would almost certainly have died. The Washington Children's Hospital was one of the most advanced in the world. They determined that I had not polio but a rare case of Guillain-Barré syndrome, the disease that came to public attention in the late 1970s when a number of Americans became infected from vaccines designed to halt the swine flu epidemic. Compared with the dreaded polio that crippled so many of my generation – including two close friends and two children from our Ottawa neighbourhood – this disease was more often fatal but less likely to leave a survivor with permanent damage. By the summer, I was walking on crutches, and by the fall, I was able to resume my schooling.

During this period, my father's career was moving rapidly ahead. As the "minister" or second-in-command at the embassy, he had an opportunity to renew old acquaintances and forge new friendships that were to stand him in good stead. When Norman Robertson was reassigned to Ottawa, Dad filled in as the chargé d'affaires, or acting ambassador, for better than a year until the replacement arrived. His network of contacts expanded, in part through the school my sister, Heather, and I attended. One of her classmates at Sidwell Friends, a Quaker-run private school, was Tricia Nixon, whose father, the US vice-president, became the object of some admiration at a school dance when the alarm on his wristwatch sounded – a novelty in those days that would be regarded as rather poor taste today.

My academic performance was mediocre at best, perhaps in part because of the confusion caused by my illness and the transfer from Ottawa to Washington. Instead of French, I took Latin, mainly because the spinster who taught the subject organized a Roman orgy towards the end of the year at which the girls, in unbelievably skimpy outfits, waited hand and foot upon the toga-clad boys lounging on gym mats. This sybarite decision was to prove costly on my return to Canada, as I tried in vain to catch up two years of French studies over one summer and graduated with a very weak knowledge of that founding language.

My English, on the other hand, was good, although the Canadian students at the school were derided by the American teacher of English for our failure to subscribe to the American way of spelling and pronunciation. She changed her tune when I placed ahead of my schoolmates in a nationwide English test, and the next three spots were also taken by Canadians. This confirmed me in the belief I still hold dear that Canadians speak better English than Americans. It also convinced me of the value of national testing.

In 1959, Dad was recalled to Ottawa as an assistant undersecretary of state for external affairs. The terminology was a bit bewildering, particularly for his mother, who tried unsuccessfully to conceal her disappointment that after all this work her precious son was no more than an assistant to a secretary. In fact, it placed him squarely in the ranks of the top management of Canada's foreign affairs, with particular responsibility for economic matters and relations with the United States. This was no easy task.

The John Diefenbaker years were turbulent and troubled. It became increasingly clear that the charismatic Tory leader had not the foggiest notion of how to run a government. The disarray extended into foreign affairs, as was most apparent in Dief's dealings with the shining new American president, John F. Kennedy. As one of the established authorities on affairs with the United States, Dad was very much involved in trying to smooth this tormented relationship.

The most terrible moment came at the height of the Cuban Missile Crisis in October 1962. Never had the two superpowers been so close to nuclear war. After one sleepless night, Dad mentioned, very quietly, that he had not expected to see the morning. Canada was powerless to determine events, despite Dief's futile gesture of refusing to "scramble" the Canadian air forces. (As we later learned, they scrambled anyway.)

Dad played a central role in the Columbia River Treaty negotiations. British Columbia premier W. A. C. Bennett dreamed of harnessing the northern rivers of the province to generate energy and cash to fuel economic development. Typically, we turned to the Americans to provide the financing, in exchange for certain rights over the power generated from this natural resource. The initial negotiations were conducted by the federal Conservatives, led by Justice Minister E. Davey Fulton. The Conservative government collapsed in 1963 before the deal could be closed.

The incoming Liberals decided they could do better. They were persuaded that an entirely new and quite different arrangement was required. Dad was one of the key officials given the difficult assignment of renegotiating the done deal. The result was an upfront cash payment from the Americans for the rights to the power generated by dams to be built on the system. I was suitably impressed when Dad brought home a copy of the cheque. The amount seems ludicrously inadequate today following the dramatic escalation of energy prices. It did, however, give Bennett the funds he needed to invest in infrastructure to stimulate the growth of the provincial economy and to develop the Peace River Valley.

No sooner had Mike Pearson taken office than Canada was given a short, sharp lesson in its dependence on the United States. In mid-1963, the Kennedy administration announced the imposition of a tax on foreign loans of American capital, the so-called interest equalization tax. Foreigners were taking advantage of the much lower costs of borrowing in the American market, and the US authorities were concerned over the capital outflow. The tax was designed to make these borrowings less attractive.

The main impact was felt in Canadian financial markets, and it was devastating, as American lenders were discouraged from buying Canadian federal, provincial, and corporate bonds. The Canadian dollar came under great pressure as the normal inflow of funds from the United States reversed, drawing down Canada's gold and foreign exchange reserves overnight. Dad rushed down to Washington with other senior officials, seeking relief. They pointed out that Canada was not contributing to the Americans' balance of payments problems. We ran a substantial deficit on our current account – the combination of our trade in goods and services – that our borrowings were required to finance.

Following a script that was to be used many times in the future, the Americans were most apologetic. They had no idea it would have this impact on Canada. It was most regrettable that Canada had been "sideswiped" in this manner. Etc. But they were not prepared to admit their mistake and reverse their policy without concessions from Canada.

Three tumultuous days later, it was agreed that Canada would be exempted from the tax, in exchange for promising not to increase our reserves of foreign exchange, principally US dollars. This decision attracted little attention, despite its profound impact. Combined with the pegging of the Canadian dollar, it transferred the ultimate management of Canadian monetary policies to Washington. To run an independent policy, we would have to allow either an adjustment in the exchange rate, which had been pegged the year before, or a shift in our exchange reserves, which were now capped. We had lost our freedom to manoeuvre. A Canadian economist later observed that this one act put into the hands of the U.S. president more control over our economy than he had garnered from the past twenty years of growth of American investment in Canada.

In recognition of Dad's growing role, a new position was created in 1964, that of deputy undersecretary, to designate him as the clear second-in-command at External Affairs. His particular focus remained economic relations with the United States. My parents had finally scraped together enough cash for a down payment on an old three-storey house beside the Rideau Canal that runs through the heart of Ottawa. Their schedule was gruelling, typically including at least one official dinner or reception almost every night. Dad nonetheless found the time most evenings to go for a walk along the banks of the canal with me and my dog. This was our precious opportunity to discuss the events of the day. Our debates were sometimes heated, as my teenage opinions clashed with his voice of experience. Perhaps the most important lesson I learned was to respect opposing points of view without taking disagreements as personal attacks.

During this period, I was experiencing the usual struggles of growing up. At high school in Ottawa, my interests were not academic. The principal took me to task for performing far below my alleged potential. Still recovering from my paralysis, I was unable to be very active in sports. My main distinction was as the star of our debating team, whose coach valued my contribution enough to give me an undeserved passing grade in Latin. I became the chess champion of my school and then of the city's high schools, leading our team to victory against the local rivals and winning a few minor tournaments on my own.

I continued to disappoint at Carleton University. Carleton had the great advantage that it was only a few miles from our home. (It seemed farther in the winter when the biting cold would turn my blue jeans into stiff cardboard on the long walk across the open field to the campus.) I could just barely pay my way through school by living at home and working in a variety of summer jobs – as a labourer repairing sewers in the national capital, a crewman aboard a Hudson's Bay supply ship in the eastern Arctic, a miner of uranium deep underground in northern Saskatchewan. These jobs paid for my tuition and books and gave me a little spending money – including $300 to buy my first car, a battered convertible that had seen many and better years. They also provided a change in perspective from the cloisters of academe.

My academic record was barely adequate. Despite the inspiration provided by the head of the economics department, H. Scott Gordon, my scholarship in that field was less than distinguished. In my final year, I got into the habit of reading through the night and sleeping through the next day's classes. This may have given me some appreciation of the great themes of economic theory but did little to endear me to my professors. After four years, I settled for a simple bachelor's degree. Even that was a close call, as I could not be bothered to write most of my final exams.

Instead I majored in extracurricular activities, participating in all facets of student government. At one point, I was the ranking member of the legislative assembly, the chief justice of the student court, the associate editor of the student newspaper, president or vice-president of half a dozen student clubs, past president of the debating union, and leader of one of the campus political clubs. Friends joked that this was all part of a deep plan: if I was uncovered embezzling student funds through one or more of the clubs I ran, I could block conviction by the court, suppress coverage in the newspaper, and ensure that the legislative assembly kept the money flowing. In fact, this was a superb education in the way things really work – at least as valuable as the formal education I was receiving. Above all, I learned that power and influence gravitate to those who are prepared to make the commitment in time and effort to get things done. In retrospect, I do not regret for one moment the choices I made at that time.

I was strictly non-partisan or, to be more precise, multi-partisan. In my first year at Carleton, I was chosen to lead the New Democrats to victory in the model parliament election. In my sophomore year, preferring opposition to government, I ran as an independent with a motley crew – the Federated Independents, we called ourselves – and had the misfortune to win again. In my third year, I led the Liberals, who, as chance would have it, swept in on a landslide due much more to the appeal of Mike Pearson than to my poor powers of persuasion. These and other extracurricular activities ensured that

I enjoyed an extra year as an undergraduate, and I seriously considered rounding out my experience by leading the Conservatives. Just at that point, a coup was mounted in the campus Conservative club, which toppled the president on grounds of incompetence. This was the first suggestion I had heard that this was grounds for political disqualification. I decided that this new standard was too tough for me and gave the leadership a pass.

During my first year at university, I met Margaret Armstrong, a petite, dynamic woman with an utterly wicked sense of humour. We did not attend the same classes, as she was studying French while I was in economics. She was a much better student, who actually attended classes and took notes.

Marg and I saw a great deal of each other over the following three years. Above all, we found we could talk for hours about everything from the personal to the philosophical to the political. When I lingered at Carleton for a fourth year, she stayed to work in the library, and we continued to spend time together. Finally the light dawned, and I realized this was the woman with whom I wanted to spend the rest of my life. In early 1966, I proposed.

To my delight, she agreed. The next step, remembering that this was the 1960s, was for me to ask her father for her hand in marriage. I was summoned to dinner at her home, like a lamb to the slaughter. After all, I had no money, no job, and no degree, although I hoped to scrape through with a pass B.A. in a few weeks' time.

I had barely met her parents. Earle Armstrong was a bank manager and looked every inch the part to my terrified eyes. He was very close to Margaret, his only child and the apple of his eye. Peggy was a strikingly attractive mother, whose photograph had been taken by Yousuf Karsh in her early days in the Eastern Townships. As the meal came to an end, the womenfolk – Marg, her mother, aunt, and grandmother – suddenly disappeared, leaving me alone with "Army." Nearly overcome at my temerity, I somehow blurted out my request.

"By all means, son," Army replied. "Marg likes to be where the action is. I am sure you will be very happy."

Ours was not a long engagement. I had written to a number of newspapers looking for work but the only response came from Arthur Irwin, the publisher of the far-off *Victoria Daily Times*. Irwin had enjoyed a distinguished diplomatic career and must have known my father, although he never mentioned the connection. During a visit to Ottawa, he interviewed me for a position as a cub reporter. His only question was what I knew of Sir Wilfrid

Laurier. Fortuitously, I had just read a new biography on the great man and was therefore able to display an impressive knowledge of the subject. He offered me a job on the spot, at a salary considerably below what I had been making as a summer labourer. I instantly accepted.

On two weeks' notice, Peggy arranged a beautiful wedding for her daughter. The ceremony was performed by the Reverend Dr. Frank Maclean, who had been my father's minister and mentor decades earlier in Andover. Following a reception at the Armstrong home, Marg and I, with all our belongings packed in two suitcases, boarded the train for the west coast.

When we changed to the transcontinental *Canadian* in Sudbury, an urgent call came over the station loudspeaker as we were making our way across the tracks. I rushed off, leaving Marg to fend for herself and all our luggage. It was a false alarm – the revellers back in Ottawa simply wanted to wish us well. The incident defined our relationship – I would spend the next few decades rushing about, leaving Marg to manage all the important matters on her own. I am not alone in wondering how she has put up with me over the years.

Marg and I settled into Victoria, and there I spent a fascinating year as a journalist with the *Daily Times*. Not content to be relegated to the role of cub reporter, I set out to make my own mark. For a neophyte, I was given a remarkable amount of leeway. I wangled interviews with visiting dignitaries ranging from John Kenneth Galbraith, the Canadian-born Harvard economist, to Cheddi Jagan, the past and future president of Guyana. My favourite was Alexander Kerensky, the premier of Russia who had been overthrown by the Communists a half-century before. A frail old man with trembling hands, he still could not comprehend what had transpired. The least pleasant was James Meredith, whom I had greatly admired as the black man who broke the colour barrier at the University of Mississippi. As I reported, Meredith was himself a racist, urging that whites and blacks work together in a united purpose – to oppose the yellow peril.

Long before the environment was a popular issue, I did a series of articles on the pollution of British Columbia's air and water. It earned me national recognition as well as the wrath of Premier Bennett when I exposed his government's cover-up of the dumping of arsenic-laced mine tailings into the lake that provided the drinking water for the Vancouver Island town of Campbell River. It was all very stimulating despite the long hours and pitiful pay packet.

In 1966, Robert Winters, Canada's minister of trade and commerce, passed through Victoria. His deputy minister was Jake Warren, a dear family friend who had offered the toast to the bride at our wedding. A man of great charm and eloquence, Warren was already one of Canada's outstanding trade officials. He had narrowly escaped death as a naval officer in World War II when his ship was torpedoed in the North Atlantic. After service with the Departments of External Affairs and Finance, he had become deputy minister at Trade. He would later serve as Canada's high commissioner to London, ambassador to Washington, then ambassador for multilateral trade negotiations before retiring to the vice-chairmanship of the Bank of Montreal.

Jake invited us to dinner at the Empress Hotel, an offer we accepted in a flash. He had more than good food on his mind. In the course of the best meal we had enjoyed in months, Jake shared his problem with us. In Winters, Jake had a minister who was a key figure in the Pearson government and, very probably, a candidate to succeed Mike at the next leadership convention. As a good deputy, Jake had a vested interest in having his minister maintain real clout in the political process. Despite his other fine qualities, however, Bob Winters was not a great communicator, as I had seen for myself earlier in the day, when I had covered an industry association convention that Winters had nearly put to sleep. Nor was his political staff much help – his office was a shambles, with a poor or non-existent relationship with the department.

Then came the punch line. Would I consider joining the minister's staff as special assistant? My reaction was immediate, tempered only by my enormous respect for Warren: Not a chance. Simply put, I was having too much fun where I was. Life was not without its problems: on my income, we lived in little more than a slum (two rooms, sharing a bathroom with the neighbours and the roaches); the rain seemed never to stop, giving Marg a continuing case of bronchitis; and Victoria, with one in five residents over the age of sixty, was not a city designed for a young couple. Nonetheless, I had no interest in returning to the east to enter a world of politics I really knew little or nothing about. Marg, somewhat reluctantly, agreed that we should stay in British Columbia.

Several weeks later, I was approached again. Winters would like to meet me to size me up and, if he liked what he saw, to persuade me to sign on for the duration. The sweetener was that he would be coming to San Francisco in a few weeks and would fly me down to meet him there. The clincher was that my parents, whom I had not seen since our wedding day, would be coming to San Francisco at the same time. The opportunity to visit with them was too tempting to refuse although, as I made clear, I had no intention of joining Winters's staff.

Despite my cynicism, I was impressed by Winters. The son of a fishing skipper in Lunenburg, Nova Scotia, Winters had reached the top levels of international business. He had graduated from MIT in engineering and served with distinction in World War II before entering politics as a protégé of C. D. Howe. He had subsequently enjoyed a successful career in business, serving as CEO of BRINCO and as a director on an incredible number of corporate boards.

Winters was a striking figure of a man, erect in posture with a handsome and imposing head and a deep baritone voice. He kept in excellent condition with regular visits to the tennis court. He was impeccably attired in his trademark blue suit. The great man was the embodiment of courtesy with this scruffy youngster applying for a job he really did not want.

Following my brief interview with the minister, I had a wonderful couple of days in San Francisco with my parents. My mother then accompanied me back to Victoria for a highly enjoyable visit. All had worked according to plan. Or so I thought, and assured Marg.

Then the heat was turned up. On the one hand, my old friend Jake pressed his need for reinforcement for his minister. On the other, the minister's executive assistant, Tony Abbott (later a minister himself), kept making the offer more attractive. I would have a greatly expanded mandate with pay increased to match. When the salary offer reached the munificent sum of $10,000 (two and a half times my pay as a legislative correspondent), my publisher, Arthur Irwin, tipped the balance. As an old political warhorse himself, he told me, "Only a fool would turn down an offer like that, and I have no need of more fools on this newspaper." I took the hint and returned to Ottawa in early 1996 to spend the next eighteen months as Winters's political assistant.

It was while Marg and I lived in Victoria that my father was named Canada's ambassador to the United States. (To thoroughly confuse the Americans, he succeeded another, unrelated Ritchie, the distinguished diarist Charles Ritchie, in that post.) It was a natural appointment, building upon his long and close involvement with Canada-US affairs since World War II. He had established a network of professional and personal friendships that gave Canada extraordinary access to the movers and shakers in the administration, on Capitol Hill, and in the media. His greatest secret weapon was my mother, who possesses a truly exceptional ability to put people at their ease.

Today, it is fashionable to look back nostalgically at the 1960s – particularly for those who did not live through those times. For Canadians, it was enthralling but horrifying to live next to this great nation in terrible turmoil, culminating in the momentous events of 1968 as the Vietnam War and the civil rights movement exploded the old assumptions.

The embattled president, Lyndon Johnson, was central to this national agony. As it happened, during my parents' earlier posting, Mum had been deeply involved with the Capitol Speakers' Club, an institution that brought together the wives of senators, congressmen, diplomats, and other dignitaries. One of her good friends was Lady Bird Johnson, wife of the then senator. When they returned in the ambassadorial slot, the link proved highly valuable in understanding this extremely complex figure. He was a boor and a bully, and his pursuit of unattainable objectives in Vietnam destroyed his presidency and very nearly his country. My father was outraged at Johnson's attitude towards Canada's prime minister, Mike Pearson, whose attempts to bring America to its senses were denounced as treasonous cowardice. But Dad was also very conscious of Johnson's strengths, particularly in domestic policy, and had great respect for his forceful leadership.

Perhaps my parents' closest relationship was with the Acheson clan. Dean Acheson was one of the outstanding figures of American statesmanship. He had served presidents from Roosevelt to Johnson, and his advice was held in high esteem. On one occasion, when Marg and I drove down from Ottawa to visit my parents, we joined them for a visit to the Achesons' country retreat. Over lunch, Dad asked Acheson if one president stood out in his memory. Without hesitation, Acheson named Harry Truman as the most outstanding of these world leaders – perhaps in part because of the good judgment Truman had shown in relying on Acheson as his secretary of state.

I use the term "clan" advisedly. The Achesons' daughter, Mary, was married to Bill Bundy, who served as Johnson's assistant secretary of state for Far Eastern and Pacific affairs at the height of the war. Bill's brother, Mac, had been national security adviser to Jack Kennedy and then Johnson. At Christmas 1967, Marg and I joined my parents at a carol singing at the Acheson town home, a few miles from the Canadian embassy residence. It was an idyllic setting: Christmas lights reflecting on the new-fallen snow, at least four generations of the family gathered together, many with fine voices, merrily carolling "Peace on Earth, good will toward men." Bill's singing was only slightly hindered by the broken nose he had suffered when Air Force One hit an air pocket on the way home from Honolulu, where, as we later learned,

16

the decision had been taken to escalate the war and extend the bombing to Hanoi and Cambodia.

After an hour of this, Marg called me aside to tell me that she could not stomach any longer the contrast between the carollers' words and their deeds. We walked back to the Canadian residence through the snow. I am no apologist for the terrible errors these men made and the horror they inflicted on other countries and, ultimately, their own. Nonetheless, I remain convinced from having known some of them that their intentions were as good as their judgment proved bad.

Back in Ottawa, my work for Robert Winters filled a period of intense activity, particularly after Pearson announced that he would be stepping down as leader and Winters threw his hat into the ring. Among other duties, I wrote more than a hundred speeches in a twelve-month period. One of the most interesting was on foreign ownership of Canadian industry. Winters was responsible for the collection of data on the performance of foreign-owned companies in Canada and had enunciated a set of voluntary guidelines for good corporate citizenship. This provided the material for a speech I drafted in which Winters went beyond the rhetoric of his nationalist colleagues, who had been so influenced by Pearson's former finance minister, Walter Gordon, to review the actual data. It showed that most of these foreign-controlled corporations were behaving better than most comparable Canadian-controlled companies in everything from buying Canadian to supporting research and development in this country. The speech caused a bit of a stir and helped to draw the battle lines for the convention.

Although I was not a card-carrying Liberal Party member, let alone a delegate, I attended the leadership convention in April 1968. I was in the back room, under the stands in the Ottawa Civic Centre, when Winters came within 125 votes of edging out Pierre Elliott Trudeau and becoming prime minister of Canada. It was an exhausting rollercoaster experience, to come so close to victory only to fall short. For me, the drama was heightened as the television networks periodically switched away from the convention floor to show Washington in flames in the aftermath of the assassination of Dr. Martin Luther King. The smoke could be seen from the ambassador's residence.

After the convention, Winters expected to be asked to play a central role in the new government, perhaps as deputy prime minister. Trudeau was having none of it. Winters retired from politics to head the Brascan corporate empire and asked me to accompany him. It is hard to imagine the path my career might have taken if I had accepted his offer to join the private sector. In the event, tragically soon afterwards, he died of a heart attack following a strenuous tennis match.

Instead, after Winters's departure from politics, I was recruited into the Department of Trade and Commerce by his deputy minister, Jake Warren. Today the political staff are guaranteed preferences in civil service jobs at their existing levels and salaries, but in those days it was highly unusual for any political aide to enter the civil service. My salary was set a few hundred dollars below what I had received as a ministerial assistant a year and a half before – about half what I had been offered by the Toronto advertising agency that had run Winters's campaign. But I had been bitten by the public policy bug and told myself that a brief period in the government service would be good experience.

I left a spacious top-floor office and a private secretary and moved downstairs in the old West Memorial Building to a dim grey cubicle created with temporary partitions that magnified the sound. I had no secretary but instead commandeered a reliable old manual typewriter on which I could draft my notes to send to the typing pool to clean up. I was looking forward to spending a few years in the bureaucracy before moving on to a career in business or journalism. Little did I imagine that I would spend the next two decades of my life as a public servant – a life sentence by any measure.

2

A Long Apprenticeship

At Carleton University, Scott Gordon, Steve Kaliski, and other professors had schooled me in the classical analysis of the costs of protectionism and the benefits of free trade. Much of the fundamental work had been done by Canadian theorists, notably the great Harry Johnson. Their message was clear:

- It was unequivocally preferable to have the free movement of goods.
- Consumers gained from a broader range of choices at more competitive prices.
- Producers gained from the economies of scale that came with serving larger markets with more specialized products.
- The overall result must be higher national income and higher real incomes for workers and consumers.

There were, of course, important theoretical qualifications – particularly when there were high levels of unemployment, when incomes were more unevenly distributed, or when trade was only partially freed. These modified the theory but did not alter the fundamental conclusion that free trade should generally be of benefit, particularly for a smaller, highly export-dependent economy.

If this was true, why was the trading world characterized by high tariffs and other barriers to trade? The answer was that certain special interests, notably inefficient producers, stood to gain from maintaining high levels of protection that raised the prices they could extract from consumers at home. In Canada these reactionary forces were embodied in the Canadian Manu-facturers' Association and various agricultural unions who were prepared to fight tooth and nail to protect their monopolies. The general public, consumers and workers, could less afford to promote their interests and were usually out-gunned by the protectionists. Furthermore, while the theoreticians could and did argue for unilateral tariff disarmament, so long as other countries, notably the United States, maintained restrictions against Canadian exports, the more prudent and practical course was to lower our import restrictions only if other countries reciprocated.

To listen to critics on the left today, one would think that free trade was invented by the large industrial corporations and shoved down the throats of the powerless citizen, worker, and consumer. It bears repeating: free trade has been advocated by economists for more than a century and a half as an instru-ment to benefit the consumer and raise workers' incomes. It has been stri-dently *opposed* over most of this history by the business establishment, led by the monopolists and the cartels who stand to gain most from protectionism.

This case for freeing trade was powerful stuff, supported by both theory and practice. The theory was as robust as economic analysis could ever be. By 1967, the practice had been reflected in the economic expansion that had flowed from the previous twenty years of tariff reductions. We had also expe-rienced the impact of the opposite policy of high tariffs, particularly the infa-mous Smoot-Hawley tariffs of the United States that had deepened if not caused the global depression of the 1930s. It was rare in economics to find such an incontestable practical demonstration of fundamental theory.

During my time with Robert Winters, I had little opportunity to delve further into the theory of freeing trade. It was taken as a given. The Kennedy Round was under way, the sixth and in some ways most substantial round of tariff-cutting negotiations under the GATT. When the results were announced, they were widely hailed as a triumph of Canadian negotiation. We had gained lower tariffs across the board for more than $3 billion of our exports and reduced tariffs, selectively, on around $2.5 billion of imports.

What was less trumpeted at the time was that this "multilateral" agree-ment, involving dozens of countries, was, for Canada, essentially a two-way deal with the United States. Over two-thirds of the concessions we gained were in access to the American market. The Europeans had refused, in a final stand-off, to offer any specific concessions of value to Canada and thus failed to reach agreement of any sort with us. (The British were not, at that time, part of the common market in Europe and gave us special access to their market already under the system of Commonwealth preferences.) The Japanese were not a major factor; certainly, they had offered nothing of interest to Canada in these negotiations.

When I was subsequently recruited into the Trade Department, I was fascinated to pore over the departmental files on trade policy issues. Carbon copies on onion-skin paper were kept of all the key documents in a central records system. (Today, despite the elaborate computer technology, most of the records are not accessible and, indeed, in some cases simply disappear from the institutional memory banks.) One of the treasures I encountered was a series of papers prepared by the brilliant if somewhat erratic Jack Firestone, economic adviser to John Diefenbaker.

On the basis of rather tendentious analysis, Firestone advocated the policy that Diefenbaker later announced: Canada was too dependent on the United States (which bought more than half of our total exports); he was therefore determined to redirect our trade so that 15 percent of our exports then going to the US would go instead to Britain. It did not take long with pencil and paper for me to calculate that the net result had been that the proportion of our exports going to the United States had fluctuated very little during the Diefenbaker years.

In due course, after much to-ing and fro-ing, the British decided to join their traditional continental rivals in the Common Market, turning their back on Canada and their other former colonies. Instead of being inside the wall of the Commonwealth, we would now be outside the much higher wall of the European Common Market. Our exports would face the Common External Tariff, the vicious protectionism of the Common Agricultural Policy, and a host of other restrictions. I was assigned to do some work on the implications for Canada. As expected, over the next decade Britain dropped from being Canada's second-best trading partner to one of the pack of distant also-rans. Henceforth, our only link with the British "motherland" would be a shared embarrassment over the increasingly disturbed antics of the royal progeny.

In response, Canada had no choice but to look southward and attempt to improve its access to the giant American market. Despite academic advocacy, there had been no political support for an across-the-board free trade arrangement with the United States since Prime Minister W. L. Mackenzie King had repudiated a deal negotiated secretly in 1947. Sectoral initiatives met with more success. There was a special agreement to cover the production and trade of military equipment. To lower costs to farmers, agricultural equipment was allowed to move freely across the border. To facilitate the flow of petroleum, Canada was exempted from the heavy duty the Americans slapped on imports of oil from other countries.

By far the most important initiative was the Auto Pact, the single most successful sectoral trade deal ever negotiated. It was signed by Pearson at LBJ's Texas ranch in 1964. The pact took advantage of a unique set of circumstances to set the framework for the operations of the Big Four (later the Big Three) auto companies, all American-owned, which completely dominated the industry on both sides of the border. It was an ingenious sort of corporate free trade, under which these companies, but not their customers, could move vehicles and parts freely across the border, provided certain conditions were met. In Canada's case, these conditions or safeguards required the companies to achieve an overall level of Canadian content in their vehicles and to assemble one car in Canada for every car they sold in our market. This agreement had been negotiated by a small team of senior officials including my father, with the lead taken by Simon Reisman, then deputy minister of industry.

It was soon clear that the agreement would have a significant impact, although no one could have fully predicted the extraordinary benefits it would bring to Canada in the following quarter-century. The Americans took the position that the company commitments to Canada were strictly temporary in nature and the entire pact could be repealed on six months' notice. The Canadians persisted and kept the commitments alive for the next thirty years.

Despite these developments, the conventional wisdom of Canadian trade policy was that we were committed to freer but not free trade, and only on a multilateral basis in which the United States was only one of our many trading partners. This was a basic article of faith with my father and his contemporaries in the government.

In the summer of 1968, when I joined the Trade Department as what was called a commerce officer, my bosses assigned me to review a number of recent studies on the issue of free trade and write a report. They probably intended merely to keep me busy while they decided what to do with me. I took them seriously. Instead of fobbing them off with some kind of book report, which is all I imagine they expected, I plunged into studying the issue in depth.

The research material was plentiful. Major studies of free trade between Canada and the United States had recently been commissioned by the influential Canadian-American Committee of business leaders. Two distinguished

Canadian-born economists, the brothers Wonnacott, Ron and Paul, had done a seminal project on the issue. Meanwhile, Harry Johnson, perhaps the greatest economist of his generation, born in Canada and teaching at Chicago and the London School of Economics, had joined forces with a number of leading academic figures in the United Kingdom and the United States to make a forceful case for a North Atlantic free trade area to encompass Canada, the United States and Europe in one great duty-free zone.

In a few weeks of feverish work, well into the wee hours, I produced my report. I dwell on it here not because it had much impact on official policy – it did not – but because it shows my thinking at the time. Backed by studies on free trade groupings, traditional multilateral negotiations, sectoral free trade, and, last but not least, Canada–United States free trade, my lead paper set the tone, *Towards a Realistic Trade Policy for Canada*. It began in these uncompromising terms:

> In reality, the trading world of today bears little resemblance to that envisaged by the GATT. It is a world of regional blocs, dealing with an unprecedented volume of trade through the extensive use of all manner of discriminatory arrangements.

Canadian policy-makers condemned these regional groupings as being restrictive of trade, diverting trade away from other countries outside the group. In fact, a growing body of evidence demonstrated that the main growth of trade was occurring *within* and *because* of these regional groupings. To cap it all off, "compared with most nations belonging to formal regional trading blocs, Canada's regional trade is *more* important, and our foreign trade *less* important, to our overall economy."

Our regional (i.e., continental) trade was already heavily dependent on a network of discriminatory special arrangements covering better than a quarter of our trade – autos and parts, oil and gas, and defence products – that were particularly vulnerable to American policy manipulation. Our investment flows were also overwhelmingly continental, as American investment in Canada was more than four times greater than all other foreign investment combined and Americans controlled well over one-quarter of all Canadian industry, with control concentrated in oligopolistic companies. This meant that "an unprecedented proportion of Canada's trade . . . is governed not by market forces but by decisions taken in the foreign head offices of corporations owned and managed primarily by foreigners."

What should be done? My preferred option was *not* free trade with the United States. Instead, I strongly supported the concept of North Atlantic free trade that was being aggressively promoted in Britain and the United States as a final attempt to keep the Six of continental Europe from closing the gates to their fortress.

My assessment of the Canada–US free trade option was based on a critical examination of the basic research, notably the massive study by the Wonnacott brothers. I conceded that there were "clear *a priori* grounds for anticipating [that] substantial net benefits would flow to Canada from free trade with the United States," but I did not believe we were ready.

The economic models assumed free trade would narrow if not eliminate the gap in productivity between Canadian- and American-based firms. How? I was afraid we would see the less efficient Canadian firms simply going under, with the resulting losses of output and employment in Canada. US immigration laws would keep these displaced workers from following the jobs that headed south. The corrective mechanisms through the trade balance and the exchange rate would be slow to work and were, in any case, paralyzed for the moment by the recent monetary arrangement. In the end, a new equilibrium might be reached, but not without substantial temporary and in some cases permanent dislocation for the workers, firms, and communities most directly affected. Even if the overall gains outweighed the specific losses, there was no basis in past experience to expect the losers actually to be compensated by the winners.

Rereading this paper nearly thirty years later, I would change very little in this assessment. The study's emphasis on the difficult adjustment that free trade would bring and the crucial importance of business preparedness to tackle new markets proved prescient. In the mid-1980s, the fundamental questions underlying the basic choices remained very much the same as I had described them in 1968. But by then, I had concluded that some of the answers had changed.

Over the next few years, Canada continued to preach multilateralism, while struggling to escape continental realities. I was assigned to the delicate area of overseeing our international trade in natural resources and was made chief of the division set up for this purpose. Soon our group confronted American interests across an array of commodities. These opening skirmishes were highly instructive for a neophyte negotiator.

As the issues heated up, I found myself working closely with my deputy minister, Jake Warren, and carrying out the directions of an interdepartmental committee of senior deputy ministers. This frequently involved drafting instructions for our ambassador in Washington, my father. On more than one occasion, he and I privately discussed the issues in advance to avoid possible misunderstandings.

Canada's most important commodity export was crude oil. Eastern Canada, through to the Ottawa River, was supplied with oil imported from overseas. The prairie provinces, dominated by Alberta, supplied the rest of the country behind a protective policy wall along the Ottawa River and moved increasing volumes to the United States, all from the reserves of the Western Sedimentary Basin. This was before the OPEC crisis of the early 1970s, when the base price for oil was only $2.50 per barrel. The US in those days had an import regime that imposed the equivalent of substantial duties on all crude oil imports – except those from Canada, which were exempted on the grounds that these shipments came "overland" under an agreement between the two countries. This anticipated that Canada would supply specified volumes of crude oil to the crucial market east of the Rockies (Districts I to IV under the American control system).

Circumstances were changing rapidly. There was great excitement over massive new supplies that appeared to be available from the Far North, where the giant pools discovered in Alaska's Prudhoe Bay might well be matched by "elephant" fields in the Mackenzie Delta and the Arctic Islands. Proved reserves were being depleted as fast as they were found, but the industry believed – and had convinced the regulatory body, the National Energy Board – that "possible" reserves were astronomical, even without tapping the synthetic crude of the tar sands. The predictable response was to make every effort to preserve and expand export markets, particularly in the neighbouring United States. Our shipments rose to more than 100,000 barrels per day over the agreed level.

Meanwhile, American producers from the southern states were gearing up to take the Midwestern market back from the Canadians. A huge pipeline extension into Chicago was nearing completion. In the late fall of 1969, I accompanied the top brass of the National Energy Board on a visit to Washington to scout out the terrain. On our return, the vice-chairman of the board wrote a very comforting report that concluded that it was in the United States' best interest to maintain and indeed increase imports of oil from Canada.

I prepared a report for my own deputy minister that looked beyond these warm words to the harsh *realpolitik* of the American oil industry. I forecast that with the opening of the Chicago Loop pipeline at the beginning of 1970, the Americans would insist that our exports be limited to meet the residual requirement in the Midwestern market, even if this meant imposing restrictions on these imports. My deputy minister circulated it to his colleagues, among whom it provoked serious controversy. My report was denounced by the board chairman as unauthorized and alarmist.

The Americans insisted in February 1970 that imports of Canadian oil must be brought under control. After much seesawing back and forth, negotiations were held in Ottawa in the historic council rooms of the East Block. The opposing teams sat in high-backed leather chairs on opposite sides of a huge oval table. The Canadian side was headed by our ambassador, my father. It included the key deputy ministers with an energy board official, Roland Priddle (later chairman of the board), and me as technical advisers. The army of Americans was headed by Phil Tresize, an old friend of my father's from the State Department, and a swarm of representatives from other agencies.

The American position was simplicity itself. Canada had abused its privileges under the "overland exemption," which had become a major political irritant to the Americans. Either Canada would agree to limit its exports of oil to levels dictated by the Americans, or the United States would apply its own controls at a much lower level. The first day of negotiations was then largely consumed by the chairman of the NEB, Bob Howland, explaining patiently to the visitors that their proposition made no sense whatsoever, as Canada was simply filling the needs of American consumers, particularly the refiners of the northern tier of states. It was their demand that had increased our shipments to well over 450,000 barrels per day to the area east of the Rockies. That Howland was dead right cut absolutely no ice with the Americans.

Finally, a "compromise" was mooted. Provided the president paid some public recognition, in an upcoming statement, to the reliability and security of supplies from Canada and their critical role in supplying American requirements, Canada would agree to limit our exports rather than face draconian American import restrictions. There remained the little matter of the number. Phil Tresize repaired to the American embassy to contact the White House to get the green light to propose an export level to the Canadians.

When the Canadians were alone, Jake Warren turned to me, the most junior officer present, and asked, somewhat rhetorically, what I thought Tresize would propose. Without hesitation, I spit out a number: in the jargon,

400,000 barrels per day to Districts I to IV. Taken aback a little by my definitiveness, Jake pressed on: What would have been the much lower number Tresize would have imposed if the Americans had been forced to apply the controls on their side of the border? I gave the same answer, 400,000 barrels per day.

There was a moment of silence and then some muttering as the mandarins realized the significance of what I had said. It implied that the whole negotiation was nothing but a sham and that Canada was not, in reality, gaining anything by agreeing to cooperate with the Americans in taking the politically difficult decision to apply export controls. The tension in the room mounted.

My reasoning was simple: I estimated that once the Chicago Loop opened up, the Americans believed they could supply all but 400,000 barrels of their daily crude oil requirements. I conceded that they were probably wrong, as the northern tier refiners would not be satisfied, but I argued that that was immaterial. The American negotiators had only one number in mind. I was rude enough to suggest they had no need to go through the charade of consulting the White House to arrive at that figure, which had undoubtedly been set long before they left Washington. My guess was that Tresize was probably using the break to have a drink with his colleagues. The mandarins were not amused. Howland was indignant.

Looking back, I am staggered by my temerity but confess to enjoying such a delicious moment of truth. The Americans returned and Tresize solemnly advised the Canadians that, after consulting with the White House, it had been agreed that the language we had sought would be incorporated in the presidential statement and, as a gesture of friendship and good faith, Canada would be allowed to control our oil exports at a level of ... 400,000 barrels per day to Districts I to IV. The deal was struck, and afterwards some of the Canadians consoled themselves with the thought that if Canada had not agreed, the controls would have been set by the Americans at a much lower level. Who was to say they were wrong?

The sequel was even more revealing. Because of a White House foul-up, President Richard Nixon did not use the language Canada had bought and paid for. The cabinet, at that point, felt they could not honour our part of the arrangement and impose the politically unpopular export controls, which would have made them targets for the ire of Canadian producers and American consumers alike. As threatened, the administration then moved to impose formal controls on imports from Canada. The level was set at 395,000 barrels per day, a token reduction out of pure, face-saving American spite.

As it happened, the controls proved completely unsustainable. The northern tier refiners rebelled. The moment Canadian exports reached the control level, the level was raised, and raised again, until the whole nonsense was finally abandoned entirely. The ultimate fallout was even more ironic. Barely three years later, when surging US demand led Canada to introduce oil export controls, the Americans were highly indignant.

I drew a number of important lessons from this experience. Most important, I came to formulate Ritchie's Axiom: In dealing with foreigners, American negotiators have a mandate to receive, but not to make, concessions. In other words, domestic political considerations determine what, if anything, they can offer – in this case, 400,000 barrels per day. The talks then turn around what the negotiators can extract from the other party – in this case, the agreement that we would apply the controls on ourselves.

Seen in this cruel light, negotiating with the Americans is often nothing more than an elaborate stork dance. Nothing we can do is likely to get better terms from them; if we are remotely intelligent, we will therefore offer them only what we propose to do anyway, in our own interest. Unfortunately, this axiom is not widely understood, and it takes some time to train new governments in its application.

Another dispute arose over our exports of sulphur, a by-product of the sour natural gas in such plentiful supply in our Western Sedimentary Basin. The more gas we produced, largely to supply growing American requirements at the much lower prices that prevailed before the OPEC revolution, the more sulphur we produced. Unless we could sell the stuff, we were obliged to stockpile it in brilliant yellow mountains that shot up across the prairies in the early 1970s. As a result, our producers were not sticky about the price and, indeed, might have almost been prepared to pay to have it taken off their hands.

This was not good news for the economically inefficient but politically powerful sulphur producers of New Mexico, who used an expensive process to mine the stuff from the ground. As prices plummeted to $4 per ton and less, they reacted in the traditional way – by crying foul and attempting to close down their competition. It was alleged that Canadian sulphur was being unfairly traded and must therefore be heavily penalized and restricted. They had powerful allies on Capitol Hill.

This was, of course, precisely the reasoning that would have shut down the oil industry to keep the whaling vessels afloat, or outlawed the automobile to preserve the buggy whip industry, all essential to national security. Despite its illogic, this reaction had political force and posed a real threat to the Canadian industry.

I was heavily involved over the following year in an elaborate effort to divert the Americans' attention. We proposed an international agreement on sulphur. We even convened conferences, first in Montreal and then in Vancouver, involving producer and consumer interests from North America, Europe, and Asia. These were elaborate events, orchestrated with opening statements, election of officers, protracted negotiations over communiqués, the whole kit and caboodle. It was my first introduction to international diplomacy, and it was fascinating. The national stereotypes fit surprisingly well: the Japanese kept to themselves and could not make a move without instructions – which never came – from Tokyo; the Europeans moved in packs and the commission representative could not decide anything on his own; the Americans, on the other hand, were tough but straightforward to deal with and fun to party with after the meetings were done for the day. By the time these international negotiations had, mercifully, fallen through, the price of sulphur had begun to turn upward, never to look back.

Two aspects of this whole affair stayed with me. First, I developed a healthy disrespect for all commodity price forecasts. This stood me in good stead when I opposed policies, including the later National Energy Program, predicated entirely on the soundness of just such a price forecast.

Second, and more important, this dispute brought home the extent to which "fair trade" is in the eye of the beholder. In all countries, including Canada, the most elaborate and elegant rationales can be developed to justify the most self-serving protectionist activities. In this, the Americans are in a class by themselves. Indeed, they have institutionalized the business to the point where they appear almost to believe the nonsense they are spouting to justify the most stringent protectionist actions. There was absolutely no legitimate basis for restricting imports of sulphur from Canada. No matter. Provided some spurious rationale could be found, the American political system would rally round and put the importer on the defensive against charges of unfair trade.

Another dispute sealed the fate of the Canadian uranium industry. From the discovery of "pitchblende" in the Canadian North to the present, the Canadian uranium industry has existed largely in response to American requirements, military and civilian. To supply the war effort in the 1940s, and then the Cold War build-up, the Canadian industry was established and expanded until it supported the economies of whole communities and regions. One of the main centres of production was the open-pit mine at Elliot Lake, Ontario – which happened to be in the riding of Prime Minister Pearson. Another was at Uranium City in northern Saskatchewan, where I had spent four months underground as a miner to help pay for my university education.

The Canadian ore was milled on site, converted to yellowcake (uranium hexafluoride), and then enriched to the purity required for most nuclear activities. The enrichment process was extremely expensive and of considerable military significance, as it was essential to the production of weapons-grade material. Although a handful of other countries had a limited enrichment capacity, the bulk was located in the United States. Most uranium export contracts called for the yellowcake to be enriched in American facilities for sale in the United States and overseas.

As American sources of uranium were developed, the producers began to throw around their political weight. As a first step, foreign uranium was determined to be unreliable as a source of supply for American military purposes. This devastated the Canadian industry that had, of course, been built to serve these purposes. There remained the civilian and export markets. The primary uranium industry persuaded the administration, on grounds of national security, to place a total embargo on the use of American facilities to enrich foreign uranium for export. That put the icing on the yellowcake.

This did not immediately shut down the Canadian industry. After all, the CANDU reactor we had developed did not require such highly enriched uranium to operate. But for a number of reasons, including financial, the CANDU system lost ground in the international reactor race, and with it shrank that channel for Canadian uranium sales.

For me, this issue went beyond the abstractions of international trade rules. The result would determine whether entire communities would live or die. From my months working underground at the Eldorado mine at Uranium City, I knew just how precarious was such a town's grip on survival.

I developed a compelling case that the American embargo went far beyond what could be justified on legitimate national security grounds. The issue went to the GATT, where we won our case and the Americans were told to clean up their act. After much foot-dragging, the embargo was loosened, only to have an American court put it back in place at the request of the domestic producers.

By the time the embargo was finally neutralized in the mid–1970s, it was too late. The bloom was off the nuclear rose as the atomic power industry had ground to a halt, largely as a result of its own greed and incompetence. Elliot Lake became a senior citizens' community, as its industrial workforce departed. Uranium City had no alternative vocation.

Later, around 1980, when I was running the operations of the Ministry of State for Economic Development, we were faced with the closing of the mine and thus the town. I was able to help ensure that all the available assistance was provided, but I was terribly aware that it was not enough. This was the fate of the families of the tens of thousands of workers who were drawn to an industry created to meet a great purpose, only to be cast on the rock pile when it served the interests of American producers.

During this period, I was privileged to work under the direction of a highly controversial character, Mel Clark, director general of one of the trade policy offices. Clark was a self-proclaimed Canadian nationalist who wore his beliefs on his sleeve. His bureaucratic style was much like his downhill skiing: barrel-chested, clad in a black ski outfit, he would bellow "Track!" as he roared down the slope with little regard for the social niceties. As a public servant, he was refreshingly outspoken. I admired him for his forthrightness and shared his views, up to a point. Beyond that point, a healthy suspicion of American power and motives could become paranoia.

Clark's peculiar passion was water. He was absolutely convinced that the Americans were engaged in a masterful, unrelenting campaign to gain control of Canada's rivers and lakes. This fear was heightened to a fever pitch when his former boss and nemesis, Simon Reisman, joined forces with a group promoting the so-called Grand Canal project to channel water from the Canadian North to the cities of the United States. The project went nowhere, foundering on the Americans' lack of interest, which Clark, naturally, suspected was a ruse designed to throw us off our guard. Later, when the oil disputes that I have described reached their height, Clark constructed an elaborate analysis to explain that what the Americans really wanted was Canadian water.

Clark was also a committed multilateralist who believed profoundly in the theology of the GATT. In the Kennedy Round of the 1960s, he had served on the Canadian team, as he was to do again in the 1970s in the Tokyo Round. In the interim, he was the keeper of the faith, never tiring of preaching the need for Canada to be prepared to play a leading role in the multilateral trade game. In 1971, he asked me to leave the resource trade arena to head the department's GATT division.

I shared a belief in the value of the GATT for Canada. After all, my father had been one of its architects. My support was, however, much more practical than theological. I saw the GATT less as a set of sacred precepts carved in stone and more as an institution permitting nations to pursue their self-interest aggressively without unleashing open trade war. This was certainly the way the Americans operated under the GATT, respecting its principles when it served their interests and ignoring them when it did not. When, for example, the GATT ruled that the uranium embargo was contrary to their obligations, it was years before the Americans took corrective action.

The rules did, however, generally serve the interests of the United States and the other economic superpowers. It is not widely understood that the GATT rules overwhelmingly favour the interests of the big market. Other countries must pay to gain access to that large market through vital concessions of their own. Once accepted into that market, importers must play by rules that are heavily stacked in favour of the home team. The rules are, of course, largely written by the Big Three – Europe, Japan, and above all the United States.

Different powers achieve their purposes in different ways. The Japanese, for example, built their industry on a unique system of governmental and private discouragement of imports. The much-vaunted Japanese industrial strategy was, in large measure, the skilful operation of an elaborate system of controls on imports of products and technologies, operated by the Ministry of International Trade and Industry in a highly mercantilist fashion. Meanwhile, consumer attitudes, distribution systems, cross-ownership of corporations, and a host of other factors made it exceedingly difficult to penetrate the Japanese market successfully. Needless to say, none of these restrictions were addressed by the GATT.

The much-touted liberalization of the European Community, culminating in the mid-1980s with the "single European market," did indeed go a long way to free trade *within* the market. At the same time, it kept imported products out. The most obvious example is agriculture, where the infamous Common Agricultural Policy is the epitome of the most egregious protectionism, keeping out the produce of efficient nations such as Canada while promoting the exports of its inefficient producers, notably the French. This iniquitous program was tolerated under the GATT as the price of European adherence. It was increasingly obvious, however, that the calculus of international trade could not easily accommodate industrialized Europe as a net *exporter* of subsidized agricultural commodities. The numbers simply could not add up.

The great exponents of freer trade, the Americans, went a long way to lower their tariffs and open their markets to imports. They then put up new and frequently more restrictive barriers in the name of "fair trade." This was achieved through laws that are, on the surface, designed simply to ensure that imports do not take illegitimate advantage of America's generosity in opening its markets to injure American producers.

So much for the theory. In practice, these "fair trade" laws have become what one American commentator called "the fair trade fraud." The application of these principles has been corrupted beyond recognition by American legislative, legal, and administrative processes ruled by self-serving Washington trade lawyers and the special interests they represent. The system operates like the Inquisition of old, in which the proceedings are heavily stacked against the defendants. Foreign companies are punished, through the imposition of anti-dumping duties, for behaving exactly like their American competitors. Imports from foreign countries are penalized with countervailing duties for allegedly benefiting from policies and programs often identical to or less generous than those enjoyed by their American competitors. In some cases, imports are simply penalized for being too successful, and thus disrupting the cosy American market.

Despite the view, widely held by Canadian businesspeople, that we act like a nation of Boy Scouts, Canada does not come to the table with clean hands. We have shown considerable ingenuity in devising new forms of protectionism. Perhaps the best example is our marketing boards, which force up the prices paid for poultry and milk in Canada by keeping imports to an absolute minimum. The fact remains that Canada's protectionism is much less damaging precisely because we have a relatively small domestic market and are so dependent on foreign sales. If we restrict imports, this is unlikely to have a lethal impact on foreign producers for whom Canada is an additional but not essential outlet. And if we misbehave, we risk serious consequences for the 40 percent of our total production that is exported.

During the year I spent heading our GATT division, the *realpolitik* view of the GATT was strongly reinforced by events. I took up my new job at the beginning of August 1971, starting with a trip to Geneva with my minister, Jean-Luc Pepin, for some comforting speeches about the future of international trade liberalization. On my return, I promised my wife we would finally be able to take a proper summer holiday. After all, very little progress was being made in the GATT talks.

Fifteen days later, President Nixon unleashed his economic program, with devastating effect on Canada. The American dollar was cut loose from its historic basis and a system of import restrictions and export incentives was introduced. The centrepiece was a regime of substantial surcharges that applied to imports from all countries, notably America's biggest trading partner, Canada. Another device introduced a substantial tax incentive (the domestic international sales corporation, or DISC) designed to induce companies, notably those with subsidiaries in Canada, to export from the United States. The impact was staggering.

So much for any hope of summer holidays. We were immediately plunged into a full-scale trade war. As usual, the initial reaction in some quarters was that there must be some terrible mistake – the Americans could not have intended to include Canada in their sights. It soon became apparent that Canada was indeed one of the principal targets. At that time, we suffered a huge deficit on our current account, the sum of the inflows and outflows of goods, services, interest, and dividend payments. To the raging American bull, Treasury Secretary John Connally, what mattered was only our trade in goods – our merchandise trade balance – and on that account we were selling more to the Americans.

The American actions were contrary to their obligations under the GATT. We made much of this as we joined forces with the Europeans and Japanese – who were particularly shaken by what they styled the "Nixon-shokku" – to press the Americans to lift the restrictions. There were intensive discussions in Geneva, with little result. Bilateral discussions were more interesting but unproductive. Truce was declared on American terms. The surcharges were lifted. We introduced our own measures to counter the American export incentives. The lesson, however, had been all too clear: if and when the Americans wished, they could effectively close their border and shut down Canadian industry, the GATT be damned.

It is an article of the multilateral faith that trade liberalization is like riding a bicycle: if we stop moving forward, we will all fall down. Thus the Nixon-shokku heightened the importance of the Tokyo Round of trade negotiations under the GATT. (GATT rounds were named after a prominent American – Dillon, Kennedy – or the location of the meeting at which they were launched – Annecy, Tokyo, or later Uruguay.) Earlier rounds had lowered tariffs substantially from their postwar heights. These had culminated in the Kennedy Round, in which Canada stood aside from the across-the-board tariff-cutting, tailoring our tariff concessions to our own requirements. This had led to considerable criticism from other countries. Canada had been a "free rider," they claimed. They were determined that the next negotiations would not see a repeat performance.

Like its predecessors, the Tokyo Round was mainly about cutting tariffs on industrial goods. It largely ignored agriculture, given European and Japanese obduracy and the Americans' own special exemption permitting restrictions on these products. It left aside the growing trade in services, which now represented well over half the employment of the developed countries. It attempted, without much success, to put some limits on the use of such devices as countervailing or anti-dumping duties, especially by the United States, to penalize successful imports on grounds of "fair trade" – measures that had become increasingly important as normal tariffs declined in value.

I led the Canadian delegation to the first GATT working party charged with tackling these "fair trade" restrictions. It was an interesting experience. I was very much the new boy on the block. I lacked the GATT experience of a number of my colleagues, including one diplomat who had a remarkable ability to go through an entire bargaining session – sitting bolt upright with his eyes open – sound asleep. On behalf of Canada, I aggressively staked out our position: we were prepared to see a range of government assistance out-lawed, but insisted that special consideration be given to regional development and support for research and development.

The Americans were not buying what I had to sell. They were determined to have a free hand to go after any and all government support for imports into their market, and they alone were to be the judge. I hoped this was simply their opening position.

The Europeans weighed in on Canada's side in this discussion, given their massive regional development assistance programs. The Japanese, as usual, kept their heads down and waited for instructions from Tokyo. It was not an auspicious start for negotiations aimed at achieving a breakthrough in this difficult area.

My GATT experiences fed a growing fascination with the negotiating process itself. Naturally, I picked up a great deal from my betters in the government service – my father, Jake Warren, and Simon Reisman – and from my involvement in negotiations with the Americans and others. I analyzed these experiences in the light of some of the numerous "how to" books on the subject. My best teachers were probably car salesmen. Trained in the dealership system for American automobiles, these are the real professional negotiators. I badly overpaid for my first new car but got it back on subsequent rounds. As the saying goes, "You get what you negotiate, not necessarily what you deserve."

Much of the deal-maker's art is generic, applying as much to private or commercial transactions as to great affairs of state. Perhaps the most important lesson was the need to do one's homework to determine whether there are, in fact, the makings of a deal. I liked to think of this in terms of the diagrams we used in classes on symbolic logic. One circle represented the area within which a party to the negotiations was better off than before. If this overlapped with the corresponding circle of another party, the common territory defined the scope for a deal. Anywhere in that overlapping area would see both parties gain. The negotiations could then begin to focus on who would gain the most.

Negotiators with a high degree of knowledge and self-confidence can often reach agreement very quickly. They identify the area where both parties stand to gain substantially and make an initial offer close to that point. Insecure negotiators, who lack confidence or information, are often obliged to niggle their way to a deal. Their initial proposal is absurdly "low-ball," offering the other party little or nothing for fear of ending up with an agreement that is too generous to the other side. They have no clear idea where they want to end up. Instead, they simply resist the other party's demands until they are satisfied that there is no more "give." I observed that the best Canadian negotiators, and most of the Americans with whom I dealt, fell into the first category: they knew what they wanted and were not afraid to go straight to a balanced deal.

It also became apparent that in negotiations, as in chess, the initiative was highly important. The party that could seize the initiative enjoyed a great advantage over the party that was simply trying to give up as little as possible. This was sometimes a matter of negotiating style. More often, it was dictated by the circumstances. In many of the negotiations in which I was involved, Canada was inescapably on the defensive against the onrushing Americans. The classic case was the assault by John Connally on Canada's "unacceptable" trade surplus with the US. However unreasonable we judged Connally's position to be, we were clearly on the defensive, facing the inevitability of making concessions.

Finally, my experience highlighted the absolute importance of ensuring that one was facing a negotiator with real authority to make a deal. In buying a car, my test was very simple. If the salesman could make the deal, I was paying much too much. The only one with the true authority was the sales manager or, in some cases, the owner himself. Only when I was dealing directly with him would I make my best offer. Otherwise, the risk was that I would play my best cards to reach a tentative deal with the salesman, only to have him come back from some distant office to report that the manager had turned the offer down as too rich. At that point, I would have no choice but to up the ante and thus pay too much, or walk out of the showroom. The fact that this is one of the oldest tricks in the book does not mean that it does not work, time and again.

With the Americans, it very much depended on the personal status of the negotiator. But even the most senior official in the administration could always keep in reserve his "sales manager" – the US Congress. The deal would be negotiated, initialled, and even sometimes signed with the administration, only to have the American negotiators return to report that they had tested the mood on Capitol Hill and it would take a few more concessions to make the agreement fly. These lessons were all to be reinforced by the great negotiation that lay in the future.

My father, meanwhile, had returned to Ottawa in 1970 to head his department as the undersecretary of state for external affairs, Canada's top diplomatic post. He was somehow persuaded by management consultants that virtually everyone with any operational responsibility should be permitted to report directly to him without having to pass through levels of bureaucratic hierarchy. The resulting workload was absolutely crushing.

One Saturday in September 1974, my mother called to tell us that Dad had suffered a mild heart attack. He had been feeling unwell the previous afternoon and had, most uncharacteristically, returned home early, although his discomfort had not stopped him from taking several telephone calls from the office. When the problem persisted, he drove himself into the local hospital, where they soon determined he had suffered a coronary. Marg and I rushed to the hospital but were reassured by him and by the medical staff that he was fine, as indeed he appeared. As a precaution, they kept him overnight in the intensive care ward although, incredibly, they did not give him medication to thin his blood. When we returned to the hospital the next morning, he had suffered a massive stroke. His left side was completely paralyzed.

I arranged for his transfer to the National Defence Medical Centre, where he received the very best of care, but terrible damage had already been done. His rehabilitation was slow and painful. Despite the doctors' prognosis that he would never walk again, he managed to shuffle along with the help of a cane.

He was unable to return to head the department, but, remarkably, he managed to serve his country one more time, as Canada's ambassador to Ireland, before my parents retired from the government service to live in Ottawa. Although he was severely physically disabled, and his condition naturally deteriorated over the years with a succession of medical alarms, he kept his remarkable mental faculties intact. He continued to be a source of advice and support as my career progressed. Perhaps the best summation came from a fellow diplomat, Arthur Andrew, who wrote:

> Comparisons are invidious, but it would be surprising if any of the succeeding undersecretaries would disagree that [Ed Ritchie] was the last of the breed of... "Men of Influence": persons who had appeared during the war and had contributed so much to the reputation of the Canadian public service generally and the Department [of External Affairs] in particular. They were not so much giants among lesser mortals as they were unselfish people with an intense sense of duty and some very clear ideas about the nature and destiny of their country.

The GATT Tokyo Round negotiations continued without me as I left on sabbatical in the summer of 1972. Mel Clark and my successor, Germain Denis, joined the team and moved to Geneva for the long haul. Following the common pattern, the first few years were a case of "Hurry up and wait" as the parties slowly developed their positions on the issues. Self-imposed deadlines were established, driven by American legislative requirements, to create an atmosphere of urgency at the end. As the stakes were raised, so was the profile. My former mentor, Jake Warren, was called on as a special ambassador to oversee the talks.

The negotiations had been launched in 1971 when Trudeau enjoyed a substantial parliamentary majority. They dragged on through the subsequent minority parliament and the first few years of his second majority. By 1976 the Trudeau government's unpopularity sharply limited its ability to force through important initiatives. To oversee the conclusion of the trade deal, Trudeau assigned his canniest minister, Allan MacEachen. MacEachen reviewed the negotiations with the help of an ad hoc cabinet committee. In practice, MacEachen called all the shots. He was not enamoured of what he saw.

As the head of the policy office at Industry, Trade and Commerce, the position I had taken up in 1973, I was commissioned to present a paper assessing the economic impact to provide a context for final decisions on the negotiating result. My task was to bring it all together in an analysis that would be acceptable to senior officials and intelligible for ministers. The paper was relatively brief but was supported by voluminous appendices with econometric printouts and sectoral studies. Basically, it presented the classic case for trade liberalization that I had first studied at university. It asserted that the same was likely to hold for the Tokyo Round results. The benefits would be structural, improving our overall competitiveness over the long term. They could be significant for certain firms in certain industries that were identified. The overall impact would be relatively modest and swamped by the current swings of the business cycle, from boom to recession.

The impact would, nonetheless, be very serious for workers directly affected by production cutbacks and plant closings. We had done some pioneering studies of the effects of such closings, particularly in communities where there were few if any employment alternatives. The paper argued that it was essential that appropriate adjustment assistance be provided for those hardest hit. This meant substantially upgrading our manpower programs to assist displaced workers in finding new jobs, possibly in different occupations or different regions. Special attention was needed by older workers who would not, realistically, have much prospect of making the adjustment and should therefore benefit from income supplements.

The paper generally opposed adjustment grants to businesses. Their incentive to adjust was the profits they would make if they succeeded, or the losses they would suffer if they did not. If only to provide some reassurance, however, the paper did make the case for a trade negotiations "window" under an existing program to provide loan guarantees under terms and conditions designed to ensure that there would be few if any takers.

The crucial meeting of deputy ministers to review this assessment was scheduled for a Monday in the summer of 1976. I was staying with the family at our cottage in New Brunswick. I calculated that it would be a simple matter to catch the early-morning plane from Moncton to arrive in Ottawa in plenty of time to attend the meeting and return that evening. Unfortunately, that very weekend, the air traffic controllers shut down the system over the issue of bilingualism.

I was just able to get the last ticket on the overnight train, the *Ocean Limited*, leaving Moncton at 3 P.M. on Sunday. Extra cars had to be added to carry the overflow from the airlines. Painfully slowly, we chugged through the dark woods of central New Brunswick, with frequent thumping and bumping stops. After a sleepless night, I faced a sprint through the Montreal station, catching the train to Ottawa as it started to move. I was met at the Ottawa station by a colleague and we raced downtown, reviewing the material as we went. We made it with a good five minutes to spare. The presentation went well and the interdepartmental committee was very complimentary. That eased the discomfort of realizing that I was stuck in Ottawa for the duration of the strike.

This assessment and the accompanying proposals were later accepted by the government but there remained serious reservations about the whole Tokyo Round negotiations. It would have been difficult for the government to turn down the deal that had been signed with our trading partners, but MacEachen was finding it hard to accept. I watched the unfolding of this dilemma in late 1978 from a new vantage point as the deputy secretary for operations of the newly created Ministry of State for Economic Development (MSED). The Liberals were saved by the bell. Time ran out. Trudeau had no choice but to call an election, which he lost narrowly to Joe Clark and the Progressive Conservatives in May 1979.

When the Tories arrived in power, approval of the Tokyo Round deal was one of the top items on the agenda submitted by the bureaucrats. My new job required me to brief the cabinet on all economic development issues to come before them. I soon found the Conservatives were no more enthusiastic than their Liberal predecessors. The decisive argument proved to be: We can always blame it on the Liberals. On that basis, the deal was endorsed by the government. It had been a close call.

When Trudeau swept back to power in 1980, freer trade remained high on the agenda. The Liberals were badly torn by the issue. Historically, the Grits had been the party of free trade opposing the Tory program of protectionism. It was the revered Liberal Sir Wilfrid Laurier who had fought, and lost, the great political battle in 1911 over reciprocity with the United States. In the late 1940s, Mackenzie King authorized John Deutsch, a senior mandarin with the Finance Department, to negotiate a free trade agreement with Americans, only to back away at the last moment. The Liberals had also been responsible for the agreements on agricultural machinery and petroleum and, of course, the Canada-US Auto Pact.

There was a competing strain in Liberal thinking, an economic nationalism that was often accompanied by a heavy dose of anti-Americanism. Walter

Gordon had resurrected this mindset and had deeply influenced such younger followers as Herb Gray, Donald Macdonald, and Lloyd Axworthy. To this group, the Americans simply held much too much power over Canadian economic decisions, controlling vast segments of Canadian industry. Opening up markets in the United States was secondary to protecting the industrial heartland stretching from Windsor through Hamilton and Toronto to Montreal and Quebec City.

This had led to restrictions on foreign takeovers of companies in Canada through the Foreign Investment Review Agency (FIRA) and was to lead to such overt discrimination as the National Energy Program, which aggressively promoted Canadian acquisition of the energy sector – at the height of the market, just before the bottom dropped out, taking many Canadian enterprises down with it.

I was uncomfortable with both policies despite the central role close friends had played in their articulation. When the task force of officials had been recruited to work with Gray on FIRA in the late 1960s, I was able to plead the pressure of other work. In reality, I had been persuaded by my experience with Bob Winters that corporate performance was much more important than, and not necessarily related to, nationality of ownership and control. When I ducked, my friend and colleague Roberto Gualtieri spent the next few years on the project.

The brainpower behind the National Energy Program in 1980 came largely from another close friend, Edmund Clark, assistant deputy minister at Energy, Mines and Resources. When he showed me an early draft on a personal and confidential basis, I was highly critical – not of the nationalist objectives, which I readily shared, but because it clashed with my appreciation of the North American energy market. Given my earlier experience with commodity forecasts, I was deeply skeptical of the wisdom of basing any policy on an indefinite increase of 3 percent per annum in the real price of crude oil. Of course Clark, a brilliant and dedicated public servant, had not invented the program but was implementing with great skill the commitments made by his minister, Marc Lalonde.

Ironically, the opponents of this anti-Americanism within the Liberal Party were also concerned over the growing importance of the US market for Canadian exports. Gordon's nemesis, Mitchell Sharp, was the most articulate exponent of a so-called third option of neither building walls against the Americans nor integrating the continental economy but instead promoting links with Europe and the Pacific. The concept had political power: it provided respectable common ground for those who disliked Americans and those who were committed multilateralists to join in promoting closer economic ties overseas. In economic terms, it was no more successful than Diefenbaker's misguided efforts to divert trade away from the US and towards the British motherland. By the end of the Trudeau years, our dependence on the American market had reached unprecedented levels.

To balance political wishes with economic realities, the Trudeau government reluctantly gave its blessing to sectoral free trade with the United States. Building on the unique experience of the Auto Pact, it proposed to negotiate free trade agreements to cover the products of other industries, from farm machinery to industrial chemicals. The driving force was Ed Lumley, at that point the minister for international trade, the junior portfolio at the External Affairs Department. He was running counter to the deep convictions of his own deputy minister, Bob Johnstone. Supported by the head of the American desk at External Affairs, Derek Burney, Lumley oversaw the preparation of a paper charting trade policies for the 1980s. He then personally presided over a broad consultation with other departments and with old trade policy hands now outside the government.

By then, I was the associate deputy minister responsible for the operations of the Department of Regional Industrial Expansion (DRIE), the newest incarnation of the industry portfolio. I was impressed by Lumley's initiative, taking personal charge of policy formulation over the opposition of his own senior staff. I knew that a number of his officials dismissed him as a glorified industrial development commissioner, referring to his early history. Lumley had made a success in business with a Coca-Cola franchise before turning to politics. From development commissioner, he quickly became the mayor of Cornwall, then its member of Parliament. He was chosen to serve as parliamentary secretary to the finance minister, Jean Chrétien, who had treated him with the same respect Chrétien had earlier received from his mentor, Mitchell Sharp. I detected a keen strategic mind under his prematurely white hair. This did not keep me from expressing serious reservations about the negotiating feasibility of such sectoral arrangements.

In the fall of 1982, Lumley was promoted to minister of DRIE. For the next two years, we worked closely together to bring about an extraordinary range of industrial development projects, in the aerospace, automotive, forest products, and other industries. He more than lived up to my high expectations as a hard-driving and extremely effective minister. The team was completed with the arrival of Bill Teschke as the senior deputy minister in the portfolio.

With his short-cropped grey hair and military demeanour born of his time in the air force, Teschke was a career public servant who had, in his own quiet way, earned an extraordinary reputation. His qualities of judgment tempered the energies and enthusiasms that Ed Lumley and I brought to our tasks.

Meanwhile, Gerald Regan, the former premier of Nova Scotia, took over the international trade portfolio. In Regan's name, the discussion paper Lumley had initiated was published. It was entitled *Canadian Trade Policy for the 80s*. It proposed negotiations to free trade in selected industries.

The sectoral negotiations were launched with the Americans. They soon foundered. The problem was painfully obvious. In some industries, the Americans were considered simply too strong for their Canadian competitors, who feared being swamped with imports. In those industries where Canada might enjoy an advantage, the American producers were not prepared to see their domestic market opened wide. No industry offered a balanced deal, at least in the eyes of the weaker sisters in the sector, nor was it politically possible to explicitly trade off one sector for another. It became increasingly evident that the only way to achieve a balanced negotiation was to cover the whole economy through a comprehensive free trade arrangement. That was political anathema to the economic nationalists.

As I told my staff, I still expected that a Liberal government would, at some point, launch comprehensive trade negotiations with the United States. Meanwhile, however, Trudeau had run out his string. He handed over the reins of power to the man he despised, John Turner, with only months left in the mandate. He loaded Turner with a bagful of odious patronage appointments, to which Turner added some of his own before leading his party to a humiliating defeat in the general election in September 1984. I was told that Turner took it all in stride, until he received the news that Ed Lumley had gone down to personal defeat in his seemingly unassailable Cornwall seat.

That appeared to put an end to free trade with the United States for the foreseeable future. After all, the Conservative leader, Brian Mulroney, had made clear where he stood. "Free trade with the United States is like sleeping with an elephant," Mulroney said, drawing on the old cliché. "It's terrific until the elephant twitches, and if the elephant rolls over, you're dead." As Mulroney told *Maclean's* magazine, "Canadians rejected free trade with the United States in 1911. They would do so again in 1983." Whatever the future held, one thing was clear: the party of business was not about to negotiate a free trade deal with the Americans.

❦   ❦   ❦

During the period when the politicians are on the campaign trail, it is standard practice for the federal bureaucracy to keep busy by preparing for the aftermath. In every department, a set of briefing books is prepared to familiarize the new minister with the department's policies and programs. Odds are good that there will be a reshuffling of portfolios even if the government is returned to office. In most cases, some thought is also given to the implications of a change in government. What are the opposition's political priorities? What changes in direction, what new initiatives, can be expected? This is standard operating procedure.

In the Department of Regional Industrial Expansion, we also profited from having briefed the opposition critics, led by Michael Wilson. (When, out of habit, I called Wilson "Minister," he was delighted and told a chemical industry audience that evening that the writing was on the wall when the mandarins already talked as if the Tories had won the election.)

In 1984, we went one important step farther. The top officials of both DRIE and the Finance Department had come to the view that we faced growing structural problems undermining Canada's international competitiveness. The Finance Department team was led by the deputy minister, Mickey Cohen, and one of his assistant deputy ministers, Gerry Shannon. During the period before and during the election, Bill Teschke and I had a number of intensive discussions with Cohen's group about the problem and possible solutions. We were not about to sit around for months, as we had when Joe Clark came to power, waiting for the Conservatives to chart bold new directions for the economy. This time, we were prepared.

Grand policy changes, like rivers, spring from many sources. It is no coincidence, however, that much of the work we did over that summer found its way, with little change, into Michael Wilson's much-touted *New Economic Agenda* that fall. The new finance minister's November economic statement pointed the way to greatly expanded trade relations with the United States. This was far short of "free trade" but a considerable step beyond the new prime minister's wariness of the sleeping elephant. It did serve to overcome some of the built-in resistance in the Finance Department to any measures that would cut tariffs – and government revenues.

Ironically, I had a more serious problem with my own minister, Sinclair Stevens. Stevens was a funny duck. Short and balding, he was intensely partisan with a highly developed scepticism of the motives of others, including the prime minister, his colleagues, and above all the career bureaucrats who had worked for the Grits. Stevens had a reputation as a conservative but revelled

44

in control of the government apparatus. At one of our first meetings, I had briefed him on DRIE. I gave him a choice. I could tell him what we were doing, how we could do it better, or what we should be doing. "Tell me what we should be doing," he said.

I then explained that we should not be dishing out hundreds of millions of dollars in grants to industry. Our studies had consistently demonstrated that these grants did not create employment, except for politicians and bureaucrats. A grant might cause a project to be relocated or it might bring it on stream a little sooner, but any project that would not proceed without a government grant would almost certainly fail, taking the taxpayers' money with it.

Stevens was badly ruffled. This was much too radical for his taste. After years of struggle, he had finally taken the helm of a great spending department and was not about to shut it down. We quickly moved to discuss how we could give away the money more effectively. I did not make that mistake again.

On free trade, Stevens was nervous as a kitten. His concern was visceral – he had spent too long fighting against the Liberal free traders and on behalf of the protectionist Canadian manufacturers to be comfortable with any suggestion of free trade with the United States. Despite his conservative rhetoric, his instincts were highly pragmatic. Given the choice, he tended towards government interventionism through trade protection and industrial subsidies. It would take a great deal of persuasion to bring him around.

During this period, the Canadian business community was undergoing a conversion on its own road to Damascus. There are many theories about why this happened. The business school literature was starting to spread the gospel of globalization, which had the intellectual force in the business community that economic determinism had enjoyed among the Marxists – it made the outcome appear inevitable, as national markets were ripped open by the forces of technology and international competition. At the opposite pole, the economic nationalists saw the movement towards free trade as the product of a dark conspiracy led by American capitalists and executed by their Canadian lackeys. As if to prove the point, the committee established to study trade issues by the big business lobby group, the Business Council on National Issues, was chaired by an American, Alton Cartwright, who headed the Canadian operations of an American multinational, General Electric.

The cynic in me suggests that this change of heart was very much stimulated by an artificially low Canadian dollar, dropping to an all-time low of less than 70 cents US in 1986. At that level, Canadian manufacturers were all competitive geniuses. They found to their delighted surprise that they could match and beat their American competitors on their home ground. I suspect this made them much less resistant to the idea of dismantling tariffs at the border. Their very success made them vulnerable to increasing American protectionism, often directed specifically at Canada, which had been accentuated by the relatively severe recession in the United States.

In later revisionist history, the various business groups – the BCNI, the Chamber of Commerce, the Canadian Manufacturers' Association, the small business federation – put forward competing claims to have fathered the Free Trade Agreement. My recollection is somewhat different. For example, the BCNI ultimately presented a very cautious proposal that Canada and the US should negotiate some form of "trade enhancement agreement" to oversee trade links and disputes between the two countries. The Chamber of Commerce and the Canadian Manufacturers' Association both presented their own modest proposals, far short of comprehensive free trade. The important development, as far as I was concerned, was that these groups were no longer adamantly opposing freer trade with the United States. I did not hesitate to use these business groups to soften up the position of my minister and my department on the issue.

Even I was not promoting a truly comprehensive free trade agreement at that stage, in late 1984. After discussion with Bill Teschke, I prepared a private and highly confidential note for Sinclair Stevens to brief him prior to visits from the business groups.

My argument was very simple. Canada had succeeded in eliminating tariffs on most of our two-way trade with the United States through a skilful combination of multilateral and bilateral trade deals, all under the GATT rules. In fact, I would be prepared to argue that we already met the GATT test for a "free trade arrangement" – indeed, met the test much better than most of the other arrangements, including the European Common Market when it was first formed.

Our problem was that there was no joint machinery to oversee this trade relationship, leaving the Americans free to treat Canada no better, and sometimes worse, than other, much less dependent trading partners. The Americans were gearing up for trouble, as some 200 protectionist bills were making their way through the US Congress and some were bound to pass. Thus we and the Americans could simply declare that we had a free trade arrangement in place and proceed to establish special bilateral machinery to supervise the relationship, resolve disputes, and push towards free trade in those sectors that were still restricted.

Stevens was not enthusiastic. He was not anti-American, far from it. Indeed, his first act on taking office had been to scrap the Foreign Investment Review Agency so offensive to American business leaders. He could see the value of some improved machinery to deal with the Americans – so long as it was not called "free trade." Free trade, to him, was pure poison, a dangerous slogan and a Grit slogan at that.

The Finance Department and DRIE represented two elements of the trade policy troika. The third was External Affairs. External now also housed the trade components of the former Industry, Trade and Commerce Department. Support for a new trade initiative did not come from the old hands. A new player was gaining power and influence. Assistant deputy minister Derek Burney had seized the opportunity, after the sectoral free trade disappointment, to pre-empt the old guard and put his views directly to the new prime minister, Brian Mulroney. A briefing paper was drafted for the prime minister, making the case for opening the door to a trade deal with the United States.

Even before taking power, Mulroney had established a bond with US President Ronald Reagan, a fellow son of Ireland. As prime minister, he was determined to cement the relationship with a full-blown summit meeting between the two heads of government in the winter of 1984–85. The stage was set for St. Patrick's Day in Quebec City. An elaborate and glitzy affair was orchestrated by the PM's spin merchants, headed by Fred Doucet, a crony from Mulroney's school days at St. Francis Xavier University. But Doucet was a policy lightweight. To provide substance to the event, the PM turned to Burney.

Burney is a big burly bear of a man. I had some natural sympathy with any other guy with thinning hair and a continuous battle to keep down his weight. Burney has an exceptional mind and is a prodigious worker who does his homework. Before the free trade negotiations, our paths had not crossed very often but what I had seen was impressive. At a dinner meeting with some of the old diplomatic crowd, I took strong exception to their cavalier dismissal of Burney as a simple administrator, warning my friends that this was a talent to be reckoned with. Above all, I valued two qualities that are all too rare in senior bureaucrats: a commitment to produce results and a candid bluntness of expression. I soon recognized that he combined these with a capacity that I could not match for making the system sing to his tune.

Burney has a finely honed instinct for timing – an indispensable quality in policy-making. He seized his opportunity. He obtained a green light to explore the possibilities of some kind of trade deal as an element of the agenda for the summit. He then proceeded, in true diplomatic style, to focus attention on the communiqué to be issued after the event. The political flacks and their media co-conspirators love to cultivate the image of serious discussions among heads of government leading to imaginative new proposals. The reality could not be farther removed. In practice, such encounters are tightly scripted long in advance, working backward from the final communiqué. This was no exception.

Burney shrewdly juggled three alternative statements on the trade issue. One was a very cautious version praising freer trade without departing from traditional approaches. A more ambitious version emphasized the Canada-US relationship and saw some scope for further links. The third alternative was the real kicker – it would actually launch exploratory discussions aimed at free trade between the two countries.

Burney played a remarkably canny shell game with these three drafts. Even among the insiders, opinion was divided. I recall that Finance, represented by Mickey Cohen and Gerry Shannon, was prepared to go for the moderately ambitious version. For my part, I pressed strongly for the "launch" version, with support from Teschke and the acquiescence of Sinclair Stevens. In External, I don't believe most of the officials remotely understood the stakes involved. Apart from Burney, the departmental view remained overwhelmingly opposed to free trade negotiations with the US on political grounds.

The matter was finally resolved in a meeting of a small group of ministers and senior officials, ostensibly to finalize preparations for the summit. I represented the department and my minister, Stevens. The session was held in the cabinet chamber in the Centre Block of the Parliament Buildings. Burney had arranged to have an advance word with the prime minister. He recommended the "launch" version. The PM bought his proposal. Somewhat to my surprise, the activist version was the only draft presented. It was accepted with almost no discussion by those present. Without further ado, this became the basis for the summit declaration, which Burney worked out with the Americans.

Parenthetically, this was the *only* time, to my knowledge, that the matter was discussed among ministers before the summit that launched the process. Perhaps, when the required time has passed, the cabinet minutes will be unveiled to reveal a full discussion of the pros and cons of free trade with the Americans, arriving after full debate at a consensus overwhelmingly in favour. Perhaps, but I doubt it very much. Instead, I suspect it may prove to have been very much the prime minister's own initiative. He may have been encouraged by some old business friends, such as Alf Powis of Noranda. He was stimulated and supported by Burney. But the other ministers simply acquiesced against, in some cases, their natural instincts.

The summit that took place on March 17 was a circus. I reluctantly accompanied the very disgruntled Sinclair Stevens. He was most upset to find that he and his colleagues were there essentially as a scenic backdrop for some of the photo opportunities. Doucet had made absolutely no provision for them to play any role of substance. The Canadian delegation was lodged at the Quebec Hilton outside the walls of the Old City. President Reagan and his huge entourage were ensconced at the much more prestigious Château Frontenac. Travel between the two was very difficult, as the downtown was blocked off with barricades lined with police. It was incongruous in the extreme.

The plenary session was held in the Château, a place I knew like the back of my hand, having taken my sabbatical at the École nationale d'administration publique, just around the corner. The Château was a majestic structure, with its classic Canadian Pacific architecture and green roof of oxidized copper. The meeting was held in one of the smaller meeting rooms high above the square. It was restricted to the heads of government, a few key ministers, and their deputies. The Canadians arrived on time, only to spend the next half-hour in idle conversation. The American advance guard began to arrive as Secretary of State George Shultz showed up with some of his colleagues. There followed a procession of thugs, tall, steely-eyed, with short-cropped hair, bulges under their jackets, and hearing problems, to judge from the wires in their left ears. Then came the slim, well-tailored, but equally hard-eyed praetorian guard. Finally the president made his entrance.

I was immediately struck by the extent to which the television camera had exaggerated his stature. Reagan was much shorter than I had anticipated, not at all an imposing figure. After some pleasantries, we took our seats. The actual discussion of the trade issue was highly forgettable. My only recollection is being amused by the relationship between the two leaders. The great raconteur, Reagan told some engaging anecdotes. The prime minister consistently addressed his dear friend the president as "Ron." Mr. Reagan returned the favour by calling Mulroney "Mr. Prime Minister." This may have been a difference in style. It may have revealed the one-sided nature of the profession of intimacy.

After the meeting was over and the declaration was issued, it was down to serious business. A black-tie gala of obscene proportions was held at the

Quebec opera house. I was seated with the finance deputy, Mickey Cohen, and my associate Bob Brown. We were in the midst of an army of Tory faithful, from the commanding heights down to the footsoldiers of the party apparatus, come to celebrate their triumph. It was an orgy of bad taste, both on and off the stage. On stage, the highlight was the unforgettable singing of "Irish Eyes" by Mulroney, with little or no support from the somewhat bewildered-looking Reagan. Even worse was the moment when Canadian astronaut Marc Garneau, suited up in full space gear, rose through a trap door, enveloped in dry-ice fumes, and descended again into oblivion, to the accompaniment of the theme from *Star Wars*.

Later, to avoid the crush of pigs at the trough, Mickey and I skipped the official banquet to enjoy a very pleasant dinner at one of the many fine restaurants in the heart of the Old City. On the plane home the next morning, I found myself seated beside Garneau. He was a decent guy who told me he was prepared to submit to almost any indignity to get back up to the stars. This had tested his limit but he ultimately made his goal.

After the big bang came the whimper. The task of exploring the basis for negotiation was assigned to the respective trade ministers. On the way back from Quebec, Reagan summoned his special trade representative, Bill Brock, into the front compartment of Air Force One and offered him a promotion, replacing the recently disgraced secretary of labour. This was a real blow. Brock had begun the dialogue with Ed Lumley back in 1980. He had carefully shepherded the free trade issue along, past the congressional wolves and the Canadian sensitivities. He had made a very timely speech in Toronto that had given the initiative new impetus at a crucial time. In many respects, he was the American father of the free trade initiative. And now he was leaving the file, just as the talks got under way.

Presumably having forgotten about the trade negotiations, Reagan did not get around to replacing Brock for some months, and then he chose a comparative lightweight, Clayton Yeutter. Yeutter was a decent enough sort who saw trade through the rather distorted perspective of the agricultural sector, in which he had worked in business and in government. His reputation in the administration and on Capitol Hill was that he would do what was required to get along with his political superiors. The Canadian side was not much better, as International Trade Minister Jim Kelleher, a lawyer from the Sault, was a newcomer to trade negotiations. The preliminaries trailed on through the summer of 1985 with no clear end in sight.

❦　❦　❦

The relationship with the American superpower was an important ongoing personal preoccupation during these years. But my career had covered a much broader range of issues through the 1970s and early '80s. While heading the policy shop at Industry, Trade and Commerce, I designed and implemented a set of policies and programs to stimulate Canadian industry, working hand in glove for several years with the deputy minister, Gordon Osbaldeston. I was then recruited to the Finance Department and immediately sent off to clean up a mess at the Economic Council of Canada. The council had been saddled by Finance Minister Jean Chrétien with responsibility for running an agency to monitor inflation and productivity following the removal of wage and price controls.

My assignment to the Ministry of State for Economic Development in the fall of 1979 made me responsible for the operations of a new and powerful central agency of government, where I worked again with Osbaldeston. The advice I gave to cabinet covered the entire range of economic policy proposals emerging from more than a dozen departments. It was an extraordinary opportunity to work at the very heart of the governmental decision-making process, often as the only official present at meetings of senior cabinet ministers. To complete my education, I then spent three months in 1981 at the advanced management program of the Harvard Business School, where I worked and played with 160 rising stars of the American and overseas business community.

On my return, I became chief operating officer of the new Department of Regional Industrial Expansion and its programs, which included the negotiation of billions of dollars of assistance to major projects in a wide range of industries in Canada. At the same time, I represented the government's interest in the two aircraft companies it owned, Canadair and de Havilland. These two national treasures had become badly tarnished, and I was charged with the clean-up. We wrote down more than $2 billion to recognize the losses that had been incurred under previous management, and I was able to persuade the government to inject an additional $200 million into each company to get them in shape for eventual sale to the private sector. My sidekick in this clean-up was Bob Brown, an outstanding officer I had brought over from MSED.

By the early 1980s, my planned fifteen-month stint in the public service had stretched to fifteen very productive and stimulating years. The pay was poor by private-sector standards and the hours were incredibly long. In the early years, I had often worked through the night to complete an assignment.

Even when I reached the lofty rank of deputy minister in 1982, during the first six months when I was simultaneously cleaning up the mess at the two aircraft companies while merging two government departments, I often clocked over a hundred hours of work per week, leaving little time for sleep and not much else. But the work was intoxicating and it was particularly thrilling to see on the evening news what one had laboured on during the day.

Throughout these years I had earned a reputation as a manager who could be counted on to deliver results even when this required pushing the bureaucratic machinery faster and farther than it liked. I had been promoted rapidly up the ranks, typically being the youngest person serving at each successive level. This had culminated in my appointment as a "DM" – the top government rank – at the ripe old age of thirty-seven, again the youngest of the current crop. During my three years in that slot I had earned flattering reviews from a succession of ministers. This self-congratulatory account is relevant only in setting the stage for the events that followed, events that profoundly redefined my attitudes towards the Mulroney government and the public service of Canada.

As a public servant, I was strictly non-partisan. I had happily served the governments of four prime ministers from two parties – Mike Pearson, Pierre Trudeau, Joe Clark, and John Turner. Brian Mulroney's victory did not cause me any heartburn. It was time for a period of conservative fiscal management to redress the excesses of the Trudeau era. The old gang had become jaded and new faces were required, particularly from the burgeoning west, which had been so underrepresented in the later Liberal years. Furthermore, Mulroney's election majority had been due in no small part to public revulsion over the patronage excesses of the Trudeau/Turner regime, which the Conservative leader had pledged to reform.

As soon as he took office, Mulroney met with the deputy ministers to underscore these welcome themes. I attended as the associate deputy minister, second-in-command of DRIE. Mulroney said all the right things to the officials. Then, on his way out of the building, Mulroney stopped to tell the press that he had given the bureaucrats their marching orders. They could snap into line or face "pink slips and running shoes." It was not an auspicious start.

The department's senior deputy minister and chief executive, Bill Teschke, was a man of great experience and wisdom. He saw the writing on the wall. Within the year, he took early retirement, and I took over as acting head of the department.

Meanwhile, the senior public service was in turmoil. Some, like Teschke or Treasury Board secretary Jack Manion, had taken early retirement. Others – such as Ed Clark, who went on to head Canada Trustco, and Bob Rabinovitch, deputy minister of communications, who became CEO of Claridge Inc. – were brutally terminated under the most spurious pretexts at the hands of the new cabinet secretary, Gordon Osbaldeston. I shared the anguish of my old friends and associates but I did not feel personally threatened. As the summer of 1985 arrived, I was led to believe I would soon have to choose between promotions, either taking over the department permanently or moving to head one of the central agencies of the government.

At this point, I crossed paths with Michel Cogger, Mulroney's close friend, usher at his wedding, godfather to one of his children, and the head of his Quebec campaign. My first encounter came when my minister, Sinclair Stevens, summoned me to his boardroom to hear Cogger's outrage over the way my staff were stonewalling a project in which he was involved with a Quebec businessman, Guy Montpetit. The details of what ensued became part of the court record in the subsequent trials, and a later stage of the saga was recounted by Stevie Cameron in her bestselling book *On the Take*. Suffice it to say that when I did examine the case, I found that Cogger's allegations were completely unwarranted. The officers in question had behaved according to the highest standards in dealing with a very questionable project. The more closely the proposal was examined, the more unacceptable it became.

Cogger kept up intense pressure – on the minister, his office staff, the department, and me. On numerous occasions I was reminded of Cogger's involvement and his close association with the prime minister and his staff. We stood firm in our recommendation that no government assistance be provided under any circumstance. Cogger and his clients continued to press.

I was not prepared to have my staff scapegoated and insisted on being front and centre for any discussions of the case. It was for this reason that I cut short my summer vacation to return to Ottawa on Friday, August 9, to bolster the minister's resistance to Cogger's demands. Midway through the meeting to discuss the project, I was summoned to meet with the cabinet secretary, my long-time friend and mentor, Gordon Osbaldeston, at 2:30 P.M. This was the usual prelude to a shuffle, as the cabinet secretary meets with the appointees to offer them their new jobs. My only uncertainty was whether I would be offered a choice of the two jobs suggested, or, as sometimes happened, simply given my new assignment.

Osbaldeston advised me that it had been decided that I would not remain in charge of running the Department of Regional Industrial Expansion. I asked what job I was being offered. There was no offer as such, Osbaldeston told me, but it was possible something could be found. I was dumbfounded. I asked Osbaldeston, whom I had regarded almost as a father since my own dad had been crippled by ill health, if he could shed any light on this decision. His answer was that I had been judged to be unreliable. I can now understand that he was simply carrying out orders, but at the time it came as a terrible blow from a man I had trusted and admired during the decade we had worked together.[1]

I recognized that this was clearly the end of my public service career. What form of severance settlement was I being offered? Osbaldeston appeared genuinely taken aback. Finally he mumbled that he thought he might get approval to offer me as much as six months' pay in lieu of severance, recognizing my record. This in the face of a string of outstanding and superior performance appraisals, many signed by him, over seventeen years of rapid rise through the ranks of the public service.

I will not hide the fact that I was absolutely devastated. My initial reaction was self-doubt: perhaps Osbaldeston was right and I had failed as a manager. I put the question to a man I respected and could trust to give me a straight answer, Bill Teschke. He was utterly flabbergasted at the news. He consulted with the other top deputy ministers in the system who all, without exception, professed to share his astonishment. They had expected me to be promoted, not fired.

My feelings are hard to describe. The toughest step was telling my wife and children. Marrying Marg was unquestionably the smartest thing I have

---

1. Years later, when the RCMP were assembling evidence against Cogger, they interviewed me at some length. I was then out of the government. Cogger had been named a senator by his old friend Mulroney. The RCMP had heard widespread rumours that I had been removed because I had stood in Cogger's way. Indeed, the careers of virtually every public servant who had touched the file had subsequently come to a dead halt or an abrupt end. I was not able to help them very much. I could not say with certainty that my dismissal from the deputy's post had been anything more than a coincidence. I had been told, by a close friend of Cogger's, that he had boasted that he had personally removed my name from the list of deputy-ministerial appointments that had been submitted by the cabinet secretary to the PM. This could have been simply grandstanding, for all I knew. As for others who might shed some light on the matter, I recognized that it would not be in their interest to cross the Mulroney government simply to set the record straight. My scepticism proved well founded. When charges of influence peddling were brought against Cogger, the case backfired. Cogger turned the tables on the force, accusing the RCMP of waging a vendetta against him, thereby putting them on the defensive. In an extraordinary trial in which the Crown agreed not to present any oral testimony, Cogger was acquitted by a Quebec Court judge. The case was appealed to the Supreme Court of Canada, which in the summer of 1997 ordered a new trial.

done in my life, but never was this more apparent than at that moment. She did not utter a word of complaint or bitterness, even as our tidy little world seemed to be crashing down on our heads. She immediately turned to the business of getting on with our lives.

Our daughter, Jillian, as a young teenager, faced leaving the friends she had known since kindergarten. Through her tears, she constantly reassured me that she knew it was not my fault. "It will be all right, Dad," she told me.

Perhaps the worst was our young son, Martin, whose only comment was: "Does that mean we'll be seeing more of you, please, Dad?" I realized at that point just how badly I had neglected my own family in the service of a government that clearly believed that loyalty was a one-way street.

I was very calm at my final meeting with Osbaldeston on the following Monday, twenty-four hours before the scheduled announcement of the change. His own days were numbered. Indeed, his successor as secretary to the cabinet had been chosen, in the person of Paul Tellier, who had taken over the secretary's prestigious office in the Langevin Block just above the prime minister's own suite. Osbaldeston had been shunted into a cramped little office in another building with his loyal long-time secretary, a few filing cabinets, and a kettle for boiling tea. As prearranged, he offered and I accepted the offer of a transitional assignment in Toronto on the clear understanding that I would not return to the public service in Ottawa. We have not talked since that meeting.

After my departure, my former minister, Sinclair Stevens, was ultimately forced to resign when a judicial inquiry found he had repeatedly been in blatant conflict of interest. I took some satisfaction that the judge gave the department a stamp of approval for the way it had operated under my stewardship. Stevens's successor was also forced to leave office over charges of conflict of interest. The junior minister for small business, André Bissonnette, was forced to resign to face charges of taking a bribe, only to be acquitted when a jury in his hometown accepted his argument and jailed his campaign manager instead. Again, no blame was attached to the department.

As for me, one month after my surprise chat with Osbaldeston, my family and I were unloading our possessions at our new house in Toronto. We expected to make that city our home for the foreseeable future. I planned to leave the government as soon as matters could be arranged. I had no regrets about my eighteen years as a civil servant but had no wish ever to return. Osbaldeston had stripped away any illusions I may have had about the public service.

3

Opening Skirmishes

I soon settled into my new assignment as the federal economic development coordinator for Ontario. My office at the top of the tower at First Canadian Place had a magnificent view over Toronto's harbour. The job itself was the next best thing to a foreign posting: instead of 2,500 staff across the country, I had a total of ten employees, none of whom required much direction; instead of the long hours I had given to my previous job, it was now possible to take a leisurely trip downtown in time for a few hours of networking, centring on a pleasant lunch and followed by a swim in the pool atop an adjoining office tower. My evenings and weekends were my own.

The break with Ottawa was not complete. I still followed developments from a distance. One of Pierre Trudeau's legacies was a royal commission that had spent the past few years studying development prospects for Canada under the chairmanship of former Liberal finance minister Donald Macdonald. In a curious historical echo of the Royal Commission on Canada's Economic Prospects, chaired by Walter Gordon, on much the same subject more than a quarter-century earlier, the Macdonald Commission's report was ultimately submitted to the subsequent Conservative government. At the beginning of September 1985, the final report confirmed Macdonald's earlier hints that the keystone of the commission's findings was that Canada should negotiate a free trade agreement with the United States. This added substantial bipartisan credibility to the initiative. Less noted was the commission's call for a comprehensive program of adjustment assistance for displaced workers.

On September 26, the prime minister tabled in Parliament an insipid report from Trade Minister Kelleher and announced that he proposed to follow it up with the Americans. At the beginning of October, he wrote formally to President Reagan to propose "the broadest possible package of mutually beneficial reductions in barriers to trade in goods and services," and in the next day's mail the president's response welcomed the Canadian proposal.

I was an interested but detached observer of these developments. Occasionally my work would take me to Ottawa to meet with one or more of my former deputy-ministerial colleagues. These visits also gave me the chance to spend some time with my parents, who had retired to a pleasant bungalow in the Alta Vista area of Ottawa, near the hospital complex. They maintained an incredible network of friends and continued to lead an active social life.

One evening in early November, I joined them for dinner with some friends. The group included a number of former mandarins, led by Gordon Robertson, the long-serving secretary to the cabinet under Pearson and Trudeau; Simon Reisman, former deputy minister of finance; and Reisman's business associate Jim Grandy, former deputy minister of industry, trade, and commerce. Simon had some intriguing news. He had been asked by Prime Minister Mulroney to sketch out a possible Canadian position for free trade negotiations with the United States. Simon hinted that the prime minister was considering calling him out of retirement to head up the Canadian team.

His friends knew that Reisman yearned to be back in the centre of the action, especially at the table of the biggest game in town. Our enthusiasm was tempered only by concern that the rules had changed in the decade since Simon had last roamed the upper levels of government. But Simon was so obviously interested in taking on the challenge that we all joined in hoping that he would get the opportunity. On my return to Toronto, I mentioned the incident to Marg but thought no more about it.

Simon Reisman is probably the public servant whom the public believe they know best. Curiously, his public image conceals a very different private personality. I have known Simon for forty years — as a family friend, as a top government official, as a private consultant, and finally as the chief trade negotiator. He is unquestionably one of the most powerful and explosive personalities I have ever encountered. He is not a big man but he has the physical presence of a pugnacious street brawler, ready to drop his gloves and fight for what he believes in on a moment's notice. He was feared by many, respected by most, and admired by those who were drawn to his charisma.

The Ritchies, Reismans, and Grandys briefly shared ownership of a parcel of land in the Gatineau Hills outside Ottawa. As a teenager, I was delighted on one occasion when Simon invited me to drive back to town with him in his spanking-new, gleaming white Thunderbird. Our trip was interrupted by the wail of police sirens as a Quebec Provincial Police patrol pulled us over for speeding. Simon was furious. He turned to me to back his story: "How fast was I going?" he demanded. I answered, truthfully, that I had no idea. This did not help matters and the confrontation threatened to get nasty. Finally Simon accepted the ticket and we drove home slowly. When he could bring himself to speak, his only observation was: "You are either the most honest kid I have ever met, or the stupidest."

Simon's outstanding government career is well recorded. The scrappy Jewish kid from Montreal served with distinction in the Canadian artillery in the war. He subsequently enjoyed a meteoric rise up the ranks of the Finance Department. His first love was international trade, beginning with his role in the Canadian delegation to the original GATT meetings in 1947. In the mid-1950s, he did a stint with the Gordon Commission, where he contributed two seminal studies of Canadian trade policies and export performance. When the Industry Department was formed, in 1964, Simon became its first deputy minister. He was the principal negotiator of the Canada-US auto agreement that had such a fundamental impact on the development of the Canadian industrial heartland. From Industry, Simon moved on to head up the Treasury Board, the management agency of government, in 1968. He then returned to Finance as its deputy minister for the first half of the 1970s.

In retrospect, it is clear that during this critical period the government gravy train ran completely off the rails, as the welfare state, so successfully constructed since the war, became overloaded with ever more ingenious if unproductive ways to spend public monies. Simon saw himself as Horatius at the bridge, fighting a desperate rearguard action to keep the spenders from running completely amok. But Horatius could not hold the line for ever. There is only so much a deputy minister of finance, even one possessed of Simon's remarkable persuasive powers, can achieve in the absence of support from his minister, John Turner, or the prime minister himself. Simon's victories were, in a sense, Pyrrhic, insofar as they gave additional ammunition to his enemies.

In 1975, when the Trudeau government offered a generous early retirement program to the top public servants, ostensibly to bring new blood into the senior ranks, it expected to have few takers. Simon and Jim Grandy led the charge, took the offer, and headed for the private sector, where they were an instant success.

After some years and a great deal of money as a consultant, it was obvious to his friends that Simon was getting bored. His beloved recreations, playing poker and fishing salmon, were somehow not quite enough to fill the void. He had dabbled in public policy issues in a review of the auto industry in 1978 and as a successful negotiator of land claims in the Western Arctic in the early 1980s. He and Grandy had advised John Turner during his brief prime ministership, but that game ended when the Tories came to power.

On Friday, November 8, 1985, I lunched with an old friend, Andy Kniewasser, president of the Investment Dealers' Association of Canada, at the National Club in Toronto. I was a few minutes late, having just signed the agreement to sell our Ottawa house, which had been sitting empty for four months. Kniewasser broke the news of Simon's appointment, which had come across the newswire a few minutes before. I was delighted for him. On my return to my office, there were three telephone messages from Simon, and two from Marg to say that Simon had called at home in increasing impatience to get hold of me. I was very much afraid that I knew only too well what Simon had in mind.

Simon invited me to join him in the most important trade negotiation in Canada's history. I declined his offer. After all, with the sale of our house we had just cut our last ties with the capital. He was dismayed and disappointed. He asked me to be available to give him advice and I did supply him with a list of top performers he should recruit. Simon largely took my suggestions and began assembling an outstanding team of the best talent Ottawa could muster.

There remained, however, the problem of his chief lieutenant – or lieutenants, as Simon originally envisaged two deputies to support him. Simon's list included some of the most successful of my peers – Gérard Veilleux, Derek Burney, and Gerry Shannon – individuals who may have seen themselves as more likely candidates for the top job, not the second-in-command.

Veilleux had worked with Simon in Finance some years before. He had joined the deputy-ministerial ranks on the same day I did in 1982. He had now become a senior deputy minister in his own right. He was prepared to run the show but not to play second fiddle to his old boss. (He moved instead to the Treasury Board secretariat before taking on the presidency of the Canadian Broadcasting Corporation.)

Burney, my first choice, had been instrumental in launching the negotiations but had no wish to leave his perch in External Affairs. As it turned out, he played a key role in free trade, first as the prime minister's chief of staff and then as Canada's ambassador to the United States.

Shannon, an assistant deputy minister in the Finance Department, skilfully prolonged negotiations with Simon as a way to increase his bargaining leverage in getting the job he really wanted. He became deputy minister for international trade, then was posted to Geneva as our GATT ambassador for the closing negotiations on the World Trade Organization.

I could understand their decisions. I knew Simon was not the easiest of chief executives, particularly for those who had become accustomed to running their own shows. On the other hand, I felt that one could put up with a lot from someone with Simon's extraordinary talents.

As the pressures mounted, Simon prevailed on me to contribute, part-time, to formulating the basic negotiating strategy. A meeting in February 1986 was the occasion to bring the team together to review the approach. It was held at the Château Montebello. I knew the place well, having stayed there frequently both on business and on pleasure. The extraordinary structure, built of enormous logs, had been spruced up for the summit meeting of the leaders of the Group of Seven five years before. I went there determined that this would be my swan song.

The team assembled at Montebello included the key people already appointed to the Trade Negotiations Office and a handful of outsiders including me. I found the substantive discussions thrilling, as Simon drew on his unparalleled experience to lay out his sense of the agenda for the negotiations. There were doubters and detractors, and they had every opportunity to make their case. By the close of the session, however, it was clear that Simon had a vision that I shared of increasing Canadian prosperity through a revolutionary free trade agreement.

It was also clear that Simon need a strong collaborator to complement his leadership. He applied his persuasive powers to recruit me as his second-in-command, but I held firm. Finally, out came the secret weapon: Simon's wife, Connie Reisman, insisted the two of us go for a walk around the Château despite a freezing drizzle that coated the pathways, and us, with ice. To their friends, Connie is known as the real powerhouse in the Reisman family. As we got colder and wetter, Connie pressed me to change my mind, arguing that I was the only person who combined a real affection for Simon with the toughness to stand up to him. Compared with Connie, Simon was a pushover. She was prepared to walk all night in the freezing rain.

I surrendered to the inevitable. I could not resist the opportunity to be present at the creation of a new economic relationship. I agreed, in principle, to join Simon's team as its chief operating officer, ambassador, and deputy chief trade negotiator for Canada. On my return to Toronto, my wife could barely suppress her dismay. We decided that I would commute to Ottawa until the end of the school year, when we would again pick up stakes and move. So much for my resolution never again to put the public service ahead of my family.

There followed an extraordinary two and a half years of collaboration. For the first eighteen months, Simon and I were practically inseparable. We shared a ride to the office in the morning and home at night. During the days – often running into the wee hours – we worked as a remarkably complementary team. I ran the back office while Simon was very much at the front. I was his sounding board as he agonized through every aspect of the negotiations. I supervised the production of the ammunition that he fired to great effect, at the negotiating table or in the media. I handled the parts he found boring or distasteful – keeping ministers and their deputies informed, consulting with the business community, running the affairs of the office itself – freeing him to focus on the critical high-profile matters.

Our negotiating styles were also highly complementary. Simon is an avid poker player, who wins more than his share of pots by combining shrewd assessment of his opponents with a flair for running a bluff. My game is chess, where flashy tactics are rarely a substitute for sound strategy and the objective reality of the board limits the scope for psychological gambits. Simon could put his energies into persuading his American counterpart while I tried to plan our next moves.

Later, under circumstances I will describe, Simon's attitude towards our relationship apparently changed. Mine did not. It was an extraordinary honour and privilege to work closely with one of the most dedicated and influential public servants in the long history of outstanding government service in Canada.

Once I accepted Simon's offer to serve as chief operating officer of the trade negotiations team, two things became quickly apparent. First, Simon had a much more ambitious view of the negotiations than anyone in the bureaucracy could have contemplated. Not for him a "trade enhancement agreement" to tinker with the existing relationship. To him, "free trade" meant just that, the elimination of all barriers to two-way trade between Canada and the United States. He believed he had the prime minister's blessing for this radical objective, and that was sufficient to quiet the sceptics for the present. This enormously heightened the appeal of working on the negotiations. If successful, free trade with the United States would quite simply be the most important policy commitment Canada made for the decade if not beyond.

Second, the government apparatus had been transformed during the decade since Simon had left, and he was having great difficulty in adjusting to the changed environment. There were new rules of the game, and new players holding the cards. Simon's instincts were to plough ahead, bulldozing any resistance in his path. For a short while, this tactic would produce results, but over the life of a project of this magnitude, it could prove self-defeating. The central agencies, the other departments, the provincial governments, and the business community all played quite a different role from the good old days. To survive, Simon needed all the help he could get from his friends. He would not lack for enemies.

For the next six months, I commuted to Ottawa for up to four days a week. I delegated most of my Toronto responsibilities to the able senior staff in my office while I played absentee landlord. In Ottawa, the trade team was lodged in the Jackson Building, built in the 1950s, if memory serves, on the site at the corner of Bank and Slater Streets where a natural gas explosion had levelled the previous tenants. Ironically, these were the same facilities we had used when I had set up the Ministry of State for Economic Development seven years before – except that Simon now occupied my old corner office while I wedged myself into a tiny space down the hall that had previously contained my administrative assistant. I was perfectly content to have the full-time staff take the more presentable offices, while I played *éminence grise* from my cubbyhole.

The first priority was to fill out the organization. As I had warned Simon from the outset, the prime minister may have promised Reisman his pick of anyone he chose from the public service. We had been given the same promise when we set up the MSED. In practice, getting good people would be extremely difficult: if they were ready and keen to come, it would be like pulling teeth to convince their home departments they could be spared; if they were not, we would have to do without them. So it proved.

Despite this, we were remarkably successful in attracting a first-rate team, although Simon and I both had to use up a lot of favours to get the people we wanted. We set up the Trade Negotiations Office, or TNO as it came to be called, as a very flat structure. Sylvia Ostry, the brilliant former deputy minister of international trade, was responsible for the GATT negotiations and went to some pains to keep her distance from Simon. The other officers reported to me and through me to Simon.

There was some initial resistance, as Simon had sold some of the recruits, including a few of the junior officers, on the idea that they would be working directly with him. This led to instances of understandable pique as a number of ambitious officers found they were not members of the core group and thus not directly party to the negotiations. We had no shortage of would-be generals. What we needed was front-line troops.

The core group comprised the senior officers reporting directly to me. After some reshuffling and reassignment, the team settled down to the following key players. Germain Denis, a highly experienced GATT negotiator (he had succeeded me as head of the GATT division more than a decade before), was ultimately entrusted with the crucial responsibility for the whole range of issues related to market access, the traditional centrepiece of the negotiations. Alan Nymark, an old Privy Council hand who had served as a key staffer with the Macdonald Commission, now took charge of economic analysis and federal-provincial relations, an extremely delicate facet of the project. Charles Stedman, formerly head of the automotive branch in DRIE, was responsible for sectoral analysis and relations with business through an unprecedented array of consultative committees that proved indispensable. Andrei Sulzenko began as Simon's chief of staff (they had collaborated some years earlier in a review of the automotive industry) and ultimately was responsible for the issues of investment and trade in services, two new areas of negotiation.

Rounding out the team was the general counsel to the TNO, in charge of the intricate legal aspects of the negotiation. The original appointee was recalled by the Justice Department to take on a more senior job before he had the opportunity to make much contribution. His successor realized within a few weeks that he was in over his head. At that point, the deputy minister of justice, Frank Iacobucci, dropped into my office to ask me to agree to the appointment of Konrad von Finckenstein. I did my best to conceal my delight. Konrad had served as general counsel to DRIE, where he had done a brilliant job on some of the most complex industrial negotiations the country had ever seen. Unfortunately, the current deputy minister had an aversion to strong subordinates and wanted him to move out of the department. His loss was my gain. I agreed to Frank's request. After I ushered him out, I returned to my office and let out a whoop of glee.

By the time I joined the TNO, Simon had already established a public relations unit reporting directly to him. It was headed by Bruce Macdonald, a highly experienced former journalist who worked to cultivate Simon's image and get his message across. Inevitably, Simon came under attack for having appointed a team composed overwhelmingly of anglophone men. Sylvia was the only woman in the top ranks. Germain was the only francophone. Regrettably, Bruce responded that we had selected the best talent available. This was taken to imply that there were no other capable women or francophones, an unpardonable sin in this age of political correctness. Under fire, Bruce dug himself in deeper. Eventually, Simon felt he had no alternative but to cut Bruce loose. I was not consulted in that decision – after all, Bruce had been hired by, and reported to, Simon, not me – but I was very concerned about the tokenism involved.

There followed a bizarre saga of the worst form of discrimination, all under the banner of political correctitude. At an early press conference, I gave the press a detailed background briefing on the issues of the negotiation. The reporters' questions focused instead on the head count. In fact, at that point two of the five senior officers were francophones – Denis and the original general counsel. Anticipating trouble, however, Simon had authorized me to announce the appointment of yet another francophone. He had interviewed an officer from the Finance Department, and had agreed to appoint him despite reservations about his capabilities. To my great embarrassment, this individual subsequently denied having reached any agreement with Simon. I raised the matter with the secretary to the cabinet, only to be warned that the man was related to a senior member of the PM's staff and therefore untouchable. Sure enough, in the next round of senior appointments, this person was named deputy minister of another department.

Meanwhile, unbeknownst to me, my own appointment was stirring up waves. The original agreement had been clear and unambiguous: at the outset Simon would be chairman and I would be deputy chairman of a fictitious "preparatory committee"; once the Americans had been given the green light from Congress, Simon would become chief trade negotiator and I, deputy chief trade negotiator for Canada. The first stage was no problem, but once the US Senate Finance Committee approved the launch of the American side of the negotiations in April 1986, it was our turn to make our team official. A few days later, the order-in-council arrived appointing Simon as chief negotiator as planned. After some days went by, our administrator followed up with the Privy Council Office to track down the parallel order for my appointment. He reported to me with puzzlement that there was some sort of hold-up. Not to worry, I told him, and got on with business.

It must have been close to two months later that the issue surfaced again. It turned out that the problem was that some ministers were blocking my designation, not on its merits – there was apparently no question of my suitability for the assignment and my former minister, Stevens, was particularly enthusiastic – but in order to force the appointment of a high-profile Québécois as either another deputy chief or, as some would have it, as the associate chief trade negotiator. (I later learned that I was not the only victim of this tactic, which also resulted in a lengthy delay in the appointment of the deputy governor – later governor – of the Bank of Canada, Gordon Thiessen.)

Having been burned twice already on the francophone question, Simon was uncharacteristically timid on this occasion. Instead of insisting on his right to have whomever he chose as the key operating head of the organization, he tried to defuse the issue. With some bravado, I assured him that he need not worry about his commitment to me. So far, this nonsense had not impaired my ability to get the job done. If these characters could help us find someone capable to add to the team, I would be all in favour.

Who did they have in mind? Simon and I put the question to the powers-that-be in the Langevin Block. Incredibly, the first name that came back was Jacques Parizeau. This was an extraordinary revelation of the degree to which the top ranks of the Quebec wing of the federal Conservative cabinet had been captured by separatists, and not run-of-the-mill but "pur et dur" hard-liners. I had known Parizeau for years and enjoyed the play of his fertile mind, and I might have relished working with him on a professional basis. But I also recalled that he was a committed separatist who had served as René Lévesque's finance minister in the Parti Québécois government until quitting on the grounds that the party was going soft on the independence issue. The suggestion was dropped a few days later when Parizeau announced that he would be a candidate for the PQ leadership on the resignation of Pierre-Marc Johnson.

Other names were suggested, equally bizarre. Some were capable but otherwise fully occupied. Others were not remotely competent. It was explained that there was no intention that the appointee would actually play a significant role in the negotiations. It was all strictly for public consumption. I was appalled at the sheer, demeaning tokenism in these proposals.

Finally, I had had enough. Simon had made clear that while he was unhappy with the situation, he was not prepared to weigh in to help resolve it. He seemed to believe that he had enough problems. It was left to me to straighten out. If I had not already sold our house in Toronto, my first choice would have been to chuck the whole business and return to my original plan.

Before taking that step, I sat down with Paul Tellier, the cabinet secretary. I have found the perfect candidate, I told him. He is highly regarded by the professionals in the trade field. He knows Ottawa like the back of his hand, having spent more time there than in Quebec City. He is fluently bilingual. Best of all, he is available right now, but not for much longer.

Paul took the bait. "That is wonderful news. Let's get him. Who is he?" he asked.

"You're looking at him," I replied. "But if this does not get fixed immediately, you won't be looking at him any longer."

Message received and understood. A few days later, the order-in-council came through, designating me as Canada's ambassador (trade negotiations) and deputy chief trade negotiator for Canada. It was dated April 16, 1986.

Ironically, I then made history as the first deputy minister to be called before a parliamentary committee with the mandate to review his appointment. This was one of the more bizarre imports from the American system, under which the appropriate Senate committee solemnly passes on the nominations the president proposes to fill key posts, including cabinet secretaries and deputy secretaries and certain ambassadors. There, it makes some sense, given that the separation of powers means that the Congress may be quite independent of the president, and virtually all the candidates for appointment come from outside the career civil service. In Canada, of course, the opposite is true: the prime minister's parliamentary majority controls the House of Commons, and almost all deputy-ministerial and ambassadorial appointments come from within the public service. As the first guinea pig, I could obviously not give my personal views on current policies without divulging the confidential advice I gave my ministers, including some who now sat in opposition. Not that it mattered. The opposition members were much more interested in attacking the government than in attacking me personally. For that matter, the prime minister was under absolutely no obligation to be bound by the views of the parliamentary committee. The exercise was a sham and the practice was later, mercifully, dropped for all but special cases.

The Americans were having their own problems. President Reagan and Prime Minister Mulroney had formally agreed in September of 1985 to launch the actual negotiations. In Canada, that was enough to give us the green light to proceed. But in the United States, the Congress jealously guards what it considers its prerogative over international trade and commerce. It is prepared to delegate the negotiation of agreements to the administration, but they have no effect unless and until they are approved by Capitol Hill, home to the US Senate and House of Representatives.

The most formal instrument is a treaty ratified by a two-thirds majority of the Senate. This is an extraordinarily difficult process, reserved for the most critical matters. Even then, the record is not encouraging: treaties on everything from fish to the limitation of strategic weapons have failed to pass the test. Appeals to the national interest do not get very far. The American political process gives priority to local political interests. Thus senators revel in attaching their pet projects to any legislative proposal, including treaty ratification, like lights on a Christmas tree. Others have to be bribed to support the administration's proposals by the promise of dams or bridges or roads or other good works in their region. The process is quite shameless and the coin of bargaining is votes. It is therefore a game that foreign powers – without an American domestic constituency – have learned to avoid like the plague.

The alternative has been given the misnomer of the "fast track" for trade agreements. In essence, the Congress delegates its authority to permit the administration to conduct negotiations, but only within the parameters set by the Congress and subject to congressional approval. In return, if the administration meets these conditions, the legislation to give effect to this executive agreement will be put on a fast track through the legislature, which will be limited to voting approval or rejection, without amendments. This path had been followed successfully by the administration in the case of a very modest so-called free trade agreement with Israel, which enjoyed, however, a very powerful supporting constituency among American Jews.

The plan was to conduct the negotiations with Canada on the same basis. We were assured by our ambassador in Washington, Allan Gotlieb, and theirs in Ottawa, Tom Niles, that no problems were expected. Then came panic. When the proposal went to the powerful Finance Committee of the Senate, a widely publicized straw poll indicated that the majority were opposed.

It was obvious that the administration was completely taken by surprise. Their immediate reaction was to ask us to agree to negotiate even if they did not obtain fast-track authority. Simon and I were appalled and categorically rejected the suggestion. We could not agree to a lengthy negotiation with the administration only to then find ourselves plunged into what would amount to another set of negotiations to get the approval of individual senators and congressmen. That way lay madness.

It soon became apparent that we had been caught up in a power play. Capitol Hill was determined to remind the other end of Pennsylvania Avenue where the real strength lay. The administration had to promise to pay close attention to the Congress in trade matters and to be guided by a lengthy resolution from Senator Bob Dole, stipulating American objectives in the negotiations with Canada. More to the point, we suspected – and it was later confirmed – that a side deal was made with several of the key senators, including the Finance Committee chairman, Bob Packwood, to "fix" the problem of Canadian lumber – a long-running issue that will be reviewed in a later chapter. I took a detached view of all these shenanigans: it was up to the Americans to decide whether they were really prepared to negotiate a serious agreement with Canada; if not, we had better know now, not six months down the road. But having been caught with his striped pants down, our ambassador made a great show of blanketing the Hill with his persuasive lobbying to convince the senators to allow the negotiations to proceed.

Finally, the Senate committee grudgingly gave its approval. To be exact, by a 10-to-10 tie vote, it failed to disapprove of the negotiations going forward. On a later visit to Ottawa, the Finance Committee's new chairman, Senator Lloyd Bentsen, allowed as how it could have just as easily been 11-to-9 or even 12-to-8. The Congress was sending a message to the White House. Free trade was simply a pawn in this Washington power game.

While Clayton Yeutter, as US special trade representative, would have overall responsibility for the portfolio, he clearly needed an expert to conduct the real work of the negotiations – the American counterpart to Simon Reisman. There were a number of possibilities. The deputy STR was a self-proclaimed tough *hombre* named Mike Smith. As Bill Brock's right-hand man, he had played a role in getting the process started. He was, however, suspected of having been too close to Brock, who was loathed by the right wing of the Republican Party. He also made clear that he was much too important to spend much of his time on the negotiations with Canada, which were, after all, only small change in the trade policy interests of the United States as seen by the Office of the STR.

One option would be to bring in someone with high profile from the outside. This option was reportedly strongly favoured by Secretary of State George Shultz, who proclaimed that these negotiations were the most important foreign policy initiative of the Reagan administration. One outsider whose name was prominently mentioned was Julius (Jules) Katz, an old trade hand turned Washington lobbyist. Katz had been a fixture in the State

Department from the 1950s through the '70s. He had been involved in the original Auto Pact and in other big and small negotiations with Canada. He knew Simon well and there was a measure of mutual respect. It would have been a financial sacrifice for him to take the job, as he had carved out a highly successful business career as a Washington consultant. In the event, we were later told the position was never offered.

Instead, Yeutter settled on a more junior officer who was likely to be much easier to control. Peter Murphy was a tall, gangling redhead a quarter-century Simon's junior. A Rhode Islander, Murphy had been a protégé of Mike Smith, first as a negotiator of textile agreements and then as ambassador to the GATT during the long waiting period between major negotiations. In Geneva, he had suffered a serious brain hemorrhage and had been required to take a prolonged leave of absence. This period had taken a heavy toll on him and his young family. Now he was ready for action again. But was he ready for a negotiation of this scale and complexity and monumental political importance?

I had never met or even heard of Murphy before his nomination. Our man in Geneva, Murphy's counterpart there, reported favourably on his abilities, but the GATT forum was a diplomatic conclave, a far cry from the comprehensive trade negotiation we now faced. Shortly thereafter, under the cover of my job in Toronto, I attended a briefing session for Canadian business leaders in Washington. Murphy gave a luncheon speech. Afterwards, the chairman of the meeting, my long-time friend Mickey Cohen, who knew I was advising Reisman, took me aside. "This guy is real trouble," he said. "He is closed up tight as a drum." I very much respected Mickey's judgment but tried to pooh-pooh the concerns by speculating that Peter was very much finding his way through a minefield and had every reason to be cautious. But I sensed trouble ahead: Simon tended to be overpowering, even for the most self-confident of his associates; Peter was already a monument to insecurity.

The differences in approach were striking. In Canada, Prime Minister Mulroney had staked his government's future on the success of these negotiations and put our best team on the field under the leadership of a significant public figure in Simon Reisman. In the United States, President Reagan had replaced the leading promoter of the negotiations, Bill Brock, with a light-weight who had in turn named a relative non-entity to head a non-existent negotiating team. It is a telling commentary on the power of wishful thinking that the Canadians, myself included, refused to draw the obvious conclusions: the Americans were clearly not prepared to put much into these negotiations.

On April 10, 1986, Simon and I travelled to Washington to confer with the Americans, and the two chief protagonists met face to face for the first time. Simon's immediate instinct was to attempt to bond with his counterpart, Murphy, to pave the way for a successful negotiation. This had always been his operating style. I was less enthusiastic. I was not convinced that Murphy had the clout to pull off a deal of this magnitude within the administration or, much more important, on Capitol Hill. It would be a bad strategic move at the outset for Simon to allow himself to be twinned with Peter unless and until the latter had proved he could deliver. Simon's more practical view was that he would dance with whomever the other side designated. He did agree that we would initially meet with both Murphy and his boss, Yeutter.

We got together in Yeutter's office in the Winder Building, home to the US special trade representative. This unprepossessing edifice sits across 17th Street from the imposing Executive Office Building, with its baroque design. Yeutter's own office was modest and dimly lit. We sat in a circle sipping coffee and feeling one another out. As we had discussed, Simon put on the table a very simple objective: to eliminate all tariffs between us before the year 2000. Yeutter responded enthusiastically to this suggestion but I noted that Murphy kept his counsel very much to himself.

Subsequently, when we met with Murphy alone in his cramped office up under the eaves of the Winder Building, he went right to what he saw as the heart of the negotiations: the rules of origin to govern customs procedures. These are highly technical regulations that define exactly the circumstances under which various products qualify for a given tariff treatment. Simon's jaw literally dropped. Ultimately, these matters would have to dealt with, but they were hardly an appropriate starting point for a great negotiation. More appropriate, perhaps, to a textile negotiation, where enormous time and effort is spent determining the conditions under which a few shirts will be permitted into the country. The contrast could not have been more stark between Simon's grand vision of continental free trade and Peter's preoccupation with these technicalities. The meetings were very cordial but we were shaking our heads as we headed back to Ottawa on a crowded Eastern Airlines flight.

The first meeting of the two negotiating teams took place on May 21 in the boardroom of the Trade Negotiations Office in Ottawa. We had moved from our cramped quarters in the Jackson Building to take over the entire top floor of the new tower in the Metropolitan Life Building on O'Connor Street. The interior design had been supervised by Connie Reisman herself, and the results were first-class, bordering on opulent. The negotiating room adjoined Simon's own impressive corner office, which looked out over Parliament Hill. The elegant table was custom-built of light walnut and formed an elongated oval. For the occasion, the full team was marshalled, including Sylvia Ostry, who put in a rare appearance. The television cameras rolled for the launch that made headline news in Canada. The atmosphere on the Canadian side was euphoric – the great adventure was finally under way. Our American counterparts seemed quite bewildered by all the media fuss.

Simon was determined to begin by putting the negotiations in their proper context. The centrepiece of his introduction amounted to a full-blown lecture on the Canadian economy and its relation to its giant southern neighbour. This was prepared by Alan Nymark, who drew upon the tremendous experience he had gained with the Macdonald Commission. Simon had personally pored over the presentation with great care, injecting his experience going back to the earlier Gordon Commission. The intention was to set the stage for recognition of the dramatic significance of the negotiations and, specifically, the need for the smaller economy to be given more time to make the adjustment. For example, Canada might phase out its import tariffs over ten years to the American five.

Reisman and Nymark put their hearts and souls into this exposition. I regretted at the time that the television cameras were no longer present. It would have been an education and a source of pride for Canadian viewers. The Americans soon made it clear that they were bored silly. They had not come to Canada to be subjected to an academic treatise, let alone special pleading for favourable treatment.

The discussion then moved to the organization of the negotiations. We quickly agreed that the bulk of the technical discussion would be delegated to working groups once we had settled on an overall agenda. The broader questions and the most difficult issues would be managed by a much smaller meeting of the top brass. On the Canadian side, this comprised Simon, me, and our assistant chief negotiators – Denis for the policy issues, Nymark for the provincial angles, Stedman for specific industry issues, Sulzenko for the service industries. Von Finckenstein was later added to this core group. We pointedly did not include anyone from outside the TNO – no one from the provincial governments nor even other federal departments or agencies. On the American side, Murphy was flanked by his deputy, Bill Merkin, and the lead representatives of the key US departments – State, Commerce, Treasury – plus, as required, such sectoral departments as Agriculture. This would mean that the inner secrets of the negotiations would be restricted to a handful of the most senior staff on either side.

After this general order of march had been established, Simon put Peter and the rest of us on notice that, in his experience, we should not expect that a negotiation of this complexity could necessarily be completed without the direct participation of our political masters. At some point, he predicted, senior ministers and secretaries would have to be brought in or even, possibly, the prime minister and the president. This was a useful cautionary note although it seemed a little premature at that first meeting.

The final item on the agenda produced the first real confrontation. At their summit meeting in Quebec City, the prime minister and the president had agreed to a standstill on new protectionist actions while the discussions were ongoing. This is standard procedure to ensure that one party does not shift the goalposts while the game is under way. At our first meeting in Ottawa, we recalled this commitment and suggested that both sides should reaffirm their undertakings to behave themselves.

We had taken steps to live up to this agreement. Within the Canadian government, we were consulted on any initiative that might have an impact on the negotiations. Generally, we would counsel prudence. This was not the time to act unfriendly with our partner.

Peter seemed to have difficulty in understanding the concept and was not prepared to agree to reaffirm his president's solemn undertaking. The reason soon became apparent. As our first negotiating session drew to a close, Peter took Simon and me aside and mumbled something to the effect that he was working to prevent an announcement that we would not like. Pressed, he said something about cedar shakes and shingles.

No sooner had the meeting ended than we got word from Washington that the president was slapping a punitive 35-percent tariff on these imports. Murphy's representations, if any, had obviously not been sufficient to offset the domestic political considerations that had been decisive for the White House. The prime minister naturally felt betrayed. In the House of Commons he observed that "actions like this make it difficult for anyone, including Canada, to be friends with the Americans." In private, he wrote the president to remind him that this kind of action was "pure protectionism, the precise thing you and I pledged, in Québec and Washington, we would seek to avoid." We later learned that the American ambassador in Ottawa had reassured his Washington contacts that this was the usual bluster, not to be taken seriously.

I was getting a sinking feeling that our passion for free trade was not shared. Despite the president's bold declarations, the American authorities were now acting as if they were being asked to do Canada a great favour, for which they would expect to be paid in hard coin. The American behaviour was much too systemic to be simply a cunning negotiating ploy. The effect was much the same. We fully expected to gain a great deal from free trade, but so would they. If they did not understand that, the negotiations were doomed – the only possible deal with the Americans would be so one-sided that Canada could not agree. They could still come to their senses but, in the interim, time was wasting.

4

TO THE BRINK

After that rocky start, the negotiations began in earnest in the spring of 1986. Expectations in Canada had been raised to a fever pitch. The opposition was in full cry. Whenever there was a risk of hiatus, Mulroney would fan the flames. We came to dread the occasions when he would take off his granny glasses, a sure sign that he was about to wing it, away from his carefully crafted speech text. The stakes were being escalated too quickly for my taste, and the enthusiasm was too one-sided.

Perhaps it was unrealistic to hope that we could go back to the days when the cabinet gave its negotiators a mandate and then left them alone to return with an agreement. But this situation placed inordinate pressures on the Canadian negotiators: we had to maintain the appearance of progress without being able to show any tangible results. We would be accused of negotiating in secret – as if any serious negotiation could be conducted in the public eye.

In monthly sessions, usually alternating between Ottawa and Washington, Simon and I and our key assistants would meet for a day or two with Peter and the rest of the American contingent to discuss the major components of any agreement. Our work plan was impressive, covering as it did an extraordinary catalogue of issues governing the biggest volume of trade between any two countries in the world. Under normal circumstances, any one item would have been an appropriate subject for a full-fledged negotiation in its own right.

Of primary importance were the intractable issues of American unfair trade laws and Canadian investment regulations. The secondary issues in the negotiation included:

- the establishment of the free trade area, the objectives of the agreement, the obligations accepted by each party as applied to federal and state or provincial governments, and the basic principles of the deal;
- the basic rules to determine under what circumstances goods were qualified to be treated as originating in Canada and/or the US (the issue dearest to Murphy's heart);
- the schedule for the elimination of tariffs on qualified goods immediately, in five years or in ten (with Simon's proposal that Canada be given more time);
- the rules to govern all sorts of other measures applied to goods at the customs border, including the collection of duties, the drawback, waiver, or remission of duties, and a variety of other restrictions of exports and imports;
- the rules to ensure that neither country used technical standards as a roundabout way to restrict imports or exports and to encourage the sharing of technical information and test data;
- the special rules to govern trade in agricultural commodities, including agricultural subsidies and special provisions for fresh fruits and vegetables, meat, grain, and grain products, poultry and eggs, and products containing sugar;
- provisions to deal with American complaints about Canadian policies at federal and provincial levels to discourage imports of wine, beer, and distilled spirits as well as Canadian concerns about American labelling rules;
- trade in energy commodities, including rules governing import and export restrictions, export taxes, other export measures, regulatory actions, government incentives, national security concerns, and international energy obligations;
- trade in automotive products, including the future of the Canada-US Auto Pact, various duty remission programs, and import restrictions;
- rules permitting emergency action to be taken against sudden import surges, with restrictions against the partner country or against all other countries;

- a whole set of exceptions and special provisions outside these general rules regarding trade in goods, with reference to the multilateral regulations of the GATT;
- rules governing purchases by federal, state, or provincial departments or agencies, the rights to be enjoyed by suppliers from the partner country, and how these were to be enforced, as well as exceptions to these rules;
- rules on intellectual property, including copyright, trademarks, and patents, including the highly controversial issue of patent monopolies for brand-name pharmaceuticals;
- rules for the service industries overall and for the entry of business persons from the partner country to provide those services;
- special rules to govern financial services, including banks, brokerages, and insurance companies;
- the establishment of a whole set of new institutions to oversee the operations of any agreement and to arbitrate or otherwise resolve disputes between the partner governments or with other governments, companies, or individuals;
- plus a plethora of other issues requiring special treatment, from standards for plywood lumber to the rights of cable companies to retransmit foreign broadcasts;
- plus, finally, the basic housekeeping provisions about the geographic scope of the agreement, its duration, and how it could be terminated, and when and how it would enter into force.

The Canadians would prepare thoroughly for these meetings. The TNO would first brainstorm the issue in what amounted to a graduate seminar, usually with Simon in the professor's chair. These sessions introduced a new generation of public servants to the theory and practice of trade policy, arguably the most important tool of Canadian economic policy throughout the country's history. During the 1970s, the high flyers were no longer to be found in the trade policy groups in the External Affairs, Finance, and Industry, Trade and Commerce Departments. The great men of the past had gone on to other things. The younger hotshots saw their career opportunities in other, central agencies of the government. These seminars infused a new cohort of performers with the experience, knowledge, and, above all, interest of one of the all-time leading practitioners. It was my view at the time that this represented an extraordinarily valuable side product of the negotiations, one that would serve the government well in the future as these newly indoctrinated officers moved to the top policy jobs.

Once we had completed our in-house assessment of an issue, we would marshal the best intelligence available from the responsible officials and experts in other parts of the government apparatus. The resulting position paper would be presented by Simon and me to a special cabinet committee, which would agonize over the elements of negotiation. There would be consultation with the industries mainly concerned and with the provinces, particularly on matters in their jurisdiction. The final product would then be inserted in our battle plan, for the next encounter with the Americans.

The Americans would roll in to these meetings with little or no apparent preparation. Without fail, the meetings would open with "Peter's little lists," as we came to call them: real or imagined irritants that some congressman or other, through a junior staffer, had demanded Murphy fix in the negotiations. The issues ranged from the size of knotholes permitted in plywood sheathing to the way New Brunswick licensed outfitters for hunting and fishing trips. Much of this was an obvious charade: Murphy could assure the congressman that he had discussed the matter; the congressman could tell his constituent that the issue had been raised with Canada at the highest levels. Case closed, often never to be opened again.

Unfortunately, preoccupation with this trivia meant that Peter and his associates were rarely prepared to address the fundamentals. More often than not, the framework for an agreement on a central issue, such as government purchasing, would have to be presented by someone on the Canadian side. This was true even in areas where the Americans were clearly the *demandeur* – they were the ones pressing for agreement on the subject. The Canadians would end up preparing the American proposal. This was passing strange, but it was the price we accepted in order to keep the initiative. It was also painfully clear that these middle-level functionaries had no mandate even to contemplate an agreement that would require changes to the sacred policies and programs that Congress had approved with the blessing of the domestic constituency.

It became obvious that Peter was simply not plugged in to the power centres of the American system. In our case, Simon had direct access to the prime minister whenever he required. Indeed, Mulroney would occasionally call Simon to check on how things were going. I did not enjoy that kind of personal relationship with the PM. He called me, not the other way round, but I could get a message through in short order via the cabinet secretary or the PM's chief of staff. We both met regularly and often with the cabinet committee established expressly to oversee these negotiations. I convened meetings of the deputy ministers of the senior departments every two weeks.

Peter, meanwhile, operated at a distant remove. He soon was barely on speaking terms with his own boss, Yeutter. He had no access of his own even to senior staff in the White House or other departments. Officially, his work was subject to review by the Economic Policy Committee, a cabinet-level group nominally chaired by Treasury Secretary James Baker. Unfortunately, the one time it met to discuss these issues formally, Washington was gripped by a snowstorm; Peter, whose train from the suburbs was late, missed the meeting entirely.

As for Capitol Hill, Peter's soundings on what would or would not be acceptable were apparently conducted with low-level congressional staffers. On several occasions, members of our own staff made their own contacts with old friends at higher levels in the system, only to be given an entirely different picture. They urged, with the support of Ambassador Gotlieb, that we should make contact directly with the key players. Simon rejected this strategy in what I now believe was a mistaken effort to shore up Murphy.

The only full-time negotiators were Murphy and his sidekick, Bill Merkin. Merkin at least had some experience in Canadian affairs, although strictly in a supporting role with no apparent authority of his own. I was very disappointed to find that when the two chief negotiators were in a stand-off, Merkin was unable or unwilling to work with me to bridge the gap, as the second-in-command would normally be expected to do. Murphy eventually enlisted a middle-ranking lawyer from the special trade representative's office, Charles (Chip) Roh, whose main function at this stage was apparently to serve as an attack dog, nipping at Reisman's heels on command. This trio had very limited assistance from other staff of the USSTR, most of whose energies were focused in other directions, either disputes with other countries or the much sexier negotiations in the GATT.

The rest of the work was done by middle-ranking officials from other departments who had other responsibilities and other loyalties. For some, the project was important: the Commerce Department, for example, as the bastion of American industrial interests, fielded a strong team. It was headed by the Canada desk officer, Ann Hughes, a large blonde woman with a ready smile who had the misfortune to become the designated target for the wrath Simon felt, but was reluctant to express, towards Murphy. She was accompanied by the Commerce Department counsel, Jean Anderson, a sharp-faced woman who proved tough as nails. For the entire twelve months, this pair undertook a highly effective delaying action, vigilantly protecting their home turf as the guardians of American protectionist trade laws.

We had high hopes for the Treasury Department to exert a positive influence. It was represented by economists who needed no further indoctrination in the benefits of free trade for the American consumer. The Treasury duo, Bill Barreda and Peter Cornell, at least spoke the language of international trade theory. Surely they would impose on the negotiations the broader policy view that was so lacking from Murphy. Our hopes were soon dashed. Our potential Treasury allies became implacable foes as we continued to stonewall on investment issues.

The State Department was an even greater disappointment. Secretary of State Shultz was himself a distinguished economist who had strongly supported the negotiations as one of the key foreign policy initiatives of the Reagan administration. At the table, however, the department was represented by a pleasant and undoubtedly well-meaning officer, Ralph Johnson, who contributed little or nothing to the discussions.

For most of the other departments, the Canada negotiations were very much a sideshow. They were assiduous in identifying Canadian practices they disliked. They were unwilling or unable even to contemplate changes in the way the United States did business.

At one point, during a negotiating session in Ottawa, I got word that one of our staff had received an interesting telephone call. A local resident had flown up from Washington in the seats just behind Peter and his team. He had taken careful notes of their discussions of negotiating strategies and the interplay between departments. As a loyal Canadian, he was calling to share this intelligence with us. Contrary to popular belief, this is generally how the real intelligence is obtained, rather than through electronic eavesdropping or satellite surveillance. We took appropriate precautions against this high-tech espionage, but I must admit I had always operated on the assumption that, in the unlikely event that the Americans really wanted to eavesdrop on us, they probably could.

It was rather fun to contemplate turning the tables on them thanks to an attentive Canadian with a notepad. But I sent back word: Thanks but no thanks. I was concerned that if we ever took up such an offer, it would leak out onto the Ottawa cocktail circuit and from there would get back to the omnipresent American embassy in a matter of hours. More to the point, we already knew what the American negotiating objectives and strategies were. We could only wish they were more capable of implementing them.

I was genuinely sympathetic to Peter's plight. He showed considerable courage in soldiering on despite ongoing health problems. At times he appeared to be under heavy medication. I believed he was a decent man in an impossible situation. The fact remained that we needed him to perform if we were to succeed in negotiating a free trade agreement.

His experience was limited to international trade matters, mainly in the clothing sector. He had no knowledge of American domestic policies. He was terribly out of his depth in attempting to come to grips with an agreement to regulate hundreds of billions of dollars of two-way trade right across the entire economy. He could complain and demand but was unable to compromise or agree. In those few instances where he did agree on a specific point, he almost invariably reneged under pressure from back home. This is the worst possible situation for a negotiator – that he is unable to keep his commitments.

In other cases, we charitably assumed he had simply forgotten what he had promised. At an early session in Ottawa, after a tough day's meetings, Simon took Peter off for a private dinner while I invited the rest of the group, Canadians and Americans, to my house for the evening. The party was a disaster. The American visitors acted as if they had fallen into a nest of spies and were afraid to say anything for fear of being reported. It was not until the last American had departed that the party could begin, as the Canadians took me up on the offer of some very old cognac. Afterwards, my wife flatly refused to have the Americans back to our home until they had learned a few of the social graces.

The next day, however, Simon reported that he and Peter had gotten along famously. They had agreed on how they would handle a number of issues. Indeed, they had agreed on the game plan for the remainder of the meeting. We then decamped to the conference room and the session got under way. By the end of the day, Simon was quite shaken. Nothing that he had reported as agreed the previous night had been reflected at the table. It was as if his dinner discussion had never happened. Perhaps he had misunderstood?

Thereafter, I joined Simon for the private dinners while Bill Merkin accompanied Peter. It was soon clear that Simon was not losing his marbles. Time after time, agreements were reached over dinner, only to be ignored or broken by Peter the next day. Finally, things boiled over at a session in Ottawa some months later. Peter did exactly the opposite of what he had promised the night before. Simon erupted in a private aside to me.

"Should I call him out on this?" he demanded. "Should I remind him of our private agreement?"

"No," I answered, not bothering to keep my voice down. "That would be as unprofessional as what is going on at the other side of the table. It would lower you to his level."

Peter turned pale. A few minutes later, he asked for an adjournment so we could meet privately. There, he demanded to know what I meant in calling him "unprofessional." I answered that I thought my comment was clear, even if it was intended for Simon's ears only. Simon rushed to defuse the confrontation by pretending that he had never heard what I had said.

"Besides," he said, "you will be called worse by better men before this is through."

Peter blinked, unsure quite how to take this comment. The meeting resumed. And Peter again headed off in the opposite direction to what had been agreed the night before. When I asked Bill Merkin what on earth Peter was up to, he simply rolled his eyes.

"I have no idea," he said. "He keeps me guessing just as much as you."

The real explanation may have been that Peter realized just how terribly he and Simon were mismatched. It would be charitable to say that Simon had forgotten more trade policy than Peter ever knew. Furthermore, the personal chemistry could simply not have been worse. Simon is an extremely high-voltage, extroverted performer who is convinced, with good reason, that he can think and talk his way out of just about any situation. He overpowers with the sheer force of his personality. When his target does not immediately succumb, he turns up the persuasion, higher and higher.

Peter was the opposite. He talked little and communicated less. When he did speak, we would strain to make sense of what he was saying, eventually to put our own construction on his words or give up entirely. Nor were his fellow Americans any better able to follow his tortuous line of reasoning. Perhaps his taciturnity was a shrewd negotiating ploy. Perhaps he was simply, deliberately, desperately stalling for time until the cavalry could arrive with reinforcements. Perhaps, but I doubt it very much.

From the very first meeting, the Canadian media were in a frenzy while the American media seemed unaware the negotiations were taking place. This was true in Ottawa and even in Washington. At the close of every meeting, there would be a wild scrum on the front steps of the USSTR's office, the Winder Building. The crush would be so dense that the front entrance was impassable. According to the Canadian reporters, only once was an American spotted in that wild mêlée: late in the negotiations, an unshaven man in a tracksuit pushed his way into the warmth of the television klieg lights to shove his audio cassette recorder under Simon's nose. Allan Fotheringham later reported in a column that there was no tape in the recorder.

Knowing that this Canadian media crush awaited, the last hour or more of every session came to be devoted to Simon's attempt to have Peter agree to a common line to be followed with the press outside. Sometimes he succeeded. On other occasions, whether to be mischievous or simply because he misspoke, Peter would make a comment that would take Simon days to counteract.

Press preoccupation with the marriage of this oddest couple was understandable but very destructive. The media delighted in the artificial match-up of the old Canadian bear with the young American dog. It made the story so much more explicable in human terms. For Simon, it was his hour – indeed his year – of glory on centre stage. (He took great delight when a poll of editors placed him behind Rick Hansen, the wheelchair athlete, and Ben Johnson, the sprinter, as newsmaker of the year.) He was very good at getting his messages across and rehearsed his lines with great care. The problem was that he needed Peter as his foil. Peter, meanwhile, had his own agenda. He did not need the media attention as Simon did, but once exposed he rather enjoyed it. In Washington he was a complete unknown, even within the circles of power. In Canada, he was a media star, Jack the Giant-Killer one moment, the Ugly American the next.

To his credit, Murphy quickly grasped the situation and instinctively took full advantage. In the wild scrum after the first session, he baited Simon until Simon finally growled, "This is not a press conference," in a vain effort to close this Pandora's box. It was entirely a one-sided affair: Peter was able to use the Canadian media to turn up the heat on Simon by suggesting that he was taking aim at Canada's sacred cows, such as social policies and programs; Simon could only try to fend off the blows as the American media were simply not watching or listening. This imbalance continued throughout the negotiations.

Behind closed doors, we laboured mightily without making real progress. This period was bracketed by two negotiating sessions held away from our

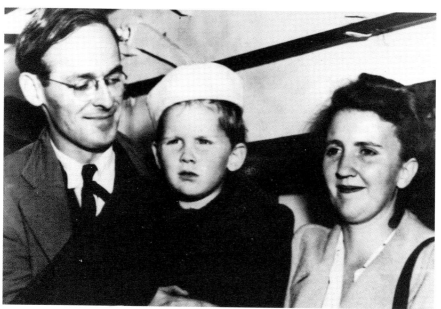

Plucked from the sea: *Bermuda Sky Queen* survivors Gordon (age three) with father Edgar and mother Gwen Ritchie in 1947. *(Author's collection)*

Reaching out: Trade diplomat Jake Warren initiated Ritchie into the world of Canada-US negotiations. *(Canapress Photo Service/René Mathieu)*

At the summit: Brian Mulroney introduces Gordon Ritchie to US President Ronald Reagan. *(Photo by Stan Behal/author's collection)*

Unconvinced: Sinclair Stevens told Ritchie he was nervous about the very idea of free trade.
(Canapress Photo Service/Ron Poling)

Super clerk: Cabinet secretary Gordon Osbaldeston, Ritchie's longtime patron, delivered the message that he was no longer wanted.
(Canapress Photo Service/Ron Poling)

Poor substitute: US Special Trade Representative Clayton Yeutter proved a weak replacement for free trade advocate Bill Brock.
(Canapress Photo Service)

Reagan made a deal to "fix" Canadian lumber in exchange for Senate votes to let the FTA negotiations begin. *(Courtesy Andy Donato/Toronto Sun)*

The punitive tariff on cedar shakes and shingles nearly killed the free trade talks at the start. *(Courtesy Globe and Mail)*

Don't say that: Peter Murphy loved to bait Simon Reisman before the Canadian media. *(Canapress Photo Service/Ron Poling)*

Slow pitch/hard ball: Murphy and Reisman played quite different games at an early negotiating session at Mont Tremblant. *(Canapress Photo Service/Ryan Remiorz)*

I have no idea: Even American deputy chief negotiator Bill Merkin was bewildered by Murphy's conduct of the FTA talks. *(Canapress Photo Service/Heather Wilson)*

Stick to the script: Ritchie looks over Reisman's shoulder at yet another media scrum. *(Canapress Photo Service/Chuck Mitchell)*

Agree to disagree: Ontario Premier David Peterson joins Pat Carney, Mulroney, and the other premiers to be briefed on the FTA, September 14, 1987. *(Canapress Photo Service/Fred Chartrand)*

SIMON AND PETER

Reisman claimed Murphy had
wanted the Canadians to show
what they had before he would
make any serious offers.
(Courtesy Andy Donato/Toronto Sun)

Inside joke: The Americans did not
understand why Ritchie hung this poster
over the negotiating table in Washington.
(Mike Hollist 1982/Daily Mail)

I ALREADY GOT
A DISPUTE SETTLEMENT
MECHANISM

FREE TRADE

DISPUTE
SETTLEMENT
MECHANISM

American producers
were reluctant to agree
to rules and procedures
which would help give
Canadians a fair shake
in trade disputes.
*(Duncan Macpherson/
Toronto Star, 1987)*

Cheering section: Quebec Premier
Robert Bourassa led the premiers in
support of free trade with the United States.
(*Canapress Photo Service/Chuck Mitchell*)

Helpful fixer: Canada's ambassador to
Washington, Allan Gotlieb, was
determined that the free trade
talks must not fail on his watch.
(*Toronto Star Syndicate*)

Breakdown: Deeply disappointed, Reisman breaks off the talks as the Americans fail to respond on the fundamentals. *(Canapress Photo Service/Bill Ingram)*

offices in Ottawa or Washington. At the end of July 1986, we held a three-day session at the lodge at Mont Tremblant, the historic resort in the Laurentian Hills. We had agreed confidentially with Peter that the agenda would centre on two highly contentious areas: agricultural trade, much of which was restricted; and how to deal with unfairly traded goods, goods that were allegedly given government assistance (subsidized) or exported below cost or below the home-market price (dumped). We came prepared for a substantial negotiation, with proposals that would involve some give as well as take from both sides.

The Canadian media were everywhere in force. They were desperate for stories, any stories, if only to justify the expense of spending a few days at a vacation resort. Somehow, they had learned and broadcast what our agenda would comprise and who would be attending. This was no great surprise, since the Americans leaked like a sieve to the press.

Early one morning, as I left my cabin to cross the garden to have breakfast in the lodge, I was pounced upon by the well-known television personality Mike Duffy, then with the CBC, with a cameraman in tow. I was flattered to rate such attention and waited with keen anticipation to see what incisive question he would ask one of the chief negotiators.

"Tell me, Mr. Secretary," Duffy asked, "is this your first trip to Canada?"

That deflated me in a hurry. Duffy had mistaken me for the American undersecretary of agriculture, Dan Amstutz, who admittedly resembled me in at least one respect, his thinning hair. I nearly pushed Duffy into the vegetable garden for his gaffe.

I was at least hopeful that Amstutz would have the authority to engage in serious negotiation of the difficult issues. Both sides substantially subsidized their farmers, but in some sectors one country was more generous than the other. Both sides restricted imports, in Canada's case to protect our sacrosanct system of "supply management" – import controls, tariffs, and other measures to keep up prices for the dairy and poultry produced by Canadian farmers. These measures were extremely sensitive politically. Indeed, Quebec had taken the position that they should not even be discussed in the negotiations. We were prepared, nonetheless, to work to find some agreement that would enable our consumers to buy better-quality food at lower prices while protecting the legitimate interests of the agricultural community.

Instead, in the sweltering heat of a meeting room in the attic of the lodge, over the noise of the creaking, ancient fans, we were subjected to a lecture on America's objectives – in the GATT negotiations then under way in Geneva.

The message could not have been more clear, or less helpful. As far as the Americans were concerned, they were holding back on any concessions, saving them to use with the Europeans in the global talks. That did not stop them from demanding unrestricted access to the Canadian market. It was obvious that the Americans had simply recycled an old script from the Geneva talks, rather than putting any real effort into the talks with Canada.

The other issue, the unfair trade laws, fared no better. The American position was very simple: If you want to sell in our market, you have to play by our rules. If our rules give our own producers an enormous home field advantage, that is just too bad. It would be unthinkable, politically, for us to propose to Congress that we change any of these laws in any respect just to accommodate Canada. This, on the issue that the prime minister had identified as the top priority for Canada in these negotiations. As he had put it, rather unfortunately, in an interview with the *New York Times*, Canada was seeking to be "exempted" from American trade laws. The Americans made clear that this was out of the question. Indeed, they were not even prepared to shunt the issue off to a working group for analysis.

As it turned out, the highlight of the meeting was a softball game – the first and last time I have played before the television cameras. At my suggestion, the teams mixed up the Americans and Canadians. At first base, I deliberately missed an easy catch that would have put Simon out and then threw the ball over the head of the astonished American at second to enable the delighted Reisman to complete the circuit. At the end, I announced the final score to be 10-to-10, to mirror the result of the Senate vote that launched the talks. It was all good fun, a far cry from the next and last time we played just over one year later.

That occasion came at the end of August 1987 at the Transport Canada training facility in Cornwall, Ontario, on the banks of the St. Lawrence River two hours' drive from Ottawa. After a year of mounting frustration, the negotiating teams played against each other, and the Americans, with the help of several young Marines on security duty, kicked Canadian butt. During the twelve months between softball games, a raft of issues had been discussed in plenary session and referred to various working groups, where the technical staff had beavered away to define the issues and the scope of possible solutions. But despite seventeen seemingly interminable plenary meetings and countless working parties, little progress had been made in reaching an agreement.

The problem was not the lack of expertise but a test of wills. The chief negotiators were locked into an endless ritual dance that had become tedious in the extreme. They paid the price for the failure of the political leadership to pin down the scope of the negotiations. On the issue of central importance to Canada, the reform of American trade laws, Murphy did not believe he had any authority to conclude an agreement. He was too terrified of the protectionist Congress to even admit that the issue could be discussed. At meeting after meeting, this produced a temper tantrum from Reisman. The first time it happened, the Americans turned pale and even the other Canadians were startled as Simon declared: "If you are not prepared to negotiate, we can call the whole thing off, right here and now."

Peter's response was to reiterate, "From my standpoint, everything is on the table." But he would continue to refuse to concede that trade laws could even be discussed.

This exchange was repeated at least once at every one of the negotiating sessions between Tremblant and Cornwall. When Simon could control his frustration no longer and would threaten yet again to walk out of the talks, the other Americans would first smile and later snigger openly at the performance. They had obviously concluded that Simon was bluffing. His ego was too committed to the success of the negotiations for him ever to contemplate admitting personal defeat.

On the other hand, the most important American objective was to force Canada to abandon the right to regulate foreign investment, long a thorn in the American side. We took the position that our mandate was to negotiate to free trade, not to free *investment* from national regulation. We pointed to the strong historical foundation for our position, as Canada had always refused to bind itself to international investment codes such as those under the Organization for Economic Cooperation and Development. We refused even to discuss investment issues throughout this long year.

This drove the Americans mad, particularly the representatives of the US Treasury, for whom this was the most important single reason for the negotiations. They could not believe that we could take this position and make it stick. After all, the proponents of foreign investment regulations had been the hated Liberals, led by Walter Gordon and then the terrible Trudeau. On gaining power, the Mulroney Conservatives had rushed with indecent haste to dismantle the National Energy Program and defang the Foreign Investment Review Agency, with Sinclair Stevens leading the charge. The Americans believed, not without good reason, that the prime minister and his colleagues had led their American counterparts to believe that they were itching for the opportunity to renounce the use of these invidious instruments for all time.

Surely the cabinet would not permit the Canadian negotiators to hold this issue hostage.

It was a classical Mexican stand-off, in which neither side could afford to move or even to blink. Meanwhile, work on the rest of the agenda slowed to a crawl. Both sides had agreed from the outset on one basic principle: Nothing is agreed until everything is agreed. Originally, Simon and I had believed this would permit the negotiations to come to a provisional conclusion on all but the most sensitive issues since, after all, none of these agreements would be final and binding until all the critical items had been resolved. Peter adopted the opposite construction. He and his minions would not agree to even the smallest detail until the entire package met with his satisfaction, including the all-important issue of investment.

To some extent, the technical staff in the working parties were able to wriggle their way around this stalemate and reach a substantial measure of agreement. The pretence had always to be maintained, however, that nothing had been agreed unless the central issues were resolved. If these lower-level agreements surfaced at the main negotiating table, there was always the risk that they would be caught up in the deadlock between Simon and Peter.

The ultimate confrontation came at the Cornwall meeting. After a tremendous build-up, the talks were going absolutely nowhere. The plenaries were going around in circles and the working groups were grinding to a halt. Before the meeting, the Canadian team had, in frustration, written up our own version of the final agreement. I had concluded that this exercise was essential to maintain the morale and the intellectual discipline of our troops. I was pleasantly surprised by the result. It was very good. Good enough, indeed, that we shared a somewhat edited version of the text with the Americans. It came to nearly 200 pages and covered the negotiating waterfront – with blanks, for tactical reasons, in the sections of greatest interest to the other side, notably investment. The Americans attempted to match our effort by stapling together some seventy pages of cut-and-paste. Needless to say, they had not included any mention of the issue of unfair trade laws. The challenge now was to reconcile the two texts and narrow the points of ultimate disagreement.

The Transport Canada training facility is a sprawling complex of meeting rooms, sleeping accommodations, cafeterias, and an impressive array of sports facilities, including an Olympic-size swimming pool and tennis courts. We did not have much time to enjoy the amenities.

The four horsemen, Peter, Simon, Bill Merkin, and I, held endless meetings. First in our suite, and then at the picnic table beside the horseshoe pitch at the training facility. The horseshoes were lousy but they were better than the negotiations. Finally Simon decided to make one last attempt to break the impasse. Our security chief lined up a large fishing boat, and the four of us headed down the St. Lawrence River. The water was choppy in the inlet and by the time we reached the main river, the sizeable craft was being rocked by the swell. Simon's passion for fishing, particularly for Atlantic salmon, is legendary, but he was after a quite different catch on this occasion. He literally chased Peter around the boat – to the seat in the stern, out onto the bow, into the cabin, and finally onto the top deck beside the pilot. He gave it his best shot.

"Peter, you have the choice of being a hero or being a bum," he warned him. "Yes, we want a deal. So does your president. How will he react when he finds out that the negotiations have collapsed because you are simply unwilling to agree to anything?"

It was a virtuoso performance, all for naught. It was as if Simon was raining blows on Peter's head and shoulders. Peter bobbed and weaved, but kept his feet. He may have been intimidated by Simon but he was much more afraid of taking a decision – any decision – that he might later regret.

It all boiled down to the issue of American unfair trade laws. This was the single most important negotiating objective set out by the Canadian government: We could not agree to allow American goods and services to flow freely into Canada when they reserved the right, at any time, on the most spurious pretext, to slap penalties on imports from Canada on the grounds that some politically influenced agency alleged those imports were subsidized or dumped or otherwise unfair. These measures of "contingent protectionism" were simply incompatible with a free trade agreement.

We could haggle over the precise formulation, but we had to have solid provisions in any agreement. We had made proposals that the Americans had critiqued, but they had refused to make any proposal of their own that came near addressing our concerns. This was the deal-breaker for Canada. In a desperate if transparent negotiating ploy, we had in response deliberately refused to talk formally about the issue of prime concern to the Americans, rules on foreign investment. (The reality was that the Conservative government was perfectly prepared to agree that Canada could not in the future take these kinds of actions, which the Tories opposed more strongly even than the Americans.)

Bobbing up and down on the St. Lawrence, Simon took the plunge.

Breaking with our game plan, he presented Peter with a proposal that went a very long way to accommodating American concerns. This was a fervent expression of good faith on his part, Simon explained. Now, in return, he needed Peter to make the long-awaited and long-promised American proposal on the trade laws.

The clock was running. The Congress had given the president authority to sign an agreement with Canada no later than January 2, 1988. But it also required that the agreement be reviewed with the Congress for a full ninety days before that terminal date. That meant the president had until midnight on October 4, 1987, to conclude the agreement. That was only a month away.

The time had come, indeed it was long past, to lay the final cards on the table. Either the Americans came forward with their proposal now, or the negotiations were ended in abject failure. Peter listened and mumbled and listened and mumbled some more. Finally he agreed that the Americans would make their final proposal on the trade law issue at one more, final meeting that we set for September 10, less than one month before the deadline.

Simon was utterly exhausted. He headed home with Connie to recharge his batteries. He was sixty-eight years old, past the age of retirement for mere mortals. He needed to gather his forces for the final push. I wrapped up the meetings and bid the Americans farewell. Before I left, I telephoned the Prime Minister's Office to report on developments. I warned Derek Burney, now the PM's chief of staff, that I was not optimistic that Murphy could deliver.

At the Washington meeting on September 10, Murphy reported that he had managed, just the day before, to meet with the Economic Policy Committee, the equivalent of a cabinet committee. They had not been prepared to have Murphy put forward the American proposal to disarm their unfair trade laws until there was clear evidence that the Canadians were prepared to accept serious disciplines on their unfair subsidy practices.

It was obvious to us that Murphy had, typically, failed to tell his colleagues of our private agreement at Cornwall and they, in turn, had briefed their bosses on the basis of the stalled discussions in the working group. The Commerce Department had successfully fended off the attempt to curb its powers. To add insult to injury, the Americans were also pulling back on a number of other important areas – they were scaling back their offer on government purchasing, wanted to delay tariff cuts on a wide range of products, etc.

At that point, I made one last effort to unblock the stalemate. To that stage, the working group on the subsidy issues had been handled by Germain

Denis. He had been unable to break down the resistance of the tag team from the Commerce Department, Hughes and Anderson. At Simon's urging, I stepped in personally to head the Canadian side at a working-group meeting convened late that evening. It was a brutal session, the tension was enormous. Partway through, Germain could not stand the pressure and abruptly left to return to his hotel.

I pushed on until we reached what appeared to be a new basis for agreement. It involved a plan to define three categories of government assistance to industry. One would be prohibited – this was the "red light" group. One would be subject to the unfair trade law apparatus – the yellow, caution group. The all-important third category would be given a green light, in effect exempted from the unfair trade laws. The key lay in the definition of the third category, which we proposed to expand to include most if not all the measures we were determined to shelter from attack.

I undertook to take this proposal home and confirm that we were prepared to agree to prohibit those measures, federal and, even more difficult, provincial, which fell into the red-light category. The Americans would confirm that they were prepared to give us the green light we required and would present a proposal to implement this plan at our next and final session, in ten days' time. With that, we headed home.

This apparent breakthrough gave the talks new life. My associates at the working-group meeting shared their euphoria with the rest of the delegation. Simon was thrilled. Again, I found myself the resident pessimist. If it seemed too good to be true, perhaps it was.

I had no doubt the plan was workable and would be very much to Canada's overall advantage. But I was by no means sure that we could convince patronage-loving politicians, at the federal level and above all in the provincial governments, to agree to prohibit any of the assistance programs they treasured. As one of the provincial representatives had commented, these programs did a lousy job of economic development, but they were highly effective at "political development." In any event, I was sceptical that the Americans would ultimately be prepared to give the green light to so many of the practices they had been condemning over the years.

When I briefed the prime minister and then the special cabinet committee on these developments, I was in for a surprise. They were prepared to accept the proposal, despite the constraints it would put on their handouts in the future. The same script was repeated at the meeting of first ministers on the weekend. At the PM's request, I sketched out the proposal for the ten premiers. While no one was asked to sign on the dotted line, there was no outcry of opposition, even from such free trade foes as David Peterson, fresh from his Ontario election victory earlier that week.

As we geared up for our return to Washington, I met privately with Derek Burney to apprise him of my concerns: I was very much afraid the Americans would not make the offer; but I was even more afraid of the reaction back home if they did. When the full implications sank in, the political leadership was all too likely to run for cover. Burney shared my concerns, but we agreed that if the prime minister was prepared to put the issue to the test we should give it our very best shot.

The final showdown was staged at the shabby old Winder Building in Washington. We had flown down the night before. Simon and I took advantage of the prime minister's offer to lend us the government's Canadair Challenger jet, usually reserved for the PM or his senior ministers. I remained pessimistic, recalling Peter's track record over the past twelve months. Simon desperately hoped against hope. He knew that this was his last chance to pull off the deal of the century. What he had told Peter applied doubly to himself: the next few days would decide if he would be a hero or a bum.

From the moment we walked into the building, we were in trouble. First, we were delayed longer than usual by security at the front door – these talks were obviously not high on the list of priorities for the USSTR. Then Murphy asked to meet privately with Simon and me before the plenary session could begin. We convened in his garret of an office.

True to form, Peter wanted us to agree to discuss other issues before he came forward with the American proposal on trade laws. This was completely unacceptable. We had already waited for twelve months. The conversation went round and round in circles as the two delegations cooled their heels in the boardroom downstairs. They had come to hate the stained carpets and the tacky furniture. The only refreshments offered were available, for two American quarters, from a Coke machine down the hall, past stacks of boxes and old desks.

Finally, in mid-afternoon, Peter relented and the session began. The Americans presented us with what they confirmed was the best offer they could make to limit the application of their trade laws against imports from Canada. It was pathetic, devoid of content, as if the meetings earlier in the month had never occurred. The green light had been switched off and the red lights were flashing. As far as I myself was concerned, that spelled the end of negotiations with Murphy and his team. If there was going to be an agreement, we would have to escalate matters to a higher level in the administration.

As soon as the meeting adjourned for the day, I headed back out to Andrews Air Force Base and hopped on the government plane. In any other circumstances, I would have revelled in the situation, with a private plane entirely to myself. Instead, I was deeply concerned, rehearsing the report I would have to make in Ottawa. Later that evening, I met privately with the PM and his chief of staff to tell them what had happened.

"What do you recommend?" Mulroney asked.

"If that is the best the Americans can do, you have no choice but to break off the negotiations," I said.

"Does Simon agree?"

"Completely."

He sighed. Although he had staked the credibility of his government on reaching an agreement with the United States, he recognized, as he had often said, that the only thing worse than no agreement would be a bad agreement.

He asked me to brief the Priorities and Planning Committee, the inner committee of cabinet, at a special meeting early the next morning. There it was agreed that we would give the Americans one last opportunity to make a reasonable offer. If they did not, we would pull the plug. It was a gutsy call, made without any hesitation. The only thing the PM asked was that I ensure that he was informed before the media got the story, so that he could defend himself.

I had little reason to love or even trust Brian Mulroney, given the earlier treatment I had suffered from his subordinates. By this time, however, he had earned my respect and even admiration. When he settled on an objective – free trade or the Constitution or tax reform – he had the courage to follow through, at enormous personal political risk. As we came to work together, I was also exposed to his personal charm at close quarters, far removed from the smarminess that marked too many of his public performances. Despite my earlier experience, I was actually coming to like the man – at a time when most Canadians seemed to be heading in the opposite direction.

Thanks to the government jet, I was back in Washington in time for the negotiating session. The Americans had no inkling of my trip or my face-to-face consultations with the prime minister and his cabinet. The meeting went from bad to worse. Having stiffed us on the issue of subsidies, they repeated the performance on the thorny issue of duties against dumped imports. Their proposal was to study the matter jointly over the next ten years.

The day dragged on. Simon showed extraordinary patience. (Within the room, that is. Outside during a break, he got into a shouting match with a reporter from the *Toronto Star*, Canada's largest-circulation newspaper, virulently opposed to free trade.) He was hoping for one last opportunity to stiffen Peter's spine over our regular private dinner meeting. Then Peter cancelled out of that as well. Simon and I spent a painful evening together weighing our options. We had hoped to have made more progress before the deal was kicked upstairs. That had proven impossible. We were running out of time.

At our delegation meeting the next morning, I alerted our team to our intention to shut down the negotiations. At the USSTR's office, Simon and I met privately with Murphy and Merkin. They were unwilling or, more likely, unable to budge.

We agreed to take a break in order to caucus. In fact, Simon and I headed off to a quiet room that our security chief had set aside. Simon was desperately unhappy to face the inevitable: we were unable to reach an agreement with Murphy. He sensed that the moment he admitted failure, the power would pass from him. It would be for others to attempt to salvage something from the wreckage, for others to get the credit if any there was. The blame would be all his. I reminded him of our first meeting with the Americans in Ottawa some fifteen months before, when he had observed that it might well be impossible to close the deal at our table without invoking the political leadership.

"Simon, my friend," I said, "it is time to walk away from this mess."

I got Burney on the telephone to reinforce my argument. Finally, after much agonizing, Simon agreed. I typed up a brief statement, in French and English, on a portable computer and photocopied a handful for the waiting media. Then Simon and I went back upstairs to give Peter the news. I will never forget his reaction: "Do you realize what you're doing to the president of the United States?" he demanded.

We were incredulous. I barely suppressed an urge to smack him. Didn't he realize what his failure to deliver had done to us, personally, and to our government and its prime minister? We turned and left without saying more. Simon went out onto the front steps of the building and made his announcement. We headed for home.

5

DOING THE DEAL

Flying back to Ottawa, I personally believed that there was only about one chance in ten that an agreement could be salvaged. Having warmly endorsed the initiative in the first place, President Reagan had promptly forgotten all about it. The team assigned by the administration was mediocre at best, completely removed from the centres of power in Washington. Encouraged by assessments from their embassy in Ottawa, the Americans were operating on the assumption that Mulroney would do anything to get a deal. They therefore had been unwilling to offer anything of real substance on the critical issues. As far as they were concerned, it was simply not worth going to war with Congress to clean up their unfair trade laws to secure an agreement with Canada.

When we shut down the talks, the Americans were utterly convinced that we were bluffing. They went so far as to reserve meeting rooms at the USSTR office for when we returned, with our tails between our legs, later in the week. The rooms remained empty. No one on the Canadian side had the stomach to continue the charade.

I was much too caught up in the sweep of these events to be entirely objective. But a good negotiator, like a good chess player, must be capable of stepping back from the fray and assessing just what went wrong, and why, and what could have been done to prevent the problem. I remained convinced that there was the basis for a deal which would substantially benefit both parties. Under Simon's leadership, the Canadian side had quickly identified the scope of such an agreement at the very first meeting with Clayton Yeutter and Peter

Murphy. This was a mark of the confidence we felt, both that we had done the necessary homework and that we had the full backing of our government.

Peter Murphy did not possess the same confidence. I had seen the symptoms before in other negotiations, where one of the players acts as if he has no clear idea where he is going. Was this because of Murphy's lack of experience? Was it because his team did not have the resources to do the necessary analysis? Was it because he feared he did not have the support of his boss, Yeutter, or the top levels of the administration or the Congress? Or was it simply Murphy's personality – deathly afraid to take a step forward because he might fall flat on his face? Whatever the reason, we knew we could not reach agreement with Peter Murphy.

The Canadian side had hoped that the difficulty was simply that Murphy was not the right man for the job. A number of our team had reached this view after the first few meetings, and Simon and I had shared our concerns with Burney and, eventually, the prime minister. On several occasions, through several channels, the Americans had been warned that there was a serious problem. At a meeting of foreign affairs ministers, Joe Clark had raised the issue of the American chief negotiator with George Shultz, only to be told that it was out of his hands. When Vice-President George Bush came to town in January 1987, he was warned of Canadian concerns that Murphy was unwilling or unable to negotiate on the fundamental issues. At a meeting of the leaders of the seven industrial powers in Venice in May 1987, Mulroney had broached the matter directly with President Reagan, who had agreed to look into the issue. Each time, the message had come back that Murphy had full authority to deal on the key issues, and the administration saw no reason to raise congressional suspicions by changing horses in midstream. Thus we had been forced for the past few months to go through the motions of negotiating with a man who we were convinced was unable to make a deal. Under those circumstances, I drew on the analogy of dealing with car salesmen and opposed any further sweetening of the Canadian offer until we were face to face with someone with real negotiating authority.

Obviously, the American perspective was very different. Murphy was understandably angry that the Canadians had gone over his head in what he saw as an attempt to undermine his credibility. As far as they were concerned, the problems lay on the Canadian side. Whatever the rights and wrongs, we had reached a total impasse.

When Simon and I met with the prime minister and Burney on our return, the mood was bleak. There was complete consensus: the Americans had not offered us the basis for an agreement. The PM never wavered in his determination not to be suckered into an agreement that fell short of our objectives. He commissioned Simon and me to get on the airwaves to explain what had happened, and why. While I played a supporting role, principally with the French media and English print and radio, Simon vigorously took the lead with English television. His bitter disappointment with the Americans showed through. My sense was that he was generally viewed as a sympathetic figure: he had fought for Canada's interests and was not prepared to surrender them to accommodate the Americans.

I recall a discussion with the prime minister where it was reported that the opinion polling data had shown a high level of support for the walkout. Those who opposed the negotiations in the first place were, of course, delighted. Those who had favoured free trade were generally relieved that we had not given in to American pressure. I commented that this sudden upsurge of support would evaporate when it became obvious that the Mulroney government had failed to put in place the cornerstone of its economic policies. Mulroney agreed with a wry smile.

The command centre in Ottawa had shifted quietly but forcefully to the Prime Minister's Office. The prime minister was very much in charge of this, the most important economic initiative of his government. He had conscripted Burney, who had been instrumental in the original Shamrock Summit Declaration, to be his top political adviser. To an extraordinary degree, Burney served as the PM's alter ego on this issue, acting with his total confidence and support, almost as his deputy prime minister – a role usually reserved for the most senior minister. The war room was established in the PMO in the Langevin Block, two blocks from the Trade Negotiations Office. In a boardroom adjoining his office, Burney presided over what seemed like a continuous strategy meeting, summoning key ministers as required.

I served as the bridge to the trade office. Simon was too exhausted and deeply depressed. What he had most feared had come to pass. He had failed to pull it off on his own, and the attention in which he had basked for nearly two years had virtually vanished overnight. He recognized, however, that it was vital that the knowledge we had built up be put at the service of the government, and he trusted me to ensure that this was done, secure in the certainty that we thought alike on all the key issues. Furthermore, as I was at pains to point out to him and to Burney, the Canadian public would not stand for any deal which Simon was not prepared to endorse. His role may have changed but his concurrence was indispensable.

The next moves were up to the Americans. The White House contacted the Prime Minister's Office to arrange for Reagan to talk to Mulroney to charm him back to the table. The PMO crisply declined: unless the president had something substantial to offer on the negotiating issues, such a call would be a waste of time. The PM solemnly advised the House of Commons that "Canada has tried vigorously, effectively and well to conclude this arrangement and the burden is now on the U.S. to deliver on its end of the bargain."

It took a long while to dawn on official Washington – at least, the handful of people who were even aware the talks had occurred – that the Canadians just might be serious. That would mean failure in the initiative that the president had described as "historic" in his State of the Union address and his secretary of state had identified as the administration's top international priority, on an equal footing with an arms control agreement with the Soviet Union. It would have implications for the current round of negotiations in the GATT, where the Europeans and Japanese might wonder how much political capital they should invest in seeking agreement with the United States when it was unable to close a deal with its closest neighbour and best trading partner. And, of course, it would, as Peter Murphy feared, be highly distasteful personally to a president who put any real value on his relationship with Canada's prime minister.

The Americans sent us what was described as a new proposal. We pored over it carefully at the TNO, and I shared our conclusions with the war room: it was a non-starter. The Americans had not moved an inch on the important issues.

Canada's ambassador, the ever-helpful fixer, Allan Gotlieb, was determined to move heaven and earth to avoid a disaster of this magnitude on his watch. He agitated for a senior political team to come down to meet with the Americans. The prime minister agreed. Simon and I would stay away to avoid any appearance of resuming negotiations. Derek Burney, accompanied by ministers Michael Wilson, of Finance, and Pat Carney, of Trade, flew to Washington on September 28, five long days after Simon had broken off negotiations.

It was an interesting trio. Burney I knew and trusted completely. I also admired many of Wilson's obvious qualities. A former Bay street financier who had served as trade minister in the government of Joe Clark, he had a patrician air that belied his self-deprecating sense of humour. He came across as a man of principle who was constant in his beliefs. If I had concerns, they centred on his firmness under pressure. I had been disappointed when

Mulroney had cut the ground out from under him on old age pensions, and I was not impressed with the actual results of his oft-stated commitment to fiscal restraint. Despite the golden opportunities of a booming economy, Canada's indebtedness grew astronomically during his period in the finance portfolio. He had a reputation for agonizing over the details while losing sight of the strategic goals. In this he was encouraged by a large entourage of political advisers who seemed to have opinions on everything and experience of very little. My main concern was whether he could hold the line in toe-to-toe negotiations with the likes of James Baker, his formidable American counterpart.

Pat Carney was the opposite personality type. A competent economic journalist in her younger days, she was nobody's fool. But the years of being the centre of attention as a cabinet minister had not been kind. They had indulged some of her less attractive qualities. She had an undeserved reputation as temperamental, prone to becoming completely unstuck under pressure, lashing out at those around her. To top it off, the physical demands of the long plane trip between her Vancouver home and her Ottawa office had taken a heavy toll on her stamina. Interestingly, I found that these outward signs concealed a very different reality. Once we had squared things away and she understood that I was not prepared to put up with her bullying, our relationship was smooth. She was unquestionably intelligent and her instincts were generally sound. Her attacks of nerves before major events were no more than the reflexes of a professional gearing up for a stellar performance. I felt she did not get the respect she deserved from her colleagues and her officials. I was careful not to commit the mistake of underestimating her.

The Canadians stuck to the script. They had not come to resume negotiations. Unless the Americans tabled a proposal that at least began to address our concerns, the negotiations were over. After an all-day meeting with James Baker they turned around and came back to Ottawa. The Americans seemed to have finally got the message, although there did not appear much they could do about it at this late date.

The one ray of hope was that Baker was finally personally engaged in the issue. If there was one power centre in Washington, he was it. Baker was a wealthy Texan who had taken to politics. He was a consummately skilful strategist. He had been instrumental in Reagan's election and had managed the White House during the first term as the president's chief of staff. He was the unchallenged second-in-command of the administration. When he moved to the post of secretary of the Treasury, he achieved the seemingly impossible on more than one occasion, negotiating international agreement on such complex issues as foreign exchange rates and persuading the US Congress to go along. Finally we were talking to someone who actually had the mandate to negotiate and the ability to deliver on his commitments.

There followed a series of telex exchanges and telephone conversations, mainly between Baker and Burney. The Americans kept reiterating their willingness to do a deal, and then demonstrating their unwillingness to propose anything that would justify our returning to the table. Finally Burney, Wilson, and Carney were shipped off to Washington again to convey our disappointment to the Americans. The meeting was shorter this time, but the result was the same. Canada's position was firm: we simply could not reach an agreement to free trade, only to have it gutted by the application of their unfair trade laws.

Both sides were by this time grasping at straws. The most promising had emerged from a conversation Allan Gotlieb had with Sam Gibbons, the crusty old congressman from Florida, chairman of the trade subcommittee in the House of Representatives. It later emerged that the exchange was interpreted very differently by Gibbons and the message was confused. In any event, garbled or not, it contained the germ of a solution.

To explain the problem of unfair trade laws, it will be necessary to touch on some of the technical issues involved. Under the rules of international trade enshrined in the GATT, most countries have agreed to reduce the tariffs and other barriers to foreign imports to their mutual benefit. But the moment imports capture a significant or sharply increased share of the protected market, the domestic producers in the host country cry foul. This is as true in Canada as it is in the United States or other countries. The domestic interests claim that the imports are competing unfairly and should be disciplined.

Two arguments are particularly common. The imports are benefiting from government subsidies or they are selling below the price in their home market or even below their costs. Thus the GATT rules have always permitted the host country to take action against these "unfair" imports: to apply countervailing duties to offset the impact of subsidies; to impose anti-dumping duties to restore the competitive price. Under extreme circumstances, other, even more direct measures may be permissible to limit unfair imports that are disrupting domestic markets.

Generally, Canada does not use these powers excessively. Not because we are more virtuous, but because we are a middle-size economy heavily dependent on foreign trade and therefore abuse the system at our peril. The Americans are in a very different situation. They possess the world's most powerful economy, its richest consumer market. Until recently, the vast majority of American businesses never felt the need to export to succeed. In the early postwar period, the American economy was at the height of its relative power, representing half of the world's total production and consumption. During this period, American business was confident it could take on all foreign competitors, and organized labour saw its advantage in supporting a more liberal trade policy. By the 1980s, however, this confidence had given way to paranoia and defeatism. The Congress, ever sensitive to the political mood, gave every sign of moving back towards the isolationism and protectionism of earlier years.

This showed up in a flood of proposed legislation to stop or restrict imports of this or that product or commodity after the 1986 congressional election. It also showed up in the administration of laws already on the books, the so-called "unfair trade" laws. The anti-dumping statutes looked very much like Canada's, but their application was often more draconian. Major cases had gone against the importer simply on the basis of unsupported allegations by the domestic producer.

Far worse from Canada's perspective were the countervailing duty laws against subsidized imports. By 1985 the United States was responsible for 80 percent of the outstanding countervailing duties in force around the world. The most frequent victim had been Canada, which had seen a wide range of industries crippled in their ability to compete in the American market. The biggest single case by far involved one commodity, softwood lumber, about which I will have more to say in a later chapter. It is enough at this point to note that while the free trade negotiations were under way, the administration had reversed an earlier decision and slapped huge penalties on imports of lumber from Canada. The Canadian industry and government were convinced that these actions were completely unjustified and that they had not been given a fair hearing by the hopelessly biased administrators in the Department of Commerce.

Thus, the stand-off that had led to the collapse of the negotiations. Murphy had kept up the game for a couple of years, but it was manifest by the end that he had simply no authority to negotiate on any issues that would involve changes in these American trade laws. This was completely unacceptable to Canada. We would be worse than fools to agree to take down our tariffs, generally higher than the Americans', in return for access to their market which they could turn around and close by the abuse of their trade laws.

We had tried for months to find some basis for meeting legitimate American concerns while protecting our interests. The problem was too one-sided to be easily negotiable. As far as the Americans were concerned, the status quo was just fine. American firms were generally not bankrupted by Canadian anti-dumping duties that covered only a small percentage of their total sales. And Canada had never applied countervailing duties to American imports, presumably because we recognized that Americans never subsidize.

This complacency was briefly shaken in November 1986 when we finally mustered the courage to slap what amounted to a 67-percent duty on imports of subsidized American corn. This certainly captured the attention of Clayton Yeutter, who had been in the American Agriculture Department and would later serve as its secretary. There was a delicious moment when the apoplectic Yeutter rushed out a press release condemning the absurdity of the Canadian decision, only to have his legal advisers explain to him that the very provisions he was condemning were routinely applied by the Americans against imports from Canada. The fact remained that Canada was much less likely to penalize American imports, and when we did, the impact was relatively insignificant for most American firms, which did not depend on the Canadian market.

For many Canadian exporters, this was literally a matter of economic life or death. Many of our firms shipped half or more of their production to the United States. They had structured their operations around that market as the best way to achieve the volumes needed to increase their revenues and lower their costs. This would be all the more true after a free trade agreement eliminated the tariffs at the border. If, the moment they were successful in exporting to the United States, their American competitors could haul them before a kangaroo court, tie them up in interminable, prohibitively expensive litigation, and very possibly get penalties applied to all imported shipments, these companies would be wiped out. Or they would be forced to move their investment, with the production and jobs, south of the border to escape these penalties.

We had tried for months to find some way to reach a more balanced set of rules. We had been prepared to agree to prohibit a large number of practices that had been dear to the hearts of federal and provincial politicians in the past, provided the Americans were prepared to do the same. They had come close to agreement and then shied away, presumably because they found they could not deliver the Congress, let alone those American states that were in the subsidy business in a very big way. Besides, our agreement would obviously not cover the Japanese and the Europeans, and the Americans had embarked on a subsidy war against these countries. If they disarmed to accommodate Canada, they would be unable to retaliate against their overseas competitors. It was obvious that we had been wasting our time.[1]

The germ of the Gibbons proposal was that Congress just might agree to some form of neutral arbitration to deal with complaints of unfairness. The unfair trade laws themselves would not be touched in either country. But there would be some bilateral mechanism to oversee their application. In the garbled form in which this originally landed on my desk, there were many questions and problems: Who would arbitrate? How could we trust them? What rules would they apply? Would their decisions really be binding? What was to stop either party from changing its unfair trade laws at some later date, to persecute importers even more? These were difficult issues that would come back to the table again and again.

At that moment, however, the central question for Canada was whether anything along these lines could possibly meet our requirements. Obviously, our first choice would be to get rid of the unfair trade laws entirely. Alternatively, we would want Canada to be "exempted" from these laws, to use the prime minister's phrase. Neither of these options was in the cards. Could we find some way to live with these laws, provided they were fairly and objectively applied? We gave the matter a great deal of thought and consulted widely with the business leadership that had been working closely with us on these matters.

The consensus emerged that while the fundamental problem was that the laws themselves were bad, and inappropriate to a free trade agreement, a large part of the problem would be resolved if only the laws were fairly applied, instead of politically manipulated as we had seen too often in the past.

My team and I could see ways in which the holes in the so-called Gibbons proposal could be plugged. Arbitration could be entrusted to a binational panel of permanent judges – after all, we were prepared to live with fair decisions. The decisions could be made final and binding on both parties. There could be rules to prevent changes in the trade laws to make them more

1. This suspicion was confirmed several years later in the GATT negotiations that led to the formation of the World Trade Organization. In that forum, the Americans agreed to a system based on the proposal discussed at that late-night working-party meeting in Washington in September 1987.

unfair. None of these protections was envisaged in the original proposal. Even if the Americans adopted the proposal as we understood it, which was far from probable, they might well refuse to accept these essential improvements. Still, it could be worth a shot.

When we met with the prime minister, he asked for our assessment. I told him that it fell short of our goals but that it might, with some work, be the basis for an agreement. Simon and Derek agreed. It was time to move to the end game. On the morning of Friday, October 2, some thirty-six hours before the deadline, we quickly assembled the TNO team and packed our bags for one final session in Washington. Simon and I were joined by Burney, Trade Minister Pat Carney, and her assistant deputy minister, Don Campbell, for the trip down. Ambassador Gotlieb would meet us on the other end, where we would be joined by Mike Wilson, who was in town for a meeting of the International Monetary Fund, and Wilson's deputy minister, Stanley Hartt. The reinforcements had arrived, and the Canadians were prepared to make one last attempt to reach an acceptable agreement before the American negotiating authority expired.

On arrival, it was apparent that there were serious divisions and mistrust even among the Canadian team. Gotlieb, in his desperate anxiety to promote a deal, was becoming meddlesome. He whisked off in the big black limousine, with the Canadian flag on the hood, with Burney and Carney, the political heavies. Campbell and Hartt grabbed the next car, and Simon and I brought up the rear. On the trip downtown from Andrews Air Force Base, we were informed that the Gotlieb plan was that the others would repair to the Treasury Department to conduct the real negotiations while Simon and I would be located in the Winder Building, on the far side of the White House, to oversee the technical staff. This was a personal affront to Simon. It was also unworkable. Contrary to the belief of some diplomats, it does help to have some idea of what you are negotiating.

Our car was the only one not equipped with a phone. In a bizarre scene, we had to race down the parkway to flag down the car ahead, occupied by Hartt and Campbell, to make use of their phone. I explained the situation to Burney and advised him that Simon and I would be joining him at the Treasury. He quickly saw the problem and agreed. We rolled in at the back entrance of the Treasury Department, relatively unnoticed after the politicians had done their media scrum. This may help explain the later accounts that stated with great authority that Simon was excluded from the final talks, banished to the STR building with Murphy. This made good reading and served the purposes of some of the more vindictive participants, but it was completely false.

What happened was perhaps less colourful but had its own drama. The Treasury is a massive building in the classical style, with white columns outside and huge vaulted ceilings inside, over broad, dark corridors. The office of Treasury Secretary Baker was on one corner near the private back elevator. His main boardroom was across the hall from the front door to his office. Across the hall from his back door was a suite of rooms with a smaller boardroom, entered through a reception area. This is where the Canadian team set up its Washington war room.

From our arrival until late that night, the two sides worked their way through the main elements of any agreement, setting aside investment and unfair trade rules for later resolution. One by one, the issues would be identified and brought to the main negotiating table to be sorted out.

We followed a simple procedure. Working from the positions we had developed over the previous eighteen months and tried to capture in our drafts at Cornwall, the responsible TNO staffer would work up a text of possible agreement with his American counterpart, indicating the language that had been agreed and, in the negotiator's traditional square brackets, the areas where the two sides were apart. The initial work-up was done under the supervision of Germain Denis for the Canadians and, on the American side, Bill Merkin. The results would be brought in to me for review in our command centre. The Americans would do their own review back in the Winder Building. When we were satisfied, the outstanding issues would be taken up in the windowless main boardroom across the hall.

At that table, James Baker sat opposite Derek Burney. In the crunch, these two had become, de facto, the political leaders of their respective sides, surrogates for their heads of government, the president and the prime minister. It was a truly extraordinary role for Burney to play, an appointed staffer presiding over a team of ministers. Beside Baker sat his deputy secretary, Peter McPherson, who was to play a crucial and unsung role in these negotiations; Clayton Yeutter; and Alan Holmer, Yeutter's deputy. They were joined by the responsible member of the American negotiating team, including on occasion, as required, Peter Murphy. On the Canadian side, Burney was flanked by Reisman, together with our key staffer on the issue. Contrary to published reports, I did not supplant Reisman in this role but joined the meeting only to relieve Simon or, on certain issues, to provide additional expertise. To provide political input, Burney was joined by Wilson and Carney, together with

Gotlieb. It was in this elegant Star Chamber that the elements were reviewed, the outstanding issues were identified, and, where any further agreement was reached, the results were sent back to the negotiators to rework.

I set up shop in the war room. As far as I could see, there was no shortage of generalist advisers to offer their opinions to Burney on the great issues. Indeed, it was a test of Burney's leadership to keep the Canadian side of the table from bickering among themselves, a test he managed with consummate skill. Instead of joining this mêlée, I positioned myself in the bridging role between these political wizards and the technical experts doing the detailed negotiations. When an element had been discussed in the main room, our staff negotiator would then report back to my command centre in the small boardroom. There we would make some sense of the often garbled outcome of the discussions in the main theatre. I would then send our negotiator back into the fray with his American counterpart – who often was working from a very different interpretation of where the top-level discussions had, or should have, come out. From time to time, the Canadian heavyweights would caucus with me in our little war room to take stock and chart the next few plays.

It was a time of testing for all concerned. We were on the Americans' home turf, dependent on them for office space and other facilities. Our experts were a couple of blocks away, in the Winder Building. They, and we, were operating with a sleep deficit and a complete lack of food or refreshments. The issues were extraordinarily complex and the pressures were enormous. Despite, or perhaps because of, these conditions, a great deal was accomplished.

A large measure of agreement was reached on the broad range of issues that came to form the free trade arrangement.

- The rules to determine whether a given item qualified under the Free Trade Agreement were spelled out for most items, although there were sticky issues in the cases of autos and parts, and textiles and clothing – these were the "rules of origin" issues with which Peter had been so preoccupied.
- All tariffs on qualified items would be eliminated in ten years, by New Year's Day 1998, and many of these would be gone five years earlier or, in some cases, immediately. This was implied in Yeutter's acceptance of Simon's proposal at our first meeting in Washington eighteen months earlier, and we had long since abandoned any hope of negotiating a longer period of adjustment for Canada.

- Rules were laid down to prevent the use of apparently technical regulations, nominally about health and safety, or the protection of consumers and the environment, to in fact discourage imports of goods and services from the partner country.
- The GATT rules to limit the use of other restrictions and taxes on imports and exports were strengthened, which turned out to be controversial mainly when Canadians learned these provisions were to be applied to energy exactly as to other commodities.
- There were agreements to cover particular issues in trade in agricultural, energy, and automotive goods, as well as an entire chapter on trade in wine and distilled spirits, which meant a direct assault on the provincial monopolies, particularly in Ontario.
- There was agreement to enable suppliers from the partner country to compete on equal terms to fill government purchase orders – although this was limited to a disappointingly small value of business by selected federal government departments and agencies, as the Americans had refused to put the bulk of their procurements, the huge military budgets, on the table.
- There was agreement to bring, for the first time, the service industries under a trade agreement, with each country promising not to discriminate further against the other's companies. It remained to determine just what industries were and were not covered and, at Canada's insistence, what guarantees Canadians would be given to cross the border to do business without being hung up by the immigration authorities.
- There were agreements on a number of other items of essential housekeeping to make the overall package workable and consistent with other international agreements.

Most of these issues had been waiting for months for agreement – waiting until the Americans fielded a team with authority to cut a deal and waiting, above all, until the really difficult matters were resolved. This was the pay-off for nearly two years of groundwork by the TNO team. Even so, it dragged on until the wee hours of the morning.

Finally we came to the difficult issue of "intellectual property rights." The Americans considered this an essential element of free trade, but I characterized it as drug racketeering. On the surface, this involved recognizing the patents or copyrights of the creators of various products. The purpose of these protections was to give the owner the right to charge whatever the market would bear for the product, without fear of competition from imitators for a very long time. The real issue was pharmaceuticals. Well over 95 percent of the drugs consumed in Canada had been developed beyond our borders by companies, often American, whose investments in research, development, and design had all been made outside Canada. With patent protection, these companies had historically gouged the consumer, particularly in Canada, where there were absolutely no offsetting economic benefits. Decades earlier, it had therefore been decided to permit other companies in Canada to copy these brand-name pharmaceuticals, producing identical generic drugs, in return for a reasonable fee, far below what had been extorted in the earlier days.

The American drug companies were outraged at this infringement of their sacred right to maximize their profits. None more than the American drug giant Pfizer, whose chief executive, Ed Pratt, in an impressive gesture of public interest, had served as the chairman of the business-labour committee advising the president on trade negotiations. This committee persuaded the administration to make this issue a top priority in the negotiations with Canada.

The industry had also lobbied extremely aggressively in Canada. They had finally persuaded the government that summer to move some distance to accommodate them with legislation that would give them a longer period of patent protection for drugs created after a certain date. Unfortunately, the anti-arthritis drug of greatest value to Pfizer had predated this deadline and so would not benefit. The American industry rejected the proposed Canadian legislation as inadequate and pressed the administration to demand more in our negotiations. The situation was not helped by a comedy of errors in Canada that resulted in the legislation being delayed into the fall when typographical errors required a reprinting of the official document, and the messenger taking the final version to Parliament lost his way and missed the legislative deadline before the summer recess. It was hard to convince the Americans that this bungling ineptitude was not a deliberate stalling tactic.

With the proposed legislation, the government had gone as far as it believed it could responsibly go. We had been authorized, however, to agree to greater patent protection for products other than plants or medicines (i.e., pharmaceuticals), which had in any event traditionally been excluded from key international agreements. We had worked with the Americans to draft an entire chapter on this subject, always with the exclusion of plants and medicines. Just before midnight, this came to the main table in the Treasury with

106

square brackets around the exclusion to reflect the disagreement. Baker howled in protest. As far as he was concerned, this was absolutely unacceptable. His reaction had been anticipated.

On reviewing this material, I had advised Burney that this was one area in which the Americans were clearly the *demandeur*. Although they wrapped themselves in a pro-market ideology and argued that it was clearly in Canada's best interest to implement these overdue "reforms," we had nothing to lose if the entire chapter was scrapped. When Baker threw his tantrum, Burney and his colleagues, as if on cue, slammed their thick black briefing books shut and walked out. Baker then stormed out, not stopping until he had jumped in his waiting limousine and it had pushed through the waiting horde of media types. This led to a flurry of stories then and later that Baker had walked out of the talks to put pressure on the Canadians. In fact, he had given it his best shot, but the Canadians had held firm, at least for these negotiations.[2]

Counting backward from the last date when an agreement could be signed on the fast track, the president had to advise the Congress of the agreement no later than midnight on Saturday, October 3. At least, that was the interpretation we had obtained from the "parliamentarian" who was the formal authority on these matters on Capitol Hill, when the Murphy team proved unwilling or unable to clarify the timetable. (An earlier calculation that had given them one more day was revised because, by convention, the president apparently did not send nor did the Congress receive such a letter on a Sunday.) After that point, the Americans would no longer have authority to do a deal with Canada on the fast track – and we had already established that without that legislative fast track, we were not interested in negotiating with them.

As far as I was concerned, that was the Americans' problem. I kept reminding my colleagues that we were under no such pressures and should not allow ourselves to be stampeded by a deadline, real, imagined, or movable, which applied to the Americans. All in vain. With Gotlieb leading the pack,

2. The Americans did get their way in the next round of trade negotiations. They pressed Canada in both the NAFTA and the GATT to give them what they had failed to get from us in the FTA: an elaborate system of intellectual property protection based on the chapter we had drafted, only to scrap; this time it was to include extended patent protection for brand-name pharmaceuticals. Mike Wilson, as trade and industry minister, not only agreed but put the necessary legislation to Parliament *before* either international agreement was concluded. The new regime gave the drug companies what they wanted but, in return, got certain commitments to restrain the increase of prices and to invest in research and development, particularly in the Montreal region.

the Canadian mindset was being shaped by the conviction that we had to get a deal before the American deadline. It was true that we expected Canada to be the biggest winner from the simple fact of free trade with the American giant. But the Americans stood to gain as well, and my professional pride as a negotiator was affronted by the weak-kneed premise that we had to somehow buy their agreement and be governed by their timetable.

On Saturday morning, the Americans tried other tactics to turn the pressure up another notch. If the theoretical deadline for the president to notify the Congress was midnight, when did matters have to be resolved, in practice? The Americans went through a weird little dance that should have fooled no one. The first step was to explain that the president was at Camp David, and therefore Baker would have to have an agreement in his hands by mid-morning Saturday in order to fly up there to get Reagan's signature on the document. Mid-morning became early afternoon, but this, it was explained with great seriousness, was the final deadline to permit Baker to get to Reagan after the latter had finished his nap but before he turned his attention to a private screening of one of those movies the old actor adored. When that deadline passed, the word came down that the definitive, final, final limit was 10 P.M., after which any deal would not be worth the paper it was written on as, presumably, the president would turn into a pumpkin. To my dismay and alarm, some of the Canadians took this guff seriously, and it achieved at least part of the effect the Americans sought in heightening the tension in our caucus.

Meanwhile, the kick-off to Saturday morning came with a private breakfast between Baker and Wilson. The meeting had been arranged before Baker's staged eruption. There were two main issues on the table. One was an agreement on financial services.

There were restrictions in both countries on the activities of the partner country's financial institutions. For example, if a securities dealer in the US was owned by a Canadian bank, it was barred from dealing in the principal American markets. On the Canadian side, there were restrictions at the federal level and at the provincial level, with particular impact in Ontario as Canada's financial centre. Typically, days before the working group on financial services had been due to meet, the Ontario government announced a series of reforms that basically gave the Americans everything they could have wanted from the province, on a platter, with nothing in return. I guess this was Premier Peterson's idea, as an anti-free-trade crusader, of how to deal with the Americans – why negotiate an agreement when you can give them everything in advance?

The working-party session had been rescheduled to give us time to regroup. Then, days before it occurred, the federal government, not to be out-done, announced *its* financial reforms, which gave the Americans most of what they wanted from us. In a display of tough-mindedness, however, Finance Minister Wilson had, in fairness, made it conditional on getting something in return, whatever that meant.

When we went ahead with the working-party meeting, the situation became even more surreal. The American team was headed by Assistant Treasury Secretary David Mulford, a financial wunderkind from Wall Street and arguably one of the most pretentious men I have ever met. He began by lecturing Reisman, from page after page of handwritten notes, on the mean-ing of reciprocity and how it was time for Canada to straighten up and fly right if we did not want the Americans to squash us like a bug. The Canadians were nonplussed. Our chief technical adviser, Bill Hood, himself a former deputy minister of finance, was absolutely furious. Simon kept his cool. Partway through the presentation, he leaned over to me and asked: "How old would you say this asshole is, anyway?" I guessed he was in his late forties. Simon did some quick arithmetic.

When Mulford finished his diatribe, Simon responded quietly by con-ceding that he did have some idea what "reciprocity" meant. Indeed, one of his first professional assignments in the government service had involved a review of the Reciprocity Agreement between Canada and the United States that had originally been negotiated in 1934 – in other words, before Mulford was born. Unfortunately, this elegant insult may have passed over Mulford's head. (Later, when Mulford showed us, with great pride, his office, in which he had been married a few months before, Simon professed to be in awe as he looked out the window facing the White House: "Why, if a fellow was in good function, he could pee all over it from here," he said to the purpling Mulford.)

Now, as we reached the final crunch, the first issue for the Wilson-Baker meeting to resolve that Saturday morning was whether the Americans would be prepared to give us anything for the changes we had so generously made. The second issue was even more politically explosive. It was Canadian control over foreign investment, embodied in the discriminatory elements of the Foreign Investment Review Agency and the National Energy Program. We had already scrapped the offending provisions of the NEP – again before the negotiations began, presumably with some hope, against experience, that the Americans would repay our generosity with concessions of their own. FIRA had also been transformed, again before the negotiations began, from an investment control agency into one for the promotion of investment, called Investment Canada. It still had the obligation, however, to review acquisitions of Canadian businesses by Americans. Most of these acquisitions were direct, when an American investor bought the business from its current owners, and Investment Canada reviewed and could disallow all cases where the price was over C$5 million – a power that had been dearly cherished by Herb Gray, who had used it to its limit. Other acquisitions were indirect, when a firm in the US bought another firm in the US, which happened to have a subsidiary in Canada – as when Westinghouse bought the appliance-maker White in the United States, and picked up White Canada in the bargain. These were also reviewable above a $50-million threshold. The screening of these indirect acquisitions drove the Americans wild, as huge transactions involving billions of dollars in the United States might be held hostage because of a small Canadian subsidiary. Furthermore, in some sectors, notably what we called the cultural industries, the government maintained the right to review all foreign acquisitions and even to force their divestiture.

The Americans wanted us to drop this investment screening entirely and treat purchases by Americans exactly as if the buyers were Canadian. Failing that, they wanted the limits raised so high as to exempt most transactions and to eliminate the special exclusions. As Mike Wilson headed in to breakfast with James Baker, we were more than a little nervous. Wilson had been carefully briefed on these issues, on the likely American demands, and on what positions and even fallback positions we might take. For example, we might be prepared to raise the screening threshold from $5 million up to $25 million for direct acquisitions. We would hold our final offer – to go all the way to $150 million – in reserve until they put some substantial proposals on the table to deal with our concerns over unfair trade laws, which they had so far failed to do. We also had proposals to raise the threshold on indirect acquisitions by a significant amount.

When Wilson came back, I thought he looked a little sheepish. They had had a very good discussion, he said. Baker had promised some consideration of our problem with Canadian bank-owned securities dealers in the United States, although it turned out that this offered very little relief. On investment rules, they had agreed to raise the threshold to $150 million for direct acquisitions and to eliminate screening entirely for indirect ones. We were dumbfounded. So much for our attempt over many months to whet the American appetite for concessions, however limited, in the investment arena. Wilson had gone right to our bottom line, without any quid pro quo.

We consoled ourselves with the recognition that these investment controls had proved largely ineffectual in the past and, in any event, even at these much higher thresholds the government had retained the right to screen investments in the cultural industries and, in other sectors, the really big ticket: strategic acquisitions that had accounted for the bulk of the dollars involved in the first place. (Wilson may have fumbled the negotiating tactics but his political instincts were vindicated later, when there was little or no adverse reaction in Canada. On the other hand, Treasury was strongly criticized for reaching an agreement that enshrined, and therefore legitimized, Canada's hated investment screening.)

This was not an encouraging start to the day. Over the next few hours, there were few victories for Canada and they were terribly hard fought by the TNO negotiators. In each and every working group, our team had become battle-toughened from months of confrontation with their American counterparts. They had struggled to keep a balance of advantages in any agreement, matching American demands with our own. They had also, by dint of greatly superior preparation and analysis, found ingenious ways to appear to give the Americans much more than was really there. Sometimes these tactics were faithfully supported at the top table, as the Americans made concessions to match our own, but in other cases the Americans were given what they demanded. Baker was relentless in pressing for advantage.

At a late stage in the afternoon, Peter Murphy and I personally went toe to toe on his favourite issue, rules of origin for clothing. The old textile negotiator was truly in his element. I bowed to the inevitable. The Americans would be allowed to maintain a tariff on clothing above a certain overall level. At his insistence, a separate tariff-free quota was also negotiated for woollen suits, which were particularly sensitive. Peter was able to present this as a personal triumph when he returned to Washington, his gift to his old friends in the textile industry.

Some in the Canadian industry read and, even worse, believed the American press on this issue. I had to meet privately with them afterwards to explain the situation. The export levels had been set far above anything we had ever been able to ship in the past – seven times as high for woollen suits. They should stop worrying about the tariff and focus on the fact that they had a free run at the American market far beyond their wildest dreams. As for those who were concerned that I had agreed, in return, to limit the old program that had helped them to cut the cost of importing fabric from overseas, they should focus their pressure on the government to eliminate the existing tariffs on these imports. They followed my advice and hit a home run. The government agreed to cut the tariffs on imported materials. Meanwhile, the manufacturers of woollen suits were laughing all the way to the bank. When the American industry finally realized what had happened, they tried, and failed, to repeal the deal in the North American Free Trade Agreement (NAFTA) and later threatened unilateral action to curb this terrible injustice.

Simon, meanwhile, had worked his magic on the similar and highly complex issues of the automotive sector. The result was to preserve the benefits for Canada of the Auto Pact, which he had personally negotiated more than twenty years earlier. The pact itself was given new life under the proposed agreement. The Americans were attempting to close out the so-called "transplant" assembly operations set up in Canada by Japanese and Korean firms and thereby make their investments in Canada uneconomic. The Americans were aided and abetted in this by the Big Three in Canada who were, naturally, taking the same positions as their head offices to the south. Also naturally, the Americans were encouraged by the auto unions, who feared the higher productivity of the non-unionized transplants.

Despite these pressures, Simon held firmly to an arrangement that would enable the transplants to survive. The original deal I had negotiated for these plants during my DRIE days permitted them to profit from a return of duties paid on their imported inputs to enable them to compete with the American companies until these transplants could qualify under the Auto Pact. The Americans made it abundantly clear that they were not prepared under any circumstances to have these companies enjoy the Auto Pact benefits, even if it meant terminating the pact itself.

Simon persuaded them to accept an arrangement that meant these companies would continue to enjoy these so-called duty drawbacks for several more years, while they built up their purchases of Canadian and American components to the required 50 percent of the total value in order to qualify under the FTA to ship the cars across the border. When Baker continued to press on this issue, we agreed to set up a panel to take another look at auto trade matters and make recommendations, not binding on either side, at some unspecified time in the future.

Canada has a system to protect inefficient poultry farmers and dairy farmers: the market in Canada is strictly controlled by a regime of production and marketing quotas that mean higher prices for these farmers, paid, of course, by Canadian consumers. The inefficient producers are thus permitted to eke out a subsistence living while the efficient producers make their fortunes.

112

Politically, this system is very popular. The restrictions are naturally supported by producers who regard it as their God-given right. Nowhere is this
more true than in rural Quebec, where the bulk of Canada's dairy farmers are
concentrated, based on their guarantee of what amounts to a 50-percent share
of Canadian consumption. (Ironically, the Quebec producers who are the
main beneficiaries of this federal system are committed and vocal separatists,
feeding on the mad illusion that the rest of the country needs their milk.) The
consumers on the other hand are not strongly represented on these issues, and
indeed the leadership of the Consumers' Association of Canada opposed
changes that would *lower* prices to their members. The entire system would
be completely unworkable if there were not a tight lid on imports to keep
much lower-priced American poultry and dairy products from flooding across
the border and smashing up this cosy little cartel.

We were, regrettably, successful in protecting these restrictions. We shut
the Americans out of our dairy business and limited them to a derisory share
of our markets, spelled out in percentages, so much for chickens, so much for
powdered eggs, etc. This was, I suppose, a negotiating triumph. It certainly
pleased the federal agriculture minister, not to mention the premier of
Quebec. It was so well protected that it survived the NAFTA negotiations and
even a subsequent challenge to its continuing legality after the negotiations
that set up the World Trade Organization. As a result, Canadian consumers
continue to pay close to the world's highest prices for those very commodities that occupy a disproportionate share in the budgets of low-income
Canadians. As a matter of national policy, I for one would welcome the
removal of these restrictions. As a negotiator, however, I did not feel the
Americans had paid us enough to be entitled to their removal.

In other cases, what was seen by many as a negotiating defeat was, in my
view, a very sound result. For example, as any lover of good wines will recall,
Canadian grape growers were doing a lousy job. They had generally settled
on some of the lowest grade hybrids to ensure a plentiful harvest, but of the
poorest grapes. Canada's winemakers were struggling to improve the quality
of their product, relying heavily on imported grapes and concentrates to offset the ill effects of the local stuff. The governments of producing provinces
across Canada had used their liquor monopolies to preserve and promote
these local wines against competition, particularly from the high-volume, better-quality California wines. They did this by marking up the prices at which
they sold imported wines much more than the local products, thus encouraging consumption of the domestic plonk. Needless to say, the Americans,

including influential backers of the Californian in the White House, were demanding the removal of these discriminatory measures.

Personally, I thought this was a great idea. I made a point of serving California wines when we entertained the American negotiators in Ottawa. As a wine drinker, I was all in favour of making a greater range of wines available at lower prices. If, in the process, it helped force the Canadian industry to upgrade, so much the better. But if it did not, this was one of the very few sectors where I would be prepared to advocate an industry-specific program of assistance to help the grape growers and winemakers adjust.

The provincial governments professed to be outraged to varying degrees. Some were prepared to defend their policies, notably in Ontario. Many felt that this was an unacceptable intrusion into provincial jurisdiction that no federally negotiated agreement could, by itself, impose. I left that issue for a later date. I was pleased to be able to persuade Pat Carney, as a minister from the other major producing province, British Columbia, that this was an area in which concession was the better part of valour.

It is now apparent that this was the best thing that could possibly have happened to the Canadian wine industry. The vineyards were replanted with much better *vinifera* stock. The wineries improved their techniques. Soon a number were breaking through into the big leagues with wines that won prizes internationally. Others took this spirit of innovation farther to beat the Germans at their own game and produce what are arguably the best ice wines in the world.

On the other hand, we were unfortunately successful in protecting the antiquated provincial regulations governing beer. Every province wants its own brewery. As the head of BC's public-sector union said to his neighbour, Trade Minister Carney, where else than at a brewery can a high school dropout make $30,000 a year? This did not strike me as a very good argument. It did impress the beer barons, who had bent to provincial demands and built many more breweries than the Canadian market could possibly require. Now they wanted these plants to be protected. The Americans went along. I did not regard this as a negotiating triumph. It is no coincidence that the protected Canadian industry has gone through hard times in the intervening years, as the leading companies have come under great financial pressure and the consumption of beer has declined, presumably in part because of relatively high prices.

Under heading after heading, agreement was reached in principle, reflected in text, and initialled by the gatekeepers, Denis for Canada and

Merkin for the United States, ready for final review and approval. For the troops engaged in the ongoing guerrilla warfare in the caverns of the Treasury Building, the level of optimism was increasing. But, as I was only too keenly aware, looming over these agreements in miniature was the brutal reality that the central issue of unfair trade laws had gone absolutely nowhere. The president had presumably finished his nap, woken up from the movie, and begun getting ready to go to bed somehow controlling his eager anticipation of an agreement with Canada.

At the main table, interminable hours had been consumed with the Canadians explaining what they required and the officials from Commerce explaining that it was quite impossible – even if they had been prepared to go along, the Congress would reject the proposal and scuttle the entire agreement.

By this stage, exhaustion was setting in. I was dead tired after perhaps six hours of sleep in the last four days, coupled with the strain of bridging the divide between the political wish and the professional reality. Through the haze of utter fatigue, I was extraordinarily proud of the team we had built up over the past two years. Without exception, they had done all that had been asked and more. Not since the war years had any group of public servants been put under such unbelievable pressure and performed so nearly flawlessly. If we failed to reach an acceptable agreement, no blame could fall on them. But their disillusionment would be almost unbearable.

By the late evening, Baker was ensconced in his office, with the Commerce and USSTR brass sweating it out in his anteroom. Our core group had gathered in the suite that had formed our war room. Burney was seated at one end of the table, by the telephone, which linked him directly to the prime minister in Ottawa. The PM had come down from his summer residence on Harrington Lake for a special meeting of his cabinet to get our final report – we had come so close on all the other issues but had fallen short of an acceptable deal. I was seated at the other end, with our top legal adviser, von Finckenstein, who had emerged as a tower of strength. The others, Wilson, Carney, Reisman, and Gotlieb, sat around the table, occasionally joined by Hartt and Campbell. The tension was thick as a London fog.

Around 10 P.M., the equally tired James Baker crossed the hall and asked to join us. He had squeezed the rock, he said, and was ready to present the final American offer. The administration was simply unable to commit itself to getting rid of American unfair trade laws or even to exempting Canada from them, thus provoking the hostility of the Europeans and Japanese. Nor could the Americans make a commitment not to make changes in these laws in the future. They were, however, prepared to make an extraordinary concession: the decisions of the International Trade Administration of the Commerce Department and the International Trade Commission could be reviewed by an ad hoc committee of Canadian and American judges to determine if they had made any errors of law or process. Although the Americans would not be bound by such a decision, it would clearly have great force. This might not be everything we had sought, but we must understand that it was unprecedented and he could make no guarantee that Congress would accept. It was the best offer he could make and the decision was now in our hands. We asked a few questions. Baker then returned to his office.

After some discussion, Burney polled the room. Carney was by then exhausted and could respond only that she needed much more time to consider the proposal, time that was obviously not available. Gotlieb saw it as a breakthrough that we had no option but to accept. Wilson thought it promising but wanted to hear what Simon and I thought. Simon turned to me. I tried to marshal my thoughts under the numbing pressure.

"This is not acceptable," I said. "The problem is unfair laws, unfairly applied. We have to keep up the pressure on them to clean up their laws. We can't build an agreement on shifting sands, which would be exactly the situation if the Americans were free to change their laws to damage us in the future. Nor can we ensure that these laws are fairly applied unless there is a tribunal that can strike down the American action with a binding ruling."

Simon fully concurred and added some comments of his own. Wilson said he did not see that we had any option but to turn it down under those circumstances. Burney got on the line to the PM to tell him of our assessment. The PM thanked us all. He asked Burney to advise Baker and then report back. Burney and I then crossed the little hall and, using a secret access code, entered Baker's personal office directly by the side door, unbeknownst to the Americans waiting in his anteroom. The atmosphere was cordial, tinged with genuine professional respect. Baker had come to know me as a straight-shooter. But his real respect and admiration were reserved for Burney, who had proven himself the peer of the man who was regarded, not without reason, as the premier international deal-maker.

Burney explained the assessment that had led us, with deep reluctance, to the conclusion that we did not have a deal. He told Baker that the PM sent his warmest thanks and high regard and would like personally to talk to the president if and when that was judged appropriate to convey directly his profound disappointment. Baker was clearly shaken. Finally he asked if he could have one more chance to shake the tree. He would ask the folks from Commerce to dig even deeper to find some imaginative solutions and would talk with the key players on the Hill to see if there was some room to move.

When we returned to the other room, the reaction was curiously mixed. How long could this go on? We lapsed into murmured conversation, with long silences. I wandered out into the hall for some air. On my way back through the outer boardroom, I was waylaid by Gotlieb, white with fury.

"You have deliberately sabotaged these negotiations," he said. "You never wanted an agreement in the first place." He was literally spitting with rage.

"Allan," I said very quietly. "We are all tired and it shows."

I pushed by him into the inner boardroom. To his credit, a couple of minutes later, Allan took me aside and gave me a full apology. He was a proud man whose only intention was to serve his country. He had not meant what he had said. He knew that no one, himself included, had given more of himself than I had to make these negotiations succeed. Etc. I accepted his apology and put the whole incident down to the extraordinary tension of the moment.

An hour later, Burney and I were invited to see Baker. He was flanked by his legal wizards, Jean Anderson of Commerce and Alan Holmer of the STR's office. He reported that he had made progress. He now offered us a number of important improvements. I took careful notes. The Americans realized that our concern over changes in their laws was dictated by experience – the interest equalization tax, the import surtax, and other examples we had cited – when the Americans had sideswiped us with measures aimed at others, the Japanese or the Europeans. They would agree that there would be no such unintentional changes in the future – Congress would have to clearly name Canada in the legislation. Any such changes would have to be compatible not only with the GATT but with the objectives of the FTA. They would also agree that they would negotiate with us for the next, say, five years to see if we could come up with acceptable ways to reform their unfair trade laws or even replace them with some other way of doing business.

Finally, and most difficult, they were prepared to agree to some form of ad hoc panels to review their administrative agency decisions. The panels would have to be composed entirely of highly respected legal experts. Their review would have to be restricted to the judicial review otherwise undertaken by the Court of International Trade. One panel's decisions would not serve as a formal precedent for decisions by other panels in the future. Most important for us, the final decision of a panel would be binding on both governments.

Burney and I looked at each other. I gave a wry grimace. Burney turned back to Baker and said we would have to take a look at this with our colleagues. We knew the clock was running. It was nearing midnight. We headed back across the hall to the inner boardroom. The atmosphere there was funereal. "The Americans have come up with some improvements," Burney announced. He had me describe the proposal. As Carney later said, she was barraged with legal opinions from men who had not practised law for years, if ever. Meanwhile, our real chief legal adviser, Konrad von Finckenstein, had popped out for a serious review with the trio of American counsel we had retained to advise us on the intricacies of the American system.

We waited until Konrad rejoined the group. Then Burney had us go through the proposal again. Our American advisers reported, through Konrad, that it should effectively protect us from sideswipes in any future changes to American trade laws. It was a very serious and rare step for Congress to go so far as to name a country as the target of its legislation, a step usually reserved for outlaw states.

As for the commitment to negotiate a new regime, we took this as an undertaking in good faith but far short of a guarantee of future success. We decided to allow for an extension of the deadline, from five years to seven, if required. If at that point the talks had not resulted in a substantial reform of American unfair trade laws as they applied to Canada, we would reserve the right to terminate the agreement. To some extent, this was face-saving. We had long ago recognized that the administration was unable at this time to give us what we wanted. Perhaps, down the road, the agreement would have worked so well that the Americans would agree to these reforms – or we would conclude that we could live without them.

Finally, and most important, how broad would be the scope of review? This was a very tricky question. In both countries, the courts were empowered to undertake a judicial review of these decisions. The new system would supplant that review but would be required to apply the same legal principles as the standards set out in the statutes. The standards were different in Canada than in the United States and in both cases were moving targets, as the courts redefined and interpreted their meaning. The Canadian lawyers advised us that the standard at home was quite restrictive: it would not permit what amounted to a new hearing with new evidence; it would not even, strictly speaking, allow the Federal Court to second-guess our agencies on the merits of their decision, although the courts had developed ways of doing this under other pretexts.

118

What about the American standard? The Canadian lawyers had no experience of American judicial review. Our American advisers thought that the American standard was a little more open, permitting a bit more fundamental review of agency decisions than the Canadians had described. Was it broad enough? Gotlieb then drew on his experience as an international lawyer to assert that the American standard was, in practice, considerably broader. It would permit the panels to overturn unfair decisions by the agencies. We turned to Konrad, our leading expert. The deciding factor for him, on advice from American counsel, was the provision that the review would take into account the entire "administrative record." In other words, the panel could if it chose look at everything that had been presented to the administrative agency. Given a little ingenuity, it could use this leverage to take hold of the substantive issues. On this highly unsatisfactory discussion of arcane technical issues turned the fate of the negotiations.

When Burney asked me to sum up the analysis, I made three points. First, I had no doubt that Baker had gone as far as he would be able to go that night. This really was the American final offer. Second, it fell well short of our more ambitious goal of eliminating the trade law impediment to the flow of goods within the free trade area. It did not exempt Canada from these trade laws nor even correct their fundamental flaws. It was, at best, a patchwork, second-best solution. Finally, it did, however, appear to plug the many loopholes in the original idea floated by Sam Gibbons. Relying on the legal analysis we had been given, the proposal should significantly reduce the problems Canadian exporters faced as a result of the misapplication of American trade laws. What Baker had managed, in just two days, was to slice at least partway through the Gordian knot that had plagued the negotiations from their outset eighteen months earlier.

Burney reopened the line to the PM and took him through these developments. Mulroney had expected the worst and had gathered his cabinet for this purpose. Now the delegation in Washington was telling him that we had the basis for an acceptable deal. He probed to determine that there was indeed a consensus to proceed. Burney was in favour. Wilson and Carney agreed. Gotlieb was naturally on side. The focus then shifted to Simon and me. We agreed. It was less than perfect but close enough to what we required that we believed we could make it work. The deal was done.

As Burney went to inform Baker, Wilson gave a thumbs-up signal in the window to the Canadian media below. They exploded in excitement. Meanwhile, back in Ottawa, Prime Minister Mulroney finally was able to meet the press in the Langevin Block to announce that agreement had been reached. It was a bit anticlimactic. It was 1:30 A.M., October 4, 1987, and all but the most die-hard news watchers had presumably had the good sense to go to bed. Besides, at an earlier point in the evening, Peter Murphy, whom we had hardly seen all day, was collared by Mike Duffy and with his unerring instinct for upstaging the Canadians had confirmed that the deal was done – presumably unaware that the negotiations were still under way upstairs.

At that point, I asked Mike Wilson to say a few words of thanks to the exhausted troops, whose work was far from complete. We gathered the team in the hall. Wilson made some very gracious observations about the contribution they had made. I made it back into the boardroom just in time for a photograph, arranged by Gotlieb with a keen eye to the history books. Wilson was flanked by Carney and Reisman in front, with Burney and me behind. We were joined by Gotlieb, Hartt, and Campbell. This group then repaired to the embassy residence where we had time for one tumbler of Scotch. As we sat in the living room that my father and mother had graced two decades before, I did not feel I could join unreservedly in the celebration. We were about to commit the country to a huge gamble in an uncertain future. Time would tell whether we had, in fact, made the right decision in closing the deal.

What about the mad rush to take Baker out to Camp David to get the president's signature? This was, as I had surmised, nothing but an elaborate ploy. The letter had been prepared well in advance, with the president's signature, to advise Congress that a deal had been reached, more information to follow. It was simply logged out of the White House and into the Congress a few minutes before midnight to avoid any future unpleasantness about the formalities of the fast track.

6

CLEANING UP

President Reagan's chief of staff Donald Regan once compared his job to that of the fellow who carries a shovel behind the circus parade, cleaning up after the elephant. That was my job description for most of the next year. The deal had been done, with great fanfare, by the political superstars just before the midnight deadline. Now someone had to head the housekeeping squad: determine just what had been agreed, turn that into a legal text that could be signed by the heads of government, and prepare and explain the legislation to make the whole thing operative in Canada and the United States.

On Sunday morning, the team moved over to the Winder building to complete the agreement in principle. Simon, Burney, and the ministers made themselves comfortable in an office down the hall. I found myself across the table from Peter McPherson, Baker's deputy, and Alan Holmer, general counsel at the USSTR. I was supported by the TNO team. It soon became apparent that we had a great deal of work to do. Our respective point men, Germain Denis on the Canadian side and Bill Merkin on the American, began to walk us back through the elements of agreement as reflected in the one- or two-page notes on each issue that had been prepared the previous day. In the last-minute focus on the central question of unfair trade laws, there had been no opportunity to review these notes in detail. Did they reflect what both sides had intended?

One glaring example of the risks we were running surfaced late in the morning. The notes packaged so helpfully by Merkin contained an "agreement" initialled by him and Denis on the issue of Canadian drug legislation. When it had emerged that there would be no broad agreement on intellectual property issues – the question that had closed the talks with a bang on Friday night – the Americans had demanded that Canada solemnly undertake to enact the pharmaceuticals legislation that was still before the House of Commons. A note had been done up and duly initialled by both point men to reflect this proposal. The moment we came to this page, I tore it out of the package. As far as I was concerned, Canada had never agreed to this. Indeed, I questioned the propriety of committing the government to force passage of legislation through our legislature. The Conservatives enjoyed a majority in the House of Commons, but the Liberals still controlled the Senate and were flexing their muscles. The Americans would have to be satisfied with knowing that it was obviously the government's intention to try to get it through.

McPherson wasn't buying it. They obviously believed that they had slipped one over on us. They were not prepared to let go. McPherson threatened to go over my head, claiming that Burney and Baker had an understanding. I sent word to Burney, who joined our merry little party. He confirmed that we were not prepared to put this proposal in the agreement. We believed that was the end of the saga. Not a chance. Later that day, when the Americans issued a press release to describe the agreement, the offending provision was still there – Canada undertook unconditionally to implement the bill. Not to be outdone, the press agents back at our embassy dutifully handed out their summary of the agreement. It, too, included the commitment. It seemed no one had taken the time to check the final package against these earlier drafts to strip out the discrepancies. Gotlieb, embarrassed, asked the journalists to return the offending pages. Not all did. Months later, when I was explaining the final agreement to the Senate, two entire sessions were devoted to this issue, as the Liberals hammered away at the inconsistency, claiming that we had agreed to usurp the prerogatives of the upper chamber.

When we were about halfway through the package of agreements, the Americans got word that Baker was planning to hold a press conference at 2 P.M. to announce the agreement. They argued that their only chance to capture press interest would be to get the news out on a quiet weekend afternoon. Apparently the American media would be unwilling even at this stage to go out of their way to pay any attention to the biggest trade deal in history. As a concession, Baker's staff offered a two-hour delay to a 4 P.M. announcement.

"Absolutely impossible," Burney exploded. "We are still a long way from having anything coherent to announce."

We laboured on into the early afternoon, cleaning up a number of cases where the Americans had, naturally, taken advantage of the home field – and their control of the typewriters – to transcribe various elements of agreement in the way that favoured their objectives. We were hopeful that we could finish the job that day, with a view to releasing the results perhaps on Monday. After all, the Americans could not proceed without us. Burney so advised the PM, who set in motion preparations for a Monday release.

Just before 4 P.M. one of my staff came in to report that the press conference was going ahead as planned. "No goddamn way," Burney said. "We are not going to be pushed on this to meet some American media schedule. If they hold a press conference, it will be without us."

But Ministers Wilson and Carney are already over there, the bewildered staffer explained. This was too much for Burney, who had masterfully kept his cool through the most difficult situations. We shut down the meeting, and he and I hitched a ride over to the Treasury Building. We made our way up to the grand conference room. The show was just beginning. It was a huge room with high ceilings, as befitted the centre of the empire. At the front of the hall, on a raised dais, stood the politicians. Baker was very much in control, with Yeutter, Wilson, and Carney as supporting cast.

I stood with Burney as he observed the proceedings with folded arms. After a nudge from Wilson, Baker called Reisman and Murphy up to the stage. Peter was wearing a highly photogenic green sweater that set off his unruly carrot-top hair. They shook hands, to the delight of the Canadian media who had defined the issue in terms of these two protagonists. (Predictably, this was the signature photo in Canada. In the United States, the coverage focused instead on Baker.) It was a grand moment, made all the more poignant for the fact that we did not yet have the agreement that they were all praising!

Then it was back to work. In trade agreements, grand designs have their place, but the devil lies in the details. Now that the agreement had been announced, there was no backing away. But both sides were keenly aware that we would have to live with the technical twists and turns buried in a stack of photocopied pages that reflected the distillation of thousands of pages of preparatory materials. The Americans saw this as an opportunity to tighten the screws: go along with our formulation, or face the embarrassment of cancelling the agreement. Now that Baker's prestige was publicly engaged, however, that was a game that two could play. It was heavy going.

The sticking points were the usual ones, the problem areas throughout the negotiations. The Americans were still pushing on pharmaceuticals, where we stood firm. They were trying to improve their deal on the cultural industries: having failed in the overall assault, they were trying to put an end to Canadian discrimination on postal rates or the retransmission of cable television signals. On the other hand, we were keeping their feet to the fire on other issues. I insisted that the agreement on trade in services had to include maritime transportation, knowing how very sensitive this was on Capitol Hill. The issue was pushed off to later clarification in an appendix to the agreement.

One serious stumbling block was the binational panels set up to review the unfair trade decisions of the American agencies, whom we considered terribly biased. We had wanted a permanent standing tribunal, but the Americans resisted on the grounds that Congress would oppose the establishment of a new bureaucracy. What was now proposed was a five-member panel chosen from rosters established in advance by the two parties. Canada would name two from our roster; the Americans would name two from theirs; the fifth would be chosen by the others from the national rosters, alternating between Canadians and Americans. This was an acceptable plan.

It was essential to us that the panels, as the final court of appeal, be permitted to look as broadly as possible at these issues. Simon was adamant that we could not achieve this with panels restricted to lawyers. In his experience, they would tend to look much too narrowly at the questions before them. The Americans were insistent: the panellists all had to be lawyers. Simon refused to have them dictate to us what kind of panellist we would name. Finally, I suggested a compromise: we could agree that the majority of the panel would be lawyers. We knew that the two panellists named by the Americans would be lawyers. We could name no lawyers if we chose. In that case, when the time came for the panellists to choose a fifth to chair the proceedings, we could agree to a lawyer to fill the slot. After all, there was something to be said for a legal expert in the chair of a tribunal to deal with these matters. Simon reluctantly agreed.

It was nearly 10 that night when we finally wrapped up the package. The dénouement came hours after the televised press conference. I had arranged to have the elements of the agreement, initialled by both sides, packaged together with a cover sheet on the top. We put two originals together, each with room for four signatures. We gathered the principals in the hall. Seated on the leather benches in the hall, using Burney's old briefcase for support, both sides went through the procedure. Burney, Wilson, Carney, and Reisman signed for Canada; Baker, Yeutter, McPherson, and Murphy for the United States. We then packed our bags and headed out to Andrews Air Force Base for the trip home.

What happened next may have been an augury of things to come. As we took off in the government jet, Mike Wilson pulled out a bottle of Scotch he had procured for the occasion, and the drinks were passed around. I had barely taken a sip when I noticed that the plane seemed to be circling over the tarmac. We were informed that the plane had developed mechanical problems and would have to return to Andrews. This was the height of anticlimax.

Back at the airport, the news was not good. It would be necessary to fly a part down from Ottawa. We had a choice: wait several more hours at the airport to fly back on the other plane; or grab some shut-eye at a nearby hotel and fly home on the repaired plane in the early morning. Burney and Wilson chose the first plan. Reisman, Carney, and I opted for the hotel. It turned out to be a strip motel with no food or beverage service at that late hour of the night. We were so tired it did not really matter.

Early the next morning, we climbed aboard the plane again and headed home, this time without incident. On arrival, we were caught up in a whirlwind. We met first with the prime minister and then with his cabinet, where the mood was overwhelmingly congratulatory – they had faced the prospect of disaster and greatly preferred the alternative. Then Simon and I held a press briefing. This was not the normal backgrounder – the cameras were turning and the television lights were blazing. Simon was exhausted but triumphant. I contented myself with strictly factual answers to the reporters' questions. I was operating on sheer adrenaline and today remember very little of this much-publicized moment of victory beyond what is documented in the press.

To my surprise, much of the media focused on what I had regarded as a nonissue, the provisions on energy. As far as we were concerned, the government owed its election in significant part to its repudiation of Trudeau's National Energy Program, so hated in western Canada. Instead, Canadian policy was now to recognize energy, particularly oil and gas, as commodities much like any others, whose producers had the right to seek the best rate of return, provided the national security was not endangered. Our agreement simply confirmed this policy, together with the renunciation of the use of quantitative export restrictions or export taxes on energy or other commodities, except in specified circumstances. In other words, it enshrined current policies but, with few exceptions, did not go farther than those policies. I could not see what all the fuss was about.

Simon and I then went to the official gallery in the House of Commons, where we were joined by Burney. Mulroney announced the agreement in principle. He said the agreement met the objectives the government had set when the negotiations began. He graciously recognized the three of us seated in the gallery. We then headed our separate ways, Simon to do his star turn with the media.

I met with a group of Canadian business leaders who had been support-ive throughout the negotiations to brief them on the results. It was a stellar cast, convened on short notice in a conference room at the External Affairs building. As the spokesman for the group, David Culver, the CEO of Alcan, warmly congratulated me on our achievement. The only sour note came from Roger Phillips, the CEO of the Saskatchewan steelmaker IPSCO, who seized at once on the fact that we had not succeeded in abolishing the American anti-dumping regime that had victimized his company in the past. I could only agree, but then I explained the progress we believed we had made in ensuring that these laws would at least be applied less unfairly in the future.

The media coverage on that first day and in the weeks that followed was decidedly mixed. We got off to a lousy start. When Pat Carney had been named minister of international trade, she had made a pact with Simon: "You negotiate and I will communicate." She was not about to be upstaged by a hired hand. This did not mean that Simon had vanished from public view — he was the media's star performer, the master of the thirty-second clip that would capture the headlines. It did mean that the TNO no longer assumed responsibility for media relations, which was now the function of Carney's department. Despite the resources at the department's disposal, the result was an unmitigated disaster, culminating in the announcement of the agreement.

To be fair, the department had an impossible task. It had not been heav-ily involved in the negotiations, which had been exclusively managed by the TNO. Indeed, Gerry Shannon, the deputy minister of international trade, had not attended the regular sessions I convened with senior deputy ministers throughout the negotiations and thus was not fully up to speed. Shannon and his staff were not on site in Washington but operated from Ottawa with hor-rendous communications difficulties. They had to rely on material faxed from the embassy, with all the delays that that involved. Some of these faxes were virtually illegible. Others were out of sequence. Others, as mentioned in the case of pharmaceuticals, were completely out of line. Furthermore, unlike the

Americans, they had to translate everything before it could be released. Finally, they were caught completely off guard when the Americans pressed ahead with the press conference on Sunday afternoon.

The Americans were first off the mark. Their communications staff had been working in tandem with their negotiating team. Thus they had released their synopsis of what the agreement contained in the mid-afternoon. It was riddled with errors of omission and commission and heavily accented with their political spin. It was hours before a Canadian version was ready to be released. Canada's self-proclaimed paper of record, the *Globe and Mail*, published the American synopsis of the agreement. This naturally coloured much of the media and public reaction. I was privately determined that we would not allow this to happen again.

This did not help matters in the political donnybrook that followed announcement of the agreement. Leading the Liberals in opposition, John Turner embarked on the crusade of his life to kill the agreement. There had been speculation at the outset that one of the factors that had encouraged Mulroney to choose Reisman as his chief negotiator was that he had been Turner's close friend and adviser. If so, the tactic failed abysmally. In the debate in the House of Commons on October 26, 1987, Turner nailed his colours firmly to the mast:

> I will fight that agreement. I will fight it to the point of running the next election on it. . . . We did not negotiate the deal, we are not bound by the deal, we will not live with this deal, and if the deal and the final contract reflects the principles and the general terms of agreement we have seen, we are going to tear the deal up.

At the Ottawa press briefing, we were informed that the Americans had said the final agreement could be completed within two weeks for signature by the heads of government. I responded that this sounded very ambitious but we would certainly do our best. What I did not say was that, in my experience, we were facing what amounted to another full round of negotiations. My caution was well based. When we contacted our American counterparts to see when their drafters would be available to meet, we learned that the author of that comment, Chip Roh, Murphy's legal right-hand man, had taken off on holidays. This was a strange way to do business but somehow came as no great surprise. It gave us more time to prepare.

When the negotiations resumed, there had been some changes in the cast of characters. With the exception of the trade law issues, the burden of negotiations at the staff level had been carried by the trade practitioners on both sides, with Germain Denis leading for Canada and Bill Merkin for the US. Now the legal advisers came into their own, playing a more substantial role. We were well served by Konrad and his outstanding staff in dealing with Roh and the American counterparts. Murphy also came back into the picture, leading the American team for the moment. Simon was more than prepared to leave him to me to handle. He was required to play a more demanding role in the media campaign.

His forbearance had its limits. One of our first sessions was up at the government facility at Meech Lake, the site of the historic negotiations of the ill-fated constitutional agreement. Peter and I worked our way through the elements of agreement in that rustic setting, complete with a blazing fire in the old stone fireplace. Despite the inclement weather, the media were out in force, lodged in the outbuilding a hundred feet down the road. Around 10 o'clock in the morning, Simon called with one question: Are the media there? I told him they were but that, by prior agreement, we had said nothing to them. Peter and I had simply brushed by them on our way in.

A few minutes later, I received a message from his chauffeur that Simon was on his way. As he emerged from his car, Simon was besieged by the press, to whom he explained that he was simply checking to see that everything was proceeding according to plan. When he arrived, we adjourned the talks for a few minutes while I took Simon aside and brought him up to date. He then left, but not before allowing himself to be caught up in another media scrum in which he announced that there would be no problem in wrapping things up very quickly. This was at odds with what I had told him, that we were making very slow progress and it would take at least another few weeks. Hours later, when our session finished with a great deal of work still undone, I went out to my car, only to be caught by the same scrum. They reported Simon's comment to me. I was somewhat taken aback. "If that's what Simon says, then that's where we are," I answered, climbing into my own car and driving off.

Unfortunately, the old pattern had repeated itself. On three technical points, Peter and I made tradeoffs. I agreed to accept his argument on some in return for his agreement on others. He then reneged on his end of the bargain, forcing us back to the starting point. Despite this we made considerable progress in cleaning up the relatively routine matters.

One apparently huge issue was not what it seemed. When the negotiations had first considered trade in services, nearly two years earlier, the immediate question was how broad the scope would be. Peter was categorical: the Americans were prepared to put absolutely everything on the table and insisted the Canadians do the same.

"Everything?" I asked.

"Everything," Peter replied.

"Even transportation? Air transport? Maritime transport?"

"Everything."

"You are absolutely sure?"

"Absolutely."

Unfortunately, this turned out to be another case in which Peter simply did not understand his situation. It became apparent that neither side had any stomach for getting into the intricate issues of bilateral air arrangements, which had developed a culture of their own. These were excluded from the FTA, although years later a modified free trade arrangement styled "Open Skies" was successfully negotiated, with dramatic results.

When the elements of agreement were later presented to Capitol Hill, the maritime lobby went utterly ballistic. This lobby is arguably the most powerful, and certainly one of the most corrupt, in the entire American system. Their most cherished icon was the Jones Act, which prohibited the carriage of products to or from the United States except in "American bottoms." This gave the American industry a total stranglehold on maritime commerce. They were not about to give it up. They not only tied up the Free Trade Agreement in the committees they controlled; they threatened, and had the muscle, to bring the whole process grinding to a complete halt by inducing the all-powerful Rules Committee to determine that the Free Trade Agreement did not, after all, meet the requirements to be fast-tracked through Congress. At our Meech Lake meetings, Peter had to reverse field. We had to take him off the hook, he said, or the whole deal would be down the tubes.

Provided we were given some concessions in return, I was prepared to oblige. I successfully kept my real problem from him. We were running into heavy weather with our own shipping industry. They had decided they liked the Jones Act so much, they wanted one of their own. A recent commission had recommended they be guaranteed control of Canada's coastal shipping, a prospect they viewed with greedy anticipation. Under these circumstances, the last thing they wanted was to open up the borders. I met privately with our transport minister, John Crosbie. He assured me, and reiterated in writing, that he would be in favour of a result that took the maritime transportation industry off the table entirely. Of course, I feigned great reluctance to Peter and only agreed once we had been satisfied on other points.

Some issues were not so easily resolved. One of the most awkward involved the automotive sector. I have described the deal Simon had negotiated. Auto Pact companies could ship vehicles across the border duty-free provided they met certain tests. For other producers – in other words, the transplants – it was necessary for vehicles shipped across the border duty-free to have at least 50 percent of their value, under a complex formula, represented by content produced in Canada or the United States. As far as Toyota and Honda were concerned, this was too high a standard, which it would take years for them to reach. As far as the rest of the industry was concerned, it was too low.

On the American side, Murphy demanded the standard be set at 60-percent North American value. This was a big step. It would require the transplants to source one more major component in Canada or, more likely, the United States. We were prepared to agree, on condition that we were allowed to continue to assist the transplants with the existing schemes that gave them back the duties they had paid on their imported components. This was the minimum required to keep the transplants operating and even growing in Canada. Peter agreed.

We could understand why the American-owned Big Three and the union would take this view. For the vitally important Canadian parts industry, the calculation was more complex. If the standard was set higher, they seemed to believe the result would be to force Toyota and Honda to buy more Canadian parts. The opposite was much more likely: they would forgo any expansion in Canada, supply the existing Canadian plants from an American base, and build their production in their US locations. The parts industry association, to our dismay, joined forces with the Big Three in demanding a higher-value-added standard. The president, an old sidekick of mine, went public with this message. It was a terrible blunder.

The result was precisely the opposite of what they had intended. Simon and I had made a special trip to Washington to sort out the remaining details with Murphy. True to form, Peter announced that he was going back on the deal on auto trade rules. It became obvious that others had convinced him he had been out-negotiated. Michigan Governor Jim Blanchard (a future ambassador to Canada) led the charge. They persuaded him that he had not needed to make any concessions to accommodate our concern for the health of the transplants. The rest of the Canadian industry would do his dirty work for him and force us to go along.

Simon held firm. A deal was a deal. If Peter was backing out of his side of the new deal, we would hold him to the old agreement, as announced in Washington. After much further waffling by our young American friend, that is exactly what happened. We had enough of Murphy's dithering and packed up and headed home that evening. This caused some consternation as the Americans had expected us to stay for at least one more day of negotiations.

With Christmas fast approaching, there remained a number of substantive disagreements to resolve. Murphy was no more able now than before to close agreements. It was time to bring back the generals. We invited the Americans to come to Ottawa, but only if Peter McPherson was prepared to head the American team. He came on Saturday, December 5, accompanied by Alan Holmer, who had been promoted to deputy US special trade representative in the interim; Murphy, who was clearly more junior although he still had a formal role and remained the media focus; and their negotiating team.

As soon as the senior players assembled at the TNO offices, it was painfully clear that the bitterness between Murphy and Reisman was going to make progress difficult. They immediately locked horns, with Simon on the attack and Peter dodging and weaving, both rehearsing old arguments. I obviously believed the problem lay with Peter. The senior Americans felt they could shut Peter out of the discussions only if his Canadian counterpart was also absent. I objected but Simon graciously accepted this as the price to pay to remove the man he saw as the last stumbling block. The convenient fiction adopted was that "procedural matters" would be discussed in a smaller group: McPherson and Holmer for the Americans and Burney and me for the Canadians. We met in a small office down the hall. The rest of the teams were set up in boardrooms: Simon and the other Canadians in the main boardroom of the trade office; Peter and the other Americans in another room well removed.

These "procedural matters" took up the rest of the day and well into the night. The four of us worked carefully through the outstanding issues, pausing occasionally to caucus with our delegation. In our case, Burney and I checked back regularly with Simon and the team. This procedure worked well, but it asked an awful lot of Simon to be put in this position simply, as he saw it, to keep Murphy from fouling things up. You could feel his discomfort building as the real negotiations went on without him in another room.

The negotiation of the final text eventually came down to a handful of issues. One was to prove important. The Americans were genuinely fearful that the arrangements they had agreed to impose on their unfair trade laws might be successfully challenged in the courts on constitutional grounds. To reduce if not eliminate this risk, the lawyers proposed an escape valve: if either side alleged that the final and binding panel decision had been seriously tainted, it could have the matter referred to an "extraordinary challenge" committee of three retired judges, not to review the decision but to determine that it had been fairly reached. The grounds were extremely narrow: essentially, one of the panellists had to be crooked or the panel had to have seriously violated its own authority; and this flaw had to be so serious that it had shaped the panel's decision and threatened the integrity of the whole system.

This was very troublesome. In explaining the deal we had made a great deal of mileage out of the fact that the panel decisions were final and binding. This new proposal gave the appearance that there was another layer in the process. The Americans were adamant: without this, there was always the risk that some judge, somewhere in the United States, would be persuaded to seize jurisdiction on the grounds that citizens had been judged by an unfair tribunal. Derek and Simon were fundamentally opposed. I allowed myself to be persuaded by the arguments from the lawyers, notably Konrad von Finckenstein. I assured Derek and Simon, and later the prime minister and the cabinet, that this was a truly extraordinary provision that, as I later said to the media, "might eventually be used once but would be so obviously ineffectual that it would never be used again." I will report later just how seriously I underestimated American litigiousness and indeed bad faith. Derek and Simon had been right and I was wrong.

This cut and thrust went on into the wee hours of the morning. To his credit, while McPherson had not spent his career in the trade field, he took his brief quickly and well. Holmer proved an able associate, much more qualified than Murphy had ever been to cut through the verbiage to get to the meat of the issues. On the Canadian side, Burney had the advantage of much greater familiarity with the issues, reinforced by the time we had spent together over the previous few weeks in clarifying the Canadian negotiating positions. It was laborious work but the process was finally coming to a conclusion.

Meanwhile, Simon's insecurity continued to mount as the negotiations continued outside his direct purview. He trusted me to know and reflect the views we shared – at least up to a point. At one critical moment late in the night, when we were all exhausted, Simon expressed some reservations about one issue Burney and I were negotiating with the Americans. If he was not fully satisfied, he snarled, he would not sign.

"Of course, you will have to sign," I said, trying to reassure him that nothing could be concluded without his agreement.

My attempt at conciliation backfired with a bang. Simon chose to interpret this as cutting the ground out from under him. He must have assumed that I was telling him that he would have no choice but to sign if he was so instructed. This may have been his own deep fear, but it was the farthest thing from my thoughts. I remained convinced that no agreement would be credible that did not have Simon's full and outspoken support. Before I realized what was happening, Simon lost it completely. Bellowing, he lunged at me. He would have taken a punch if he had not been held back by two of our largest colleagues, Burney and von Finckenstein, who quickly got between us. He then stormed off into his adjoining office.

There was a stunned silence for a moment or two.

"Jesus!" Derek said. "What the hell was that all about?" He had been spared exposure to Simon's famous tantrums in the past. Finally, I volunteered to go next door and see what I could do to straighten things out.

"You guys may not fully appreciate how much you still need Simon," I said. "If he is not out there supporting the agreement with all his energy, the whole deal is dead in the water."

I then gingerly made my way into Simon's office and had a long heart-to-heart discussion. He came back to the table and the negotiations continued. But our relationship was never the same again. Rightly or wrongly, he must have felt that my very presence was undermining his authority. He may have feared that he no longer had a monopoly of the confidence of the PM and his key advisers. Matters had not been helped by an *Ottawa Citizen* article that I had not seen, headlined "Top Public Servant Outlasts His Masters," reporting that I had emerged to overshadow Simon.

I never shared that view. It was not a question of false modesty. I knew I was pretty good at what I was doing. I am a competent negotiator. I had as sound an understanding of the issues as any Canadian alive. Together with our team, I understood how the various elements had to come together to make a sound agreement. I also would prove to be a highly credible expert witness, in print, on the air, or in the legislatures, in French as well as English. But I lacked two invaluable qualities that Simon possessed.

First, Simon had earned unparalleled credibility with the Canadian public as the tough guy who would stand up against the American bullies to protect Canada's interests. This reputation had been built up over many years – the enormously successful Auto Pact, his legendary confrontations with John Connally – and burnished by his remarkable, sometimes outrageous, performances in the media throughout the interminable period of negotiations with Murphy. It is not being disrespectful of Simon to say that many Canadians watching their evening news said to themselves: "God, what a tough little S.O.B.! Sure glad he's on our side."

The second quality may seem strange in one with such long experience in dealing with the Americans. Simon had a touching, almost naive faith in his ability to persuade the Americans to do the right thing in the end. Success has many fathers. The truth is that most of those who now claim to have been more or less responsible for the free trade initiative never in their wildest dreams envisaged such a comprehensive, all-embracing agreement. Yet this is what Simon had firmly in mind from the first private note he wrote for Brian Mulroney, even before he had been chosen as Canada's chief negotiator. Without Simon, there simply would not have been a free trade deal.

I was therefore pleased to fade into the woodwork when we finally wrapped up our negotiations at 2 that morning. The Canadian media were out in force, camped out in the cold, marbled lobby of our office tower. I skipped out ahead to get to my car for the drive home. Meanwhile, the media surged forward to surround Simon and Peter and besiege them with their questions. The scrum was still being carried on the networks when I tuned in at home fifteen minutes later. I could see Derek Burney and Peter McPherson standing together in the background. They would never receive the public credit they deserved. They did not fit into the predefined media story of a clash between David and Goliath. It reminded me of an old saying I used to impress on my staff: It is amazing what you can accomplish if you don't care who gets the credit.

With the Americans, it is never over until it is finally over. After that marathon session, we believed that it remained only to dot the i's and cross the t's. This took through Thursday noon. Understandably, the PM was impatient to get on with it. Finally I told him that he could have the final agreement in about an hour, around 4 P.M. I had no sooner put down the telephone than Konrad barged in to say that his American counterpart had just been instructed that they were not prepared to sign off the text until one more knotty issue had been resolved. It was a highly technical question to do with the retransmission by cable operators of television signals received from the United States.

The matter should have been settled long ago but for the bloody-mindedness of the technical departments on both sides of the border. Now the Americans were demanding further concessions.

That was the one and only time during these difficult negotiations that I truly lost my temper. Enough was enough.

"Tell the Americans to go to hell!" I exploded.

In twenty years of Canadian government service, much spent dealing with Americans, I had seen this stunt before. Just as the pen was poised over the paper to ratify an agreement, the American negotiator would demand just one more "final" concession. Then another. Then another final, final point that required "clarification," always in the Americans' favour. I used to joke that they must all work from a negotiator's manual that laid out three basic principles: always sit with your back to the window; keep the important issues to the last; and never, never let yourself be accused of failing to squeeze out the last drop of advantage, "leaving money on the table."

There had to be some end to the process. Now the top American drafter, Alan Holmer, was trying to delay the day of closure yet again. I took the phone and spoke to him in highly undiplomatic terms. "Ambassador, do I understand you are insisting on more changes before you can agree to the text we approved two days ago?" He confirmed that this was his unshakeable position.

"Then let me tell you mine. In half an hour, the prime minister of Canada will be meeting the press to inform them that a final agreement has been reached and that he has the text in his hand. It will be tabled in the House of Commons tomorrow and he will sign it on New Year's Day. There will be no more fooling around.

"If you don't like it, you can tell the president to scrap the deal."

There was a painful silence on the other end of the line. Finally the American conceded that he could live with what had, after all, been agreed before this one last attempt to squeeze more out of the Canadians.

Thirty minutes later, Simon and I joined the prime minister in his office on Parliament Hill. I presented him with the stack of binders that held the final agreement.

"I would like to see John Turner tear this up," I joked as the PM hefted one of the heavy binders in his hand. He enjoyed the thought so much he repeated it to the media a few minutes later. It was December 11, 1987, and the deal was finally done, the biggest trade agreement ever concluded between two sovereign countries.

On my return to the office, I broke out the champagne for a quick toast to the team that had put it all together. Then back to work. The document had to be in shape for presentation to Parliament the next day. This time, the TNO kept strict control of the process. The English text had been scrupulously vetted by Konrad and his team. The French translation had been double-checked by Germain Denis. I was called in to mediate fierce battles between the translators and the lawyers over such weighty matters as the correct French term for "animal feed." Overcoming his initial reluctance, one TNO staffer, Michael Hart, had prepared annotated introductions to each chapter, masterpieces of clarity with just the right amount of favourable spin. The thankless task of overseeing the actual production fell to another officer, Charles Garneau (the brother of the astronaut), who worked his team through the night. The result was flawless.

The next morning began with a full-dress press lock-up. This procedure, usually reserved for federal budgets, permits the media to have an opportunity to review the materials even before they are presented to the House of Commons. For this occasion, the television cameras were rolling as Simon and I conducted the briefing. I tried to keep the discussion as factual and objective as possible but it was heady stuff.

Simon was exhausted. In addition, he had been shaken by a report from his press aide on the way over that some of the media were following a story calling his personal integrity into question. The fatigue and disappointment spilled over at the press conference. Simon crowed over our success in out-negotiating the Americans. At one point, he commented that the Americans had "negotiated like a Third World country." This may have been a fair riposte to Clayton Yeutter's earlier widely reported remark that the deal could have been closed six months earlier if Simon had not been involved. But, as between old comrades-at-arms, I gave him hell as we headed for our next stop. I thought it was most unhelpful to the work we still had to do. It is a sure sign of weakness when a negotiator claims victory. It has a very damaging impact. Etc. Simon was repentant and volunteered that he would tone down his remarks in the barrage of media interviews he was doing later in the day. The penitent mood did not last long after the prime minister's wife, Mila Mulroney, called to congratulate him personally on his triumph and to cheer, in particular, his "Third World country" comment.

The press commentary was generally predictable. The media seized on some of the differences between the original elements and the final text but identified no serious issues. The one comment that really irritated me personally was when an old acquaintance, Michel Vastel, led his front-page story in *Le Devoir* with the complaint that the text handed out at 9 A.M. had been bound in the English version but loose-leaf in the French, although he admitted that the latter was bound before it was tabled in the House later that day. So that was the recognition we received for the extraordinary effort we had made, obviously without any help from the Americans, to fully respect the bilingual traditions of the country.

Three weeks later, on January 2, 1988, the formal signing ceremony took place. For optical reasons, Mulroney had no wish to be seen in Washington at Reagan's side for this occasion. Instead, the signing was done simultaneously in both countries under the watching eye of the television cameras. It was a Sunday afternoon. President Reagan did his bit from his ranch in Santa Barbara, California. Mulroney put his pen to paper in his office in Ottawa. The job of standing at his side and giving him the official documents was done by Konrad von Finckenstein. It was small enough recognition of the outstanding work he had done – and had yet to do.

7

CONNECTING THE LEVERS

Throughout the negotiations, one of my most difficult challenges was to ensure that the vast federal bureaucracy was on side. True, we had operated on the direct orders of the prime minister. Every step had been orchestrated with him and, as required, his cabinet. That did not mean that the armies of officials were marching to the same tune and in the same direction.

One of my early innovations had been the regular meetings of the senior deputy ministers who were likely to be most affected by the results of the negotiations. This initiative was strongly supported by the cabinet secretary, Paul Tellier, and the Privy Council Office was represented by one of its most senior staff, Harry Swain. Swain was now in charge of the operations of the economic committees of cabinet and realized how much simpler his task would be if there was good communication at the deputy-ministerial level. He could not have been more helpful.

Most interdepartmental committees are nominally composed of deputy ministers, but in practice they are usually represented by other, sometimes surprisingly junior officers. There are many reasons: most of these committees are not really necessary; they may be much less important to one department head than to another; such delegation is also part of the continuous jockeying for position in the pecking order. I had been the secretary to some of the more successful committees in the past and drew on that experience for this occasion. The committee was by invitation only. In most cases, the invitation went personally to the deputy minister, with no substitutes accepted. There were a few traditional exceptions: the central agencies – Privy Council Office, Finance, and Treasury Board – were permitted to and occasionally did send assistant deputy ministers instead. I also allowed Don Campbell, an ADM at External Affairs, to substitute for the deputy minister for international trade.

Once the committee was up and running, I made extensive use of this instrument for shaping the work of the entire government apparatus. I kept my colleagues fully briefed: initially on the proposals we planned to put to their ministers in cabinet; then on the progress of the negotiations; finally, on the actions needed to implement the agreement. This permitted a truly remarkable degree of coordination. At the high point in the negotiations, it was estimated that there were over 400 officials in twelve different departments engaged in some part of the preparatory work, under the overall direction of the trade office. Such a mobilization was utterly unprecedented in my experience. The amazing thing was not that this drive for results rubbed some bureaucrats the wrong way but that there was generally such a high degree of cooperation among these traditionally competing fiefdoms.

The meetings were not always deadly serious. The energy deputy, Arthur Kroeger, made one of the more imaginative contributions to the negotiations. At an early meeting of the deputy ministers' committee, he presented me with a huge poster showing a very small boy seated beside a very large elephant. I had the poster mounted and displayed in the boardroom, to the puzzlement of the American negotiators, who simply did not get it.

Potentially even more directly affected than the bureaucrats were the owners and executives of the Canadian companies whose futures would be transformed, for better or worse, by the Free Trade Agreement. Historically the principal source of opposition to any reduction of protective barriers, they had become the leading proponents of free trade. The major business associations were very active in the run-up to negotiations. These included the Business Council on National Issues, which had emerged as the leading lobbyist for big business under its dynamic president, Tom d'Aquino; the small business lobby, the Canadian Chamber of Commerce, under Sam Hughes, who later claimed paternity of the FTA; the Canadian Federation of Independent Business, led by the irrepressible John Bulloch; the Canadian Manufacturers' Association, led by Larry Thibeault; and many other associations representing exporters, importers, various specific industries, and other interests.

There were not enough hours in the day to commune with all these groups. It was essential to focus the business leadership's energies in a usable way. I drew upon my previous experience in setting up industry consultative groups back in the 1970s. We established a network of what became known as SAGITs – sectoral advisory groups on international trade. Each group was composed of the chief executives of the industry sector, from the leading firms themselves, excluding the trade associations. Organized labour had been invited to participate, but Dennis McDermott and Shirley Carr, leaders of the Canadian Labour Congress, had embargoed their involvement on policy grounds – to the dismay of some of their member unions, who found other ways to stay in touch. The secretariat and the budget for these industry groups were supplied by the External Affairs Department. The SAGITs proved invaluable as a resource to help with the negotiation of the agreement and later with its explanation to the general public.

In a radical departure from past practice, I assigned two TNO staffers to each of these groups. The desk officer responsible for that particular sector was supported by his or her boss. The team was overseen by one of my assistants, Charles Stedman. I made a point of attending at least one meeting of each of these groups myself. Over the opposition of the traditionalists, I shared our intelligence with these advisers, who were naturally sworn to confidentiality, to a degree never seen before nor, I am told, since. On no occasion to my knowledge were confidences betrayed. In exchange, they provided us with the very best information and advice they could give. As they came to understand the shape of the deal-making, they broke through the traditional business rhetoric to come up with pragmatic and imaginative ways of achieving national objectives. While they did not formally represent their industries, they carried very substantial moral authority. That enabled them to explain to their colleagues in other firms outside the consultations that this or that concession was required to make the agreement possible.

Throughout 1988, as the debate heated up over the trade agreement, my colleagues and I were often required to meet with groups across the country, in public or in private, to discuss the deal. Time after time, these meetings would be attended by one or more SAGIT members who would rise in their place to support the agreement we had negotiated. Their contribution was absolutely indispensable and changed forever the way the government managed trade policies.

In addition to the sectoral issues, there were a number of overarching questions on which it was essential to solicit the contribution of the business leadership. For this purpose, yet another committee was established, the top-level International Trade Advisory Committee (ITAC), chaired by the chief executive of Northern Telecom, Walter Light. Walter proved a superb, no-nonsense chairman, starting meetings on time and, even more rare, ending them precisely on time by keeping the discussion moving along at a steady pace. The membership was a Who's Who of the elite of Canadian business, including such icons as David Culver of Alcan, whose company had been hard hit by earlier American protectionism; Alf Powis of Noranda, who may have been the single most important influence on Brian Mulroney; and Philippe de Gaspé Beaubien of Télémédia, whom I had first seen in action at Expo 67, where he was the czar of the world media. I strongly encouraged successive trade ministers to put in an appearance at these meetings. I also attended every ITAC meeting personally, from beginning to end. This was the most effective way of ensuring that we were getting the full benefit of the experience of the leaders most directly affected, whose decisions would make or break the implementation of the agreement.

This arrangement paid substantial dividends. The quality of advice was very high, on such broad issues as the handling of the unfair trade laws. As a rule, the ITAC's advice was very well received. It certainly helped me to do my job. Unfortunately, the ITAC's advice was not always heeded. On the issue of adjustment assistance, for example, the ITAC was very supportive of measures to help workers find new employment. Their concerns were instrumental in persuading the government to set up a commission, under Jean de Grandpré of Bell Canada Enterprises, which again came out strongly in favour of such assistance. This recommendation was borne out by all the experience and analysis I had done on the subject over two decades. Most regrettably, the government took no action, despite the advice it had received and, indeed, the public commitments it had made. I believe that this was the single most serious failure in the government's implementation of free trade.

Ultimately perhaps even more important was the ITAC's identification of the pressing need for business to support the agreement once negotiated. This would not properly be undertaken by the ITAC itself, since its role was advisory to government. Many of the same players, however, in their other capacities, ensured that business did wade into the debate.

I also made an effort to be available to meet with business groups across the country. I recall one such trip in mid-1988. Following several industry briefings in Toronto, I headed on to Calgary, accompanied by my wife. There we rented a fast car to make the spectacular drive up to Jasper. While Marg headed off on a trail ride through the hills, I briefed a group of electric utility executives on the energy provisions of the Free Trade Agreement. We then hopped back in the car for a very quick trip back to the Calgary airport. The plane stopped in Ottawa on the way home, where Marg disembarked; I kept on to Dorval, where I arrived at midnight and was installed in a suite at the Holiday Inn. At 6 A.M. I reported for duty at the local cinema, where I kicked off an all-day briefing for businesspeople from the West Island. I was then driven back to Ottawa for a late-morning meeting with the cabinet.

It was at times a gruelling schedule. Despite my fatigue, I made every effort to keep my presentations factual and objective. Canadian business men and women could form their own judgments; what they needed was to understand the agreement and how it would work. I was subjected to some criticism for this dry-as-dust approach. Some would have preferred that I make a more dramatic effort to rally the troops. I preferred to leave the high-profile, media-directed activities to Simon, who put on quite a performance as the gutsy battler, rallying the converted and tearing into the critics of the agreement.

The provincial governments were another matter entirely. We could have refused, I suppose, to consult with business, and labour was free to refuse to talk with us. We did not have that option with the provinces, who are, after all, sovereign governments in their own spheres of jurisdiction. To some, including my former professor Claude Morin, later intergovernmental affairs minister in the Parti Québécois government of René Lévesque, the pendulum had swung to give much too much power to the federal central government. From where I sat, the opposite was true. Voters surely did not elect Howard Pawley premier in Manitoba to preside over Canadian foreign trade policies. Despite the erosion of federal powers under unrelenting provincial pressure over the years, the government of Canada had authority over international and interprovincial trade and commerce.

The issue had arisen before the negotiations with the Americans were even under way – and before I had agreed to join the team. This was at the time of Meech Lake, the high-water mark in federal-provincial collaboration, which may explain how, at a meeting of first ministers in the fall of 1986, the premiers had demanded a seat at the negotiating table. Their eight-point proposal included demands that the provinces would have the right to be fully consulted at every step of the negotiations; the talks would be overseen by a committee of trade ministers, co-chaired by a province and the federal government; the provinces would be entitled to name a representative to participate directly in the negotiations. This was arguably anti-constitutional; it was certainly unworkable.

Joe Clark was detailed to sort matters out with the provincial trade ministers at a follow-up meeting in Halifax. Seeing the dangers, Simon jumped on a plane and headed down to Nova Scotia. He was successful in blurring the issues enough to keep our flexibility. In the event, no provincial official was allowed in the negotiating room with the Americans.

There was, however, a need for consultation, particularly since the provincial governments assumed they would exercise a veto over the final outcome. A committee was established to enable us to coordinate with the provinces. Each premier named a personal trade representative – often a former federal trade diplomat, like Jake Warren for Quebec and Bob Latimer for Ontario, or a political crony of the premier, as in Nova Scotia or Alberta. With Simon in the chair, this group met monthly to coordinate positions. The staff work was prepared by Alan Nymark. The flow of information tended to be almost entirely one-way. Simon would hold forth, occasionally duelling with his old colleagues Warren and Latimer while the other representatives looked on in mounting irritation. Some of the provinces, notably Quebec, would contribute analysis and views of their own. Most sat on their hands. Ontario was actively obstructionist. The Ontario team was openly confrontational at the meetings, and on the few occasions when Ontario presented papers to the group the documents were leaked in advance to the press, followed by the Ontario delegation's self-serving notes on the subsequent in-camera discussion.

The real clash naturally came at the top. After the Halifax débâcle came a first ministers' meeting in Vancouver that was dominated by the lumber dispute with the Americans. Then, on five separate occasions in 1987, the prime minister convened private meetings with the provincial premiers. The first session, on March 11, was held in the cabinet room in the Centre Block of the Parliament Buildings and was restricted to preliminary skirmishing over organizational issues. The next three meetings were the scene of a historic confrontation over the issue of free trade.

These gatherings were held in the alternate cabinet chamber in the Langevin Block, just across from Parliament Hill. It became an elegant prison cell, the light streaming in from windows high up the barren walls. Mulroney sat at the head of the table with Pat Carney at his right hand taking detailed notes – which, as it transpired, her department later destroyed. Simon sat on the PM's left. I came next, beside Quebec Premier Robert Bourassa, directly opposite Ontario Premier David Peterson. The other premiers were arrayed in the usual order around the oval table. No officials were present, although there were literally hundreds in the antechambers – the intergovernmental affairs bureaucracies, the trade experts, and the political and media handlers for all eleven governments.

The first meeting was held in early July, to review the proposed Canadian positions on the various issues. The second, on September 14, brought the first ministers up to date on the negotiations following the Cornwall fiasco and before the closing sessions in Washington. The third session was convened on October 6 to review the results once the deal was completed. Despite the differing circumstances, the three meetings quickly fell into a common pattern.

The sessions began after lunch and were always scheduled to finish before the supper hour, that is, before the 6 o'clock evening news. In practice, the tension would rise as the early news deadline approached, then subside again as it became obvious the meeting would run on. The cycle would repeat as 10 o'clock came and went. The meetings typically ran for eight hours or longer. Often they did not conclude until early in the morning. (It will be recalled that the same cast of first ministers were becoming accustomed to pulling all-nighters on another burning issue, constitutional reform.)

Shortly before the session, Mulroney would meet with Burney, Simon, and me in his office in the building. It is a relatively modest office for the head of a G-7 government, but it makes up in stylish comfort what it lacks in grandeur. We would review the game plan for the upcoming meeting, and I would outline the presentation I had prepared to take the premiers through. Then we would head upstairs for the main event.

The PM would welcome the premiers with a brief opening statement to set the stage for the meeting. After the introductions, the PM would turn to me to brief the first ministers on the issues. To keep control, this took the form of a strictly oral presentation, accompanied by overheads in French and English. No paper was distributed to the first ministers, but some took copious notes anyway. Neither their notes nor their memories were always reliable. (Months later, when PEI Premier Joe Ghiz charged publicly that the issue of energy trade had never been discussed at these meetings, I quietly sent him a copy of the overheads I had used to brief him on two occasions on precisely these issues. He did not say another word on the subject.)

My presentation was punctuated by a stream of interruptions. The premiers were not trade experts. They had a great many questions as they tried to understand exactly what was being presented, and what the political implications would be back home. They frequently popped out of the room to consult with their armies of advisers in the halls and meeting rooms adjoining. Simon generally held his fire until he could stand it no longer, particularly when David Peterson would say something particularly outrageous. The PM was, I suspect, delighted to have Simon take Peterson on directly but would occasionally intervene to cool things down. At one point, I put my hand on Simon's left forearm gently to restrain him only to see Mulroney's hand on Simon's right.

Peterson emerged as the clear leader of the opposition at these meetings. He played the role of sceptic and critic, trying to catch me out on the issues or, much more important, to impress his colleagues with the political unsaleability of this or that provision. He was generally unsuccessful. Joe Ghiz, also a Liberal, later emerged as his ally but made little or no contribution at the meetings themselves. New Democrat Howard Pawley of Manitoba agonized out loud over free trade – as I gather he did about everything else – but was ineffectual and was eventually replaced at the table by his successor, Conservative Gary Filmon, who was much more positive.

The other premiers were generally supportive. Alberta's Don Getty was pleased with the energy arrangements, although some of his officials joked that he relied on BC's Bill Vander Zalm to explain the fine points. As a former agricultural economist, Grant Devine of Saskatchewan made a helpful contribution. Brian Peckford of Newfoundland was a strong promoter of free trade, although his province's interests were relatively narrow. Nova Scotia's John Buchanan said almost nothing during the meetings but could be counted on to support the prime minister (and later went to his reward in the Senate).

The leader of the free trade premiers was unquestionably Robert Bourassa, the most experienced and knowledgeable of the group. He was very much in favour of free trade with the United States for powerful economic reasons. He had the best personal understanding of the issues, the strongest team of officials, and the closest relationship with Mulroney. He provided a valuable counterbalance to Ontario's Peterson. When Peterson was behaving particularly aggressively, Bourassa would soothe him with the thought that, in the end, Peterson would wield a veto over any agreement.

This was the conventional wisdom at the time, expostulated by provincial leaders and political pundits alike. Some claimed that unanimous support of the premiers was required, in which case Peterson would indeed hold the veto. Others believed that the constitutional amending formula would apply, requiring support of at least seven provinces with at least 50 percent of the population. In that case, Peterson could still form a blocking coalition if he could rally a few other premiers to his side. He certainly made every effort in those meetings as well as in his every public utterance. His hand was naturally strengthened during the negotiations when he sought and obtained another mandate from the provincial electorate on a platform that included opposition to free trade. Our strategy was much deeper. While the PM obviously sought to enlist the support of premiers and their governments, he never formally asked them to concur. As a result, they never formally approved or rejected the agreement or any of its elements. It served the interests of both the federal and provincial politicians to leave hanging the issue of just how far the federal government could go without provincial agreement.

Mulroney would bring the meetings to a close by reviewing his handwritten summary of the results that he would propose to share with the media. This was a unique opportunity for me to see the full play of his talents in reconciling competing positions. He was truly masterful. His summation would be designed to convey the impression of substantial agreement, without ever putting a premier in a corner where he would have to repudiate the statement. This was particularly important at the October meeting following the agreement in Washington.

When each of the closed-door sessions finally drew to an end, the time came to meet the press. They were massed outside the door of the Langevin Block facing out onto Confederation Square. Microphones were set up under the intense camera lights. Railings kept the press from trampling the politicians in their excitement. The PM would lead off with his prepared statement. Then other provincial premiers would follow, announcing what they had said in the private meetings – or wished they had said, or at least wished the media to believe they had said. Some of them naturally commanded the undivided attention of the assembled media. Others were less noteworthy.

Simon, meanwhile, would go out another door on Wellington Street and then stroll through the scrum, on the off chance that someone would be interested in his comments. After they had heard from the main protagonists, the media were more than pleased to shift their attention to Reisman. This antagonized some of the premiers, but they got used to being upstaged by the old master.

One strategic problem hung like a cloud over these proceedings. How far in fact could we proceed without provincial concurrence? With Burney and Norman Spector, the cabinet secretary for federal-provincial relations, I formulated a three-stage plan after the first meeting of the prime minister and the premiers.

First, it was probable that the negotiations would narrow in scope as items fell off the table, thus reducing but not eliminating the need for us to intrude directly into areas of provincial jurisdiction. Second, we sought expressions of agreement from as many provinces as possible, including at least seven of the ten premiers, which would greatly strengthen the federal government's political hand. Third, in the end, the federal government could and should proceed on the basis of its own authority to conclude agreements, regulate international and interprovincial trade, and control aliens, i.e., foreign investors.

The first element of this strategy slowly took effect as the Americans scaled back what they were prepared to put on the table. Their original offer to include all of their government purchasing would have required us to give them reciprocal access to our federal and provincial procurements. Their final position could be fully offset by including a few federal departments and no provincial purchases. By the same token, when they backed away from the plan to prohibit certain state subsidies, it took the pressure off our provincial programs. There remained, nonetheless, important areas of provincial competence, including the regulation of services and investment and, most obviously, the provincial liquor monopolies.

We therefore had to keep up the pressure to bring key provinces on side. In the midst of the negotiations, we lost an important and loyal ally, New Brunswick Premier Richard Hatfield. By the time of our meeting in July, he could clearly see the writing on the wall. He brought with him a book recording a recent premiers' conference and had his colleagues sign it for posterity. He then went home to be whipped by his electorate, losing every single seat in the province. I was sorry to see him go, as I believed he had made a very important contribution to the province. When he died a few years later, the tributes were well deserved.

His successor, Frank McKenna, was a very different proposition. Hatfield had strongly supported both the Meech Lake constitutional accord and the Free Trade Agreement. McKenna had come out against both in his campaign. He had barely taken office when John Turner, as the national Liberal leader, joined with Joe Ghiz to twist their new colleague's arm. The view from the province-watchers in Ottawa was that this was a disaster for us. Turner had enlisted his Maritime Liberals in his crusade against free trade. It was too soon to tell if he had succeeded in bringing McKenna on side with the Meech Lake Accord, which Turner and Ghiz supported.

I was therefore conscripted to go down and test the waters in Fredericton. Norman Spector made it clear that he believed it was mission impossible, but it was part of the strategy to soften up McKenna on Meech

Lake. I took a very different approach. Unless he told me directly that he disagreed, I would assume that McKenna could be convinced that it was in New Brunswick's interests to have free trade with the United States. After all, I told an amused Mike Wilson, my family in New Brunswick have been bringing stuff across the border duty-free for years – except on the rare occasions when we were caught by the customs guards.

At it turned out, McKenna could not have been more courteous. I had a lengthy session with him, his deputy premier, and his key advisers. I gave him the full briefing on the proposed agreement and how, in my judgment, it would affect the province. It was a very low-key and productive session. In a brief private session with the premier we talked about matters of particular concern to the province that I still regarded as my own. On my return to Ottawa, I told the sceptics that McKenna had yet to make up his mind but I believed he would keep New Brunswick on side with the Free Trade Agreement. That is exactly what happened. McKenna resisted the blandishments and threats of his fellow Liberals and plumped for free trade.

Emboldened, Spector then tried to enlist McKenna's support on Meech Lake. He met with a very different reception, complete with a carefully orchestrated ambush before the media. McKenna remained firmly opposed to the accord. Indeed, it was his opposition that was the key factor in delaying ratification of the accord until the opposition had mustered its forces. At that point, McKenna attempted to repair the damage by offering compromise proposals. It was too late. The harm was done. McKenna had probably doomed his outside chance of becoming prime minister of Canada.

The Free Trade Agreement was tacked onto the agenda of a full-dress first ministers' conference on November 26 under the watchful eye of the television cameras in the conference room at the Harbour Castle in Toronto. By then we had concluded the agreement and very nearly finalized the text with the Americans. We were not yet ready to table implementing legislation in Parliament, where we knew we were in for a rocky ride. At the conference, there was very little discussion of any substance. Various premiers rehearsed their positions on camera. The line-up remained unchanged, with David Peterson leading the opposition and supported by Joe Ghiz – Canada's most and least populous provinces. No vote was taken. No formal commitment was sought nor obtained. After the meeting, we were not farther ahead, but at least we had not lost ground. The issue of provincial concurrence remained.

There was one final private session of first ministers on December 17, 1987, the week after the text of the agreement was tabled in the House of

Commons. I was summoned to Rideau Gate, the elegant guest-house just outside the gates of the Governor General's residence and across the street from 24 Sussex Drive. A few details had still to be explained. The last sticking point, as I recall, involved arrangements between the Bonneville Power Administration and BC Hydro. BC Premier Vander Zalm required some further assurances, which I was pleased to give him as we met in the cramped surroundings of the upstairs landing of the guest-house. The die was now cast. The federal government had signed an agreement. It remained to be seen whether and how the government could make it the law of the land.

My original understanding when I returned to Ottawa had been clear. I would remain until the free trade negotiations were completed. Then I was a free man. If the prime minister offered a post I liked, I could accept. If he did not offer or I did not accept, I was perfectly at liberty to retire from the public service. The negotiations were now completed, and as far as I was concerned it was time to think of moving on to other challenges outside government.

The PM was having none of it. On his instructions, Paul Tellier wrote to Simon, copied to me, to give us our new marching orders. Simon was to get out and spread the gospel. I was to serve as the senior official responsible for the next stage of the process, preparing the mass of legislation required to implement the agreement. This essential step was necessary to link the legal and administrative levers to the agreements we had made.

Simon was furious. He had done everything the prime minister had asked of him, and more, and this was his reward. The moment his enemies in the Privy Council Office believed he was no longer indispensable, they sought to cut him down to size by taking away a major part of his responsibilities. Against his better judgment, he had permitted me to take a higher profile in these negotiations. His generosity had backfired. Now I was being used against him by those who had always resented his independence of spirit, his public reputation, and his access to the prime minister. This was intolerable. He demanded that the letter be withdrawn. Tellier held his ground. In a typically bureaucratic compromise, Simon refused to concede that there had been any change in responsibilities, but did indeed do as the PM had asked and focused on delivering the message to the public, leaving me to do the housework.

I was less interested in the formalities than in getting the job done. There was plenty of work to go around. To be honest, I found the challenge daunting. Under the American system, the agreement we had just completed was no more than an executive agreement. It would have no effect unless it was put into legislation and duly passed into law. In Canada, we therefore resolved to present our own omnibus bill that would include all the changes required to Canadian law. Thus, Parliament would not be called upon to approve the Canada-US Free Trade Agreement itself. Instead, it would be asked to enact the implementing legislation. This was to be my task for the next nine months – a lengthy gestation that was not without its moments of high drama.

Shortly thereafter, an important new ally entered the play in the person of the redoubtable John Crosbie. He accepted the offer from his old adversary Mulroney to take over the hot potato portfolio of international trade. He did insist that he be recognized as a senior minister, not in any way subordinate to External Affairs Minister Joe Clark. As he put it to me with his typical bluntness, "I didn't want to spend the next two years looking up Joe's arse."

John Crosbie is a true original. Born to one of the great business and political families of Newfoundland, he served in the provincial cabinet of Joey Smallwood. When he could stand the rotten smell of corruption no longer, Crosbie left the Liberal Party and crossed over to the Conservatives. Under the leadership of Frank Moores, the Tories came to power, and Crosbie served in a number of key posts before leaving to run federally.

In the Joe Clark government, Crosbie brought down a budget in 1979 that, in turn, brought down the government. In retrospect, his fiscal plan looks pretty good, but at the time it was viciously attacked for imposing "short-term pain for long-term gain." This did not enhance Crosbie's reputation for political sagacity. When Clark opened up the leadership, Crosbie put on a strong showing until, with his usual incisiveness, he attempted to deflect criticisms of his inability to speak French by confessing that he did not speak Chinese, either. When Mulroney came to power, Crosbie had to settle for the justice portfolio and then transport. At the end of March 1988, he was named to the trade job, with special responsibility for getting the FTA legislation through Parliament.

On his first day on the job, he came to the trade office to meet with the staff. After the usual introductions, he waxed eloquent about his commitment to meeting the challenge – with the help of the superb trade team whose senior officers were seated around the table. It was my painful responsibility to explain that these were not the senior managers, they were the whole team – "What you see is what you get." Indeed, even they were in place only until they went to their next assignments, as I was under instructions to fold up shop as soon as possible and hand the job over to the huge External Affairs bureaucracy. Crosbie was flabbergasted. It turned out that Paul Tellier had held out to Crosbie the incentive of being supported by the best team in Ottawa. Crosbie and I finally straightened matters out and I persuaded the rump that remained in the trade office to put their career plans on hold for the duration. In some cases, this involved considerable personal sacrifice.

Crosbie was one of the most intelligent men I ever met in public life. He was very quick to master his brief, getting right down to the fundamental points. With this clarity of thinking came a candour that occasionally created problems. At one point, a journalist asked him whether he had read every page and paragraph of the Free Trade Agreement. The media love this sort of question, which sounds plausible to the general public but in fact is completely asinine. In each official language, the agreement required a text of 1,600 pages, many of which were columns of tariff schedules. Crosbie's answer was widely reported: "Of course not," he said. Not so reported was the remainder of his reply: "That's Gordon's job, to make sure the text carries out my government's instructions."

This was the true and honest answer but it was the wrong political answer. The media, few of whom had taken the trouble to read even the press release on the agreement, let alone the agreement itself, trumpeted the discovery that Crosbie was prepared to sign an agreement he had not read from cover to cover. The correct political answer was given by the prime minister, who claimed to have read every word, every comma, in the agreement. At least Mulroney had been closely involved in examining the major issues. I very much doubt the same could be said for opposition leader John Turner, who claimed to have read the agreement several times and then, in the subsequent election campaign, demonstrated that he had no idea what it really comprised.

Crosbie is one of the shyest men I have ever met. I realize this is quite the opposite of his public persona. His shyness was masked in public by his speaking technique. He was widely admired, and sometimes criticized, for the humour of his remarks. This was the product of enormous effort. Crosbie had diligently applied himself to absorbing the techniques of Dale Carnegie, famous for teaching "How to win friends and influence people." His speeches were laced with quotations dug up by his staff, many of them delightful gems, the first few times one heard them. This hid the fact that Crosbie was in apparent physical discomfort whenever he was obliged to make eye contact with another person. I attended meetings with him, and meetings he had with old acquaintances, including the prime minister, in which he was simply unable to force his eyelids open. Throughout the conversation, his face would be contorted and his eyelids twitching as he tried, and failed, to look the other person in the face. It is remarkable testimony to Crosbie's dedication and courage that this supremely private man could nonetheless put his considerable talents at the service of the public for some thirty years. He would have made an interesting prime minister.

Instead, he applied his impressive gifts to putting the Free Trade Agreement in place. One key element, widely overlooked, finally resolved the issue with the provinces. As a former justice minister, Crosbie quickly grasped our strategy. He understood the importance of staking out the federal turf. He appreciated the force of the legal opinions we had received from the leading experts. Contrary to the academic pundits, ancient decisions by the Judicial Committee of Britain's Privy Council, the final court of appeal before 1949, had not cast in concrete the requirement that the provinces concur in all matters in their jurisdiction. The federal government had the overriding ability to make treaties whose principal impact related to international trade. If, in order to negotiate and implement those agreements, it was necessary to touch on elements of provincial control, so be it.

It was on this basis that I had the legislation drafted to do what was required to bring the provincial governments into compliance. The delicate areas were drafted in such a way that the federal and provincial implementing legislation could be virtually identical. David Peterson believed he held the aces. If the anticipated veto failed, the other provincial governments would rally to his side if the federal government threatened to override provincial authority. With our proposed legislation, supportive provinces could neatly sidestep the issue. Premiers such as Don Getty of Alberta and Robert Bourassa of Quebec could implement the agreement in their own provinces without in any way undercutting their vigilant promotion of provincial rights. Thus the issue of whether the federal government could impose its will on the provinces would be moot.

The only case where Peterson could really make trouble was the provincial liquor monopoly, the Liquor Control Board of Ontario. If he refused to take action to implement the agreement, we would be in default to the Americans. On this narrow front, we therefore decided to make the defence of the overriding federal powers. The relevant section stipulated that the provinces were *encouraged* to take the required steps to bring their liquor monopolies into line. But if one or more refused, the federal government would impose its own regulations on these businesses under the authority conveyed by the agreement, unless and until the offending province came into line and thus permitted us to withdraw from the field. Those provinces that went ahead on their own could assert that they did so entirely of their own volition. Peterson, on the other hand, would have a serious problem.

At this point, Crosbie swung into action. He made a cross-country pilgrimage to meet with provincial premiers and explain the federal position and legislation. I accompanied him to the two key sessions. The first, with Quebec on May 6, 1988, was warm and friendly. In deference to his dam-building obsession, the premier's Montreal office was high atop the Hydro-Québec skyscraper. We quickly covered the ground and reached agreement with Premier Bourassa. I spent some time going over the fine points with his talented chief adviser, Diane Wilhelmy, who was very knowledgeable in intergovernmental matters. It was smooth sailing all the way.

The next stop was very different. Crosbie was ushered in for a one-on-one session with Premier Peterson, while I was left in the adjoining boardroom to the tender mercies of the head of the Ontario public service, Bob Carman, and his gunslingers. Bob summoned up his most frosty mien for the occasion, with the provincial deputy minister of industry, Pat Lavelle, playing the bad cop. Finally the politicians emerged from next door to report that they had agreed to disagree. This was entirely as expected. We were not dissuaded from our course.[1]

The remaining visits were handled skilfully by Crosbie, with the assistance of Konrad von Finckenstein and Mary Dawson, another senior official from the Justice Department (who later became its associate deputy minister). As a result, the way was cleared for the federal legislation to proceed, without a direct confrontation.

Meanwhile, there was the little matter of holding the Americans to their side of the free trade bargain. Just as they had to be satisfied that our bill did what was required to bring the Free Trade Agreement to life in Canada, we would apply the same test to the legislation that the administration was to put before the Congress. Unlike the Canadian bill, which the government, if it chose, could permit to be amended, the American bill would be set in concrete once it was exposed to the air of Capitol Hill. It was therefore imperative that we

---

1. Later Peterson and, much later, his successor, Bob Rae, threatened loudly and often to take the federal government to court on the issue. Neither proceeded, presumably because they were receiving the same advice we were: the province would almost certainly lose in a court battle; they were doing much better extracting concessions in the political arena and should stick to that.

be given the opportunity to review and accept their legislation before it was tabled. As the months dragged on, the Americans showed great reluctance to share their masterpiece with us. Alan Holmer protested that to show us the bill in advance of tabling would violate all the rules of the American legislature. What nonsense. It took another mini-showdown to smoke them out.

I had agreed that my colleagues at External Affairs would undertake the initial review, subject to my concurrence and then approval by ministers. Overall, the USSTR had done a reasonably professional job, given the limitations of the American legislative process, which makes Canada's look highly professional by comparison. External was satisfied. I was not. It seemed to me that there were several potentially serious problems. The Americans, in particular the denizens of the Commerce Department, were up to their usual games.

One issue could have been explosive but we were able to turn it into "sound and fury signifying nothing." Senators Max Baucus and John Danforth, who had steadfastly opposed the entire deal, were particularly incensed at the agreement we had reached to police their unfair trade authorities. In the American system, courts are guided not only by the letter of the law, which is typically very poorly drafted, but by their best guess as to the real intent of the Congress. This, in a country that boasts it is governed by laws and not by men. To assist the courts, the Congress may lay out its intentions in a statement of administrative action accompanying the legislation. When the Canadian legal team got around to examining this accompanying statement, they were immediately faced with an attempted end run around the FTA rules. It became known as the Baucus-Danforth provision, after its congressional authors. It purported to give American complainants yet another instrument to harass imports from Canada through a new form of investigation, paid for by the American government and using the force of law to oblige Canadian firms to comply at potentially significant expense.

I was furious and immediately confronted Holmer. By now, Alan and I had taken each other's measure. He was between a rock and a hard place. He had realized the Canadians would be angry and had used his legal and diplomatic talents to persuade the senators to water down their proposal to some degree. On the other hand, when I told him that I was prepared to bring the whole thing to a halt over this issue, he knew that I was not bluffing. In my judgment, this provision as it then stood could undermine what Canada considered the most important pillar of the agreement. After a great deal of very tough negotiations, we managed to agree on a formulation that Messrs.

Baucus and Danforth could trumpet to their protectionist constituents as a major victory while we could rest secure in the knowledge that the measure was entirely toothless. I was very pleased with the result and did not anticipate any problem in getting ministers to understand and agree.

As was our habit, we gathered the few key ministers and advisers in the small boardroom adjoining the cabinet chamber in the Centre Block. This is a very pleasant round room with windows facing out over the west lawn. It seats a maximum of perhaps twenty persons in solid chairs on casters at a padded round table. I explained where we stood on the Canadian legislation and reported briefly on the American draft bill. I explained that the Baucus-Danforth provision as it now stood was virtually meaningless. It conferred no new rights and powers and would not represent any threat to Canadian interests. (In the event, this assessment proved absolutely correct, as the provision was never used.) With the agreement of ministers, I would give the Americans the green light to proceed.

I had not allowed for Simon's mood swings. He had shown great restraint throughout the legislative process. He was fully occupied in fighting for the hearts and minds of Canadians on the speaking circuit. Unfortunately, he happened to be in town when this matter arose. It must have seemed a useful opportunity to demonstrate that the old bear was still around and still had a full set of teeth and claws. Without any prior warning, he jumped into the discussion with a scathing condemnation of the provision and those weak-kneed functionaries who had negotiated it. He went on at some length. He then turned to me to support his argument, apparently oblivious to the fact that I was recommending that we accept the very thing he had attacked.

I am embarrassed to admit that it was my turn to lose my cool. This really was too much. I rose to my feet a bit more abruptly than I intended. My chair smashed into the wall, gouging a great chunk out of the plaster. There was a moment of stunned silence as the ministers took in what was happening before their eyes. Finally, one of them allowed that the provision looked acceptable to him and suggested we move to the next item. The meeting came to an early end and I left without talking to Simon. I later offered to pay for any repairs to the wall or the chair but was assured by the officer from the cabinet secretariat that they would see to fixing the damage themselves.

There were other technical issues that required some negotiations and some loose ends that I would rather have tied more tightly. Overall, however, I believed that if Congress approved the draft as it had been revised,

Canada could proceed to implement our side of the deal. The prime minister subsequently advised the House of Commons of this conclusion. It only remained to turn the agreement into the law of the land. That simple step was to take the whole of 1988 and culminate in a ferocious election struggle over the issue of free trade.

8

THE GREAT DEBATE

T he initial debate was over the legislation to implement the agreement. The prime minister had made me responsible for this undertaking but the real work was done by a team of federal lawyers under the overall direction of Konrad von Finckenstein. As the senior officer of the Department of Justice, he had the monumental task of reviewing the changes that would be required to bring a dozen or more federal laws and uncounted regulations into conformity with the agreement. His team created an omnibus bill that would incorporate all the changes in a single piece of legislation. The opposition Liberals attempted to have the Speaker of the House of Commons throw the bill out and require us to come back with dozens of separate specific bills. Mercifully, he ruled in the government's favour, and the omnibus bill could proceed.

At Prime Minister Mulroney's insistence, I was called on to take an unusually high profile in the legislative process. I firmly believe that it is the responsibility of politicians to promote and defend their policies. The public servant should confine his efforts to clarifying and explaining those policies and their implementation. I advanced this principle late one night in a conversation with Paul Martin, Jr., the head of Canada Steamship Lines and a prominent Liberal. He had requested a briefing on the Free Trade Agreement, and I had arranged to drive down to Montreal after work. After a very pleasant dinner and too much vintage port back at his home in Westmount, I told him that I was perfectly prepared to explain all the twists and turns of the agreement. I would also assert my belief that it was the best deal we could have negotiated under the circumstances. It would then be for the public to decide, on the basis of the arguments of the politicians, whether that was good enough. They would have to determine whether the agreement was in Canada's interest. I could live with their decision, either way.

Martin took my point. After all, he was equally steeped in the conventions of Canadian public service through the lessons he had learned from his father, a great Liberal statesman, whom my father had served as deputy minister. But Martin maintained that I would not be able to stick to this purist position under fire. "At some point," he said, "you will have to answer the question directly: Is the agreement good for Canada?" As he foresaw, my fine scruples were often out of place in the extraordinary no-holds-barred public controversy that followed, and I came under great pressure to answer Martin's question.

But so long as I remained in the public service, I made every effort to keep my contribution as objective as humanly possible, given my role in the FTA's paternity. In explaining the agreement and its implementation, I highlighted the problems as well as the strong points, even when this gave comfort and aid to the agreement's sworn enemies – and even when I knew they would not show comparable restraint in the use they made of my testimony.

During the parliamentary process, the factual and technical questions were simply grist for the political mill as both sides sought to position themselves for the coming election. The lead role in the debate was obviously played by Mulroney. Neither he nor his critics would have had it any other way: it became the "Mulroney Agreement," for better or worse. At his best, Mulroney showed an extraordinary command of the debate. At his worst, he could succumb to extremes of partisan excess. At the cabinet level, the principal contributions were made by Finance Minister Wilson and the successive trade ministers, Pat Carney and John Crosbie. They put on a reasonably solid performance, making their case without becoming unduly provocative.

The same could not be said for all of their colleagues. The Quebec contingent was particularly weak, despite the strong support of the provincial electorate and their allies in the provincial government. Initially, Bob de Cotret was detailed to be the Quebec spokesman, but he soon faltered. Meanwhile, Mulroney's old buddy Lucien Bouchard had been recalled from the embassy in Paris and parachuted into the cabinet after the PM had pulled out all the stops to get him elected. Mulroney designated Bouchard as the government's lead batter on free trade and asked me to ensure that he was brought up to speed. Bouchard did not bother even to feign interest in trade or other issues. He was too preoccupied with his place in the great constitutional debate. Mulroney was left to carry the role of Quebec spokesman by himself.

Simon Reisman played a critical part in the political campaign but virtually none in the parliamentary process. He served as the attack dog, savaging the critics of the agreement. That may have played well on television or in the political debate outside Parliament. It was simply too hot to handle in the legislative forum. Simon did put in one appearance at the first committee meeting to review the legislation. The session instantly erupted over comments Simon had made a few days before which were interpreted – unfairly – as identifying critics of the agreement with the propagandists of the Third Reich. After that, the prime minister's instructions were clear and strict: Simon was to stay away from Parliament Hill, as that job was left entirely to me.

I was not sure whether to be flattered or insulted. The prime minister delighted in teasing me for my ability to defuse the political dramatics with dispassionate and technocratic expositions. "You are the only person I know," he once said to me at a cabinet meeting, "who speaks off the cuff in perfectly formed paragraphs." The media, for their part, came to rely on me for the information that served as background to their reports. They rarely enticed me into the dramatic sound bite that could headline their stories.

Thus, as a public servant, I found myself in the unique role of the government's chief witness in a highly charged political debate. Over the previous decade, I had appeared before a number of parliamentary committees examining the departmental estimates, proposed legislation, or other matters. This was different by several orders of magnitude. It involved dozens of appearances before several committees of the House of Commons and the Senate stretching over a period of more than ten months. The official record in Hansard makes a stack nearly six inches high. More important, the stakes were higher than I had ever experienced.

The opposition parties knew from the outset that free trade would be one of the central issues in the 1988 election. The drama was heightened by the clash between the two chambers of the legislature: the House of Commons reflected Mulroney's overwhelming victory in 1984, giving him and his party undisputed sway over the elected body; but the Senate was still dominated by a majority of Liberal appointees, the legacy of the decades that party had enjoyed in power through most of the postwar period and, in particular, for all but nine months of the two decades before Mulroney came to office. The political conventions were clear: the appointed Senate might delay but should never block the will of the elected House. But under the wily Allan MacEachen, who led the majority in the upper house, the Liberals were perfectly prepared to flout convention and to block passage of the free trade bill in the name of democracy. These political appointees had declared themselves the guardians of the public trust, ready and willing to force the prime minister to call an election over the issue.

The parliamentary committees thus became the battleground for the preliminary skirmishes in the electoral wars. This was the opportunity for both sides to test the case they would soon make to the voters. For the opposition Liberals and New Democrats, it was the time to probe for holes in the agreement. For the Conservatives, it was the occasion for testing their own defences.

At stake was nothing less than determining the next government. The pressures were unbelievable. Lloyd Axworthy led the charge for the Liberals in the House of Commons. He had thrived on political power, which he had used to full advantage to strengthen his own impregnable base in Winnipeg – the city that Lloyd built. This had enabled him to weather the electoral storms. He had stood fast against the Joe Clark breeze and held his ground before the Mulroney hurricane. A close ally of John Turner, he saw the battle against free trade as his passport back to power. This pragmatic view was strengthened by his deep-rooted anti-Americanism. He also sought to cultivate personal support as the darling of the left wing of the party. This all came together to make him an implacable foe.

I had known Axworthy for more than twenty years, since we were both assistants to Liberal ministers in the Pearson government. As an official, I had served the governments in which he had held ministerial rank under Trudeau and Turner. He was for many years the seatmate and friend of my former minister, Ed Lumley. Despite this, Axworthy and I were far from close. On a number of occasions in previous assignments under Conservative regimes, I had given careful testimony before various parliamentary committees, only to find Axworthy throwing a very different version of my statements back at the government in Question Period. This embarrassed my ministers and it personally offended me. As a result, whenever I was called to testify before a committee where Axworthy sat in opposition, I ensured that a member of my minister's staff was present to take notes and brief the minister against subsequent misrepresentations by Axworthy. Unfortunately, even that precaution failed when Axworthy, in a televised debate on the CBC, attributed statements to me that left his opponent, John Crosbie, spluttering in confusion. If I had said it, Crosbie figured it must be true, but it was at odds with everything I had told him in our private briefings. In fact, it was a manoeuvre by Axworthy to throw Crosbie off his stride, which was no mean feat.

The assault from the New Democrats was headed by Steve Langdon. From a Windsor riding, Langdon was cursed by a terrible whining voice. There were medical reasons for this condition, which was beyond his control. What was not beyond his control was the hectoring, badgering content of his public statements, which largely diminished his effectiveness. On the other hand, his chief confrère, Bill Blaikie from Saskatchewan, was quite impressive in these hearings. He came to epitomize for me some of the best traditions of Canadian public discourse. He gave every evidence of genuinely seeking to determine the truth in these complex matters. His starting point was, understandably, deep scepticism that a government led by Brian Mulroney could negotiate an arrangement in Canada's best interests. But he was prepared to listen and to learn. His questions were usually the most challenging. He was a more effective partisan for the very dispassionate tenor of his interventions.

With the parliamentary committee hearings, the free trade debate had moved to a new stage. For better than two years, the political wars had been fought in a fog. Until the agreement was concluded, both supporters and critics of free trade were unconstrained by any factual limits. The most outrageous claims could be made on either side without fear of contradiction. Once the agreement became public, however, all this changed. The government was relieved that it now had something tangible to defend. Provided – and this was a very big proviso – the agreement could stand up to expert scrutiny, the task of the free traders became much easier. Criticisms could be met with chapter and verse. For opponents of free trade, the strategy was therefore to keep the debate away from the agreement itself and focus instead on more sensational issues.

This order of battle governed the parliamentary proceedings. The first set of hearings focused on the agreement just concluded in Washington. They began on October 29, 1987. The opening day was not an auspicious beginning. Much of the time was taken up with procedural manoeuvres and name-calling. Right off the bat, the opposition proclaimed that it was not being given enough time to review this all-important agreement that had been sprung on an unsuspecting Canadian public after being negotiated in total secrecy. Axworthy and Langdon demanded that the Canadian legislature be given as much time as the American Congress. Parliament should give itself until the beginning of April to complete its initial review. This demand was deflected by the government forces, who pointed out that this first general review was only a prelude to the usual detailed examination of the implementing legislation to be tabled early in the spring. At one point, Sheila Copps goaded a hot-tempered Conservative member, Bill Kempling, into an exchange of insults in which he called her "a goddamned ignorant bitch." There followed considerable enlightening discussion of who said what and who should apologize to whom.

Somehow, through all this, we managed to take a first long look at the agreement negotiated in Washington. Trade Minister Pat Carney made a thoughtful opening statement laying out the government's assessment of the agreement. I then took the committee through a detailed presentation of its elements. At subsequent sessions, I attended with a handful of staffers to give the parliamentarians the best answers we could provide to their questions. It was then up to them, on both sides of the debate, to determine what were the strongest points to make their political case.

As always, however, the politicians and media shied away from real but complex issues. They gravitated instead to the spectacular if nonsensical. When our team was present, we were able to clarify the confusion and refute the worst of the lies. When we were not, the fun began. The opposition quickly understood that its best chances lay in making an unending stream of allegations, cataloguing yet more ways in which the agreement, through the incompetence of the negotiators or the venality of the government, would sell Canadians down the river. My staff and I did our best to brief the government spokespersons – the prime minister, the trade minister, and her colleagues – but it was a nearly impossible task. No sooner had we given them the answer to one outlandish allegation than one even more absurd came along.

I will spare the reader the full chronicle of these bizarre claims and counterclaims that provided so much entertainment for the news media at the time. A few do merit a mention, if only for their inventiveness.

To go through the motions of "consulting Canadians," the committee hit the road – and came immediately to a crashing stop. I received an urgent call from the chairman. At a hearing in Saskatoon, as I recall, a Canadian author, John Ralston Saul, breathlessly revealed his discovery that the negotiators had left a gaping loophole in the agreement, through which Mexican goods could come pouring into Canada. This was such a startling claim, made with such definitive authority, that the committee suspended its hearings to get to the bottom of this terrible problem. It was, of course, utter nonsense, as I carefully explained in a note that I faxed out to the chairman that afternoon. What I could not explain was why this august group would take seriously the delusions of a writer with absolutely no understanding of international trade, let alone the finer points of customs procedures.

At a meeting in Halifax, a high-profile sister with a religious order revealed that the Free Trade Agreement would open the Canadian border to imports from the United States of guns and pornography. Once burned, the committee this time took the precaution of checking the facts to find that this was, of course, a complete invention. The laws restricting the imports of guns, pornography, or, for that matter, other controlled substances (such as narcotics) remained unchanged by the Free Trade Agreement. The cream of the jest came when a zealous radio reporter telephoned a representative of the infamous American gun lobby, the National Rifle Association, in Washington to ask if they believed the FTA would eliminate the prohibition on carrying arms across the border. The NRA bozo was outraged: "What do you mean, there are restrictions on our right to carry arms across the border?" he blustered. "That's unconstitutional!"

A final example involved one of the long-running brush fires in the House of Commons Question Period, the sacrosanct Canadian blood supply. Some critics tried to read into the agreement that it would give American companies the right to ship their tainted blood into Canada or, even worse, to displace the inestimable Canadian Red Cross as managers of the supply in Canada. There was, of course, no such right under the agreement although, considering the horrendous revelations before the Krever Inquiry into Canada's own blood supply, it is hard to see how the situation could have been made any worse. Nonetheless, this question kept coming back again and again.

The next step came with the tabling of the legislation to turn the agreement into the law of Canada. In light of its potential impact on individuals and companies, the proposed Bill C-130 got the full treatment, including another media lock-up. This was planned for Friday, May 20. Then we got wind of the counterattack the Liberal opposition was preparing, raising endless points of parliamentary procedure to delay the bill's tabling at least over the weekend. We had no sooner put out the notice that the event would be postponed to the following week than I got a call from Wendy Mesley, a reporter for CBC Television. "What's up, Gordon?" she demanded. "Have the negotiations blown up again, or what?"

I told her of the Liberal plan and explained that once she and her colleagues had been locked up with the officials, we could not possibly get out until the bill was tabled. "Much as I enjoy your company, Wendy, I suspect three days in a locked room with me is not your idea of a good time," I said. "Besides, my wife would kill me if I missed our twenty-second anniversary this Saturday because I was locked away with you and the other reporters."

There was a long pause on the other end of the line. "Twenty-two years," Wendy said. "I don't know anybody who has been married that long. You had better put off the lock-up."

Once the implementing legislation was tabled in Parliament the following Monday, a new committee was established to undertake the detailed scrutiny of its complexities. This time, the political responsibility was carried by John Crosbie as the new minister of international trade. He opened the hearings with a lengthy statement laying out the benefits of the Free Trade Agreement for Canada.

Again, the opposition tactic was to shift attention from the technicalities of the agreement to other, more personalized and telegenic matters. Langdon launched an attack on Crosbie for not having read the agreement. This ground salt into the raw wound Crosbie had opened with his earlier honest but impolitic remark. Predictably, Crosbie reacted like a wounded animal, cornered by a pack of yapping dogs: "I do my homework, and no member of this committee need think that I do not know nor understand this agreement. I will put myself up against anyone else in the Canadian Parliament in that respect. But I am not going to say that I have read every word or every page of this agreement.

"I have dozens of experts on my staff who are knowledgeable about every facet of this agreement, and there are lawyers and economists, persons with the necessary skills to advise me.... Don't give me any crap about whether I have read the agreement."

Once the political pyrotechnics were out of the way, the committee settled down to a more detailed examination of the bill. I headed the team of officials, which now included the deputy ministers of the departments most directly involved in the implementation of the agreement. It was an extraordinary parade of bureaucratic talent. The prime minister made it clear that he held me personally responsible for, as he put it, "herding the flock" safely through the political minefield.

From the deputy minister of finance through to the head of a minor agency, I led the bureaucratic brass through their paces. By that time, I had become quite battle-hardened and felt very much at home in the parliamentary committee setting. To my surprise, most of my colleagues had enjoyed little or no exposure to this process. As a necessary precaution, my staff and I met with most of them beforehand, much as a lawyer might meet with expert witnesses. The preparations paid off.

The omnibus bill naturally cut across jealously guarded departmental boundaries and ministerial responsibilities. It was a challenging exercise in bureaucratic diplomacy. In most cases, the minister, the deputy, and the departmental officials were fully on side. They had been closely consulted throughout the negotiations and had completely concurred in the result. They were therefore more than willing to work with us to get the legislation pointed in the right direction.

There were exceptions. A couple of ministers had not been following the negotiations attentively. Their deputy ministers had been preoccupied with other issues or simply asleep at the switch. They had not expected any agreement to be reached. They were taken by surprise when the deal was concluded and in some cases professed to be unhappy with the results. Most of these issues had been resolved in the drafting of the final text of the agreement. This was the case, for example, with maritime transport. In certain other areas, however, there was still real political sensitivity.

The Energy Department had risen to prominence as the architect and enforcer of the National Energy Program. The moment the Tories took power, they reversed course. They reached a new accord with the western provinces that restored the market to its role of prime determinant of energy economics, and they took steps to bring the federal apparatus of laws, regulations, and institutions into line with their policies – against considerable resistance.

There were a number of officials in the Energy Department and the National Energy Board who believed this was all a terrible mistake that would have to be corrected down the road. They were dismayed when we reached an agreement with the Americans that committed us to treat energy more like other commodities. They feared it locked us into a regime that could, when circumstances changed, create serious problems for the country. They were not above attempting to promote their objectives through the back door, by influencing the proposed legislation or by giving ammunition, directly or indirectly, to the critics. The government stuck to its guns and eventually carried the day, but not without significant internal friction.

The Department of Communications, as the guardian of Canadian culture, presented other problems. It was a remarkable creature. To an extent I believe unmatched in any other department, this outfit defined its role as working not for the government but for its constituency. The relationship was unbelievably incestuous. The departmental officials administered elaborate programs to protect and subsidize the "cultural community" – i.e., the business men and women who made their living in publishing, film production, or broadcasting. The officials of the regulatory commission decided the fate of these business entities in their awarding or refusal of licences. These same officials typically, on leaving the government service, went to work for the very firms they had been regulating or subsidizing. Understandably, then, loyalties were at best mixed.

The minister, Flora MacDonald, was an unabashed Canadian nationalist. She was also a realist. She gave Simon and me our strict marching orders and watched closely to ensure that we carried them out to her satisfaction. She was fully satisfied with the final agreement. It was never clear that her officials were so satisfied. There was never any open opposition. At no time did these officials come out and make a reasoned case in opposition to this or that element of the agreement. They did, however, have extraordinary difficulty in getting things right and delivering what they had promised. We were never entirely sure whether this was deliberate guerrilla warfare or simple incompetence – and there was ample evidence of the latter. Some of the issues were highly technical, even arcane. They were also of keen financial interest to specific businesses.

If this was a concerted strategy in either the Energy or the Communications Department, it may have backfired in the end. If there had been grounds for insisting on different results – in the original negotiations, in the text of the agreement, or in the implementing legislation – I would have made every effort to accommodate these concerns, as we did, for example, in the case of our postal rates. But once agreement had been reached and confirmed, I was not prepared to have the government's credibility undermined by foolish games played by officials who were either too clever by half, or too stupid to follow instructions. Even worse, these attempts to subvert the results may have produced unintended consequences. Without getting into the technical details, on such points as the tests to be applied to exports by the energy board or the compensation to be paid to rights-holders by broadcasters for cable retransmission, the responsible department may have outsmarted itself and given the Americans more than I believed they had earned.

After hearing from the government experts, the committee then opened its proceedings to hear from other interested parties, generally those opposed to free trade. I welcomed this respite. It enabled me to take a few days away from Ottawa at our summer cottage in New Brunswick. The prime minister reluctantly agreed to my absence, provided I finally, after decades of resistance, installed a telephone in our cottage. I neglected to warn him that it was a party line. This led to some awkward moments as a neighbour recognized a familiar voice when he inadvertently picked up the phone in the midst of one of our conversations. Meanwhile, the committee was learning very little from the parade of witnesses. The critics preferred to keep their attacks general and ideological or even, in the case of the Canadian Labour Congress leadership, to back out of making any appearance in a forum where they could be challenged.

Ultimately, the government majority rammed the bill through the committee virtually unchanged. There were a few technical amendments, which we had ourselves introduced to clarify points here and there. There was also one amendment introduced for purely political reasons. It was designed to address the vociferous concerns expressed that the agreement would somehow allow the Americans to compel us to divert streams and rivers to meet their requirements.

My old mentor Mel Clark emerged from retirement as one of the prime movers behind this issue. He had long held the belief that the Americans' secret agenda was to get their hands on our water. When we had worked together in the late 1960s, this had been his obsession. Now he cobbled up a highly inventive argument that the agreement would treat running water as a commodity like any other. The suggestion was preposterous. But like the mole in the circus sideshow game, it kept popping up no matter how hard or how often the claim was knocked on the head.

Perhaps I took this issue too lightly because I knew the argument was totally fallacious. The tortured thesis ran as follows. Canada and the United States were adopting the so-called harmonized system of tariff nomenclature – a mouthful meaning an agreed way of listing imported items. Unlike the old system, this new regime included a commodity classification for water, in bottles or other small containers; thus water should be considered a commodity like any other and subject to the general rules. These included the rule that said that a country facing a shortage of some commodity would treat traditional customers fairly. Therefore, the Americans could require us to supply them with running water.

This sounded plausible until one looked a little more closely. Then the gaping holes in the argument became apparent, as none of these claims is true.

The commodity classification applied to bottles of water. It did not, by any stretch of the imagination, govern the diversion of rivers or other interbasin flows of water. These were up to national governments to regulate. In Canada's case, our policy was clear: no such interbasin transfers of water were permitted. Thus, even if we allowed huge diversions of water, which we expressly forbade, we could change our mind and cut off the flow whenever we, as Canadians, wanted. If the Americans didn't like it, that was their problem.

The Americans had no illusions on this score. It had never even occurred to them that anyone could make this argument until Mel and his nationalist-environmentalist friends came up with it. The Americans recognized that it was totally without merit. But once the Canadian critics trumpeted their concerns, they created a serious problem for us. They had made clear that they would be satisfied with nothing short of a formal amendment to the agreement to exclude water. Whatever their intentions, the tactics of the hydrophobes backfired on Canada.

We could, of course, have asked the Americans to agree formally to amend the Free Trade Agreement to deal with this issue, but that would have brought its own problems. The American negotiating authority had expired. They would have to go to a recalcitrant Congress to seek new authority to amend the agreement. The Congress would be outraged. If the amendment was needed to accommodate Canada, they would ask what the United States was getting in return – and be told they were getting nothing for nothing. But if the amendment was entirely unnecessary, as the administration was fully aware, they would be asking the Congress to waste its time just to placate a fringe constituency in Canada.

I came up with an alternative that I hoped would defuse the issue. The Americans would go ahead with their side of the agreement only if they were satisfied that we were, through our legislation, completely implementing our side. I persuaded the government to pass an amendment to our bill that categorically stated that water was not covered by the agreement. If the Americans then went ahead, it was clearly because they accepted this interpretation as fully consistent with the agreement. Surely this would satisfy even the most strident critics? Not a chance.

The hydrophobes did not even pause for breath. They dismissed the statement as irrelevant since it obviously did not amend the agreement itself.

They continued their attacks. The result was a fascinating study in public debate. As far as most observers – and all of the media – were concerned, what looked like a highly expert argument had been met with an equally technical response. The argument itself was much too complex for them to reach their own conclusions on the merits of the case. What they could see was that the critics were passionate in their concerns while the defenders of the agreement tended to be much more cold-blooded.

At one point, Peter Gzowski devoted an entire edition of his radio program *Morningside* to a debate on free trade. Each side had its advocate, who could call witnesses to be cross-examined. One of the most contentious issues proved to be water. Mel Clark was given a chance to lay out his position, then interrogated by the pro-free-trade advocate, a well-known Toronto lawyer, Edward Greenspan. It was brutal. Mel stuck to his guns, while conceding that others whom he respected and for whom he had worked rejected his argument as outlandish. Finally Greenspan called me to the microphone. Having heard Mel out, he asked, would I say he had "water on the brain." Much as I disliked what Mel was saying, I was not prepared to play the insults game and contented myself with restating my own assessment of the situation. Some time later, the issue resurfaced in a television program where various individuals were invited to do brief cameo appearances on selected issues. Again Mel and I were put into direct confrontation, and again I felt I had completely debunked his argument. Obviously, not everyone shared my view.

To jump ahead of the story, during five years under the Free Trade Agreement, water was never an issue between the two countries. The Americans never claimed they had won any rights under the agreement to lay claim to any sources of water from Canada. Still, the anti-free-traders trumpeted their concerns, enlisting environmental activists in their crusade. Finally, as a precondition for implementing the North American Free Trade Agreement, incoming prime minister Jean Chrétien demanded and obtained a formal exchange of letters establishing that interbasin transfers of water were not governed by either NAFTA or its predecessor agreement.

Even this failed to silence the critics completely. Until the cows come home, I could demonstrate that the Americans could not *compel* us to supply water (or privatize blood clinics or whatever). But I could never claim that the Free Trade Agreement precluded our own governments from deciding to *permit* interbasin transfers of water (or privatization of hospitals). I came to realize that on this, as on other issues, the opponents of free trade were most afraid of their own governments, federal and provincial. What they really wanted was for the agreement to prevent their own governments from acting against what these groups saw as Canada's interests.

Once the committee had approved the bill, as amended, for submission to the full House of Commons, the final parliamentary debate was anticlimactic. Given the overwhelming Conservative majority, the outcome was a foregone conclusion. In special session, the House approved the free trade legislation at the end of August 1988 and passed it on to the Senate for its approval. Meanwhile, the Senate had, in anticipation, conducted its own extensive hearings. Again, I was the principal witness for the government.

The initial hearings, under the chairmanship of Senator George Van Roggen, had been a pleasure. The senator and his committee had been among the most articulate exponents of free trade with the US. Following its own extensive hearings, the committee had called for free trade back when the idea had no support in the House of Commons. As the negotiations reached a conclusion, Van Roggen could scarcely contain his satisfaction.

Once the implementing bill was in play, however, his leaders in the Liberal majority in the Senate were having none of this chumminess with the anti-Christ. Van Roggen was summarily replaced as chair, and the hearings were conducted in a relatively combative atmosphere – compared with the usual stately proceedings of the Red Chamber. At its most vigorous, the Senate committee showed little of the strident partisanship of its counterpart in the House. Not that it mattered. Here, too, the outcome was a foregone conclusion.

I did not wait around for the charade to be played out. At the end of August, as the free trade bill cleared the House of Commons, I retired from the government service. The Liberals in the Senate blocked the free trade bill, forcing Mulroney to put the issue to the electorate in November.

Others have chronicled that remarkable election. My recollections are more personal. I was deeply shocked and offended by John Turner's behaviour as the leader of the Liberals. This was, after all, the party whose defining characteristic for most of its history had been its support for free trade against the forces of the monopolists and their Tory lackeys. Laurier with the reciprocity agreements, King with the postwar agreements (and the aborted free trade negotiation with the US), Pearson with the Auto Pact – this had been the Liberal tradition.

Turner had been very much part of this tradition, espousing free trade as recently as days before he took over the leadership. Now, in a desperate attempt to differentiate himself from Mulroney – with whom he had made common cause on constitutional issues and Meech Lake – Turner had done an about-face. He had tapped into that other wellspring of Liberal thought, the anti-Americanism of Trudeau and his protégés. He now embarked on the "greatest crusade" of his life, the fight to preserve protective tariffs and defeat the Mulroney free trade agreement.

Free trade with the United States had never been a big electoral success. At best, some 40 percent of the population appeared to favour such a deal. Another 40 percent were opposed. The rest were on the fence. At some point back in 1987, Simon had mused that the FTA would be the salvation of Brian Mulroney, who was trailing the agreement in public opinion polls. That situation had changed dramatically. At the beginning of the election, Mulroney was leading his party ahead of the Liberals in the polls. I recalled Mulroney's winning formula: if only he could get the Liberals into bed with the New Democrats, they would split the anti-free-trade vote down the middle and give the Conservatives a cakewalk home. In the first few weeks, the consensus among those with whom I talked was that the strategy was working.

Then came the televised leaders' debates. In 1984, on the subject of the patronage appointments demanded by Trudeau, Mulroney had dropped Turner to the mat with his knockout punch, "You could have said no." This time, the pundits agreed, there was no prospect of a similar decisive win by either side. As a result, the Conservative strategists followed what was known as the "low-bridge" approach – keeping the debate as low-key as possible.

Freed from the restrictions that must be respected by a public servant, I was enlisted in the preparations for the debates. Working with Derek Burney, who was now playing a highly political role as Mulroney's chief of staff, I carefully identified the most damaging issues that Turner had raised in the past, plus a few others that he had not yet deployed. I helped develop the tight but crushing responses required to keep Turner at bay. It was pretty good stuff, if I do say so myself.

Despite my briefings and, more important, Burney's strong advice, Mulroney followed the counsel of his other handlers and tried to take the high road in the debates. Burney sat in a trailer outside the arena, sending in advice to his champion. Time and again, Turner went on the attack with lines we had predicted almost to the letter. Time and again, Mulroney tried to deflect these blows with soft answers. Perhaps the most telling was when Mulroney weakly mumbled that it was, after all, only a trade agreement. It could be terminated on six months' notice. Turner could not believe his good fortune. Nor could we.

That night, the big business lobby group had arranged for a briefing on the results of the debates from one of the country's most respected pollsters, Michael Adams, the president of Environics. Adams reported that it had been a non-event. It would have little or no impact on national public opinion. But in the days that followed, his and other polls revealed that never in the history of polling had a single event caused such a dramatic swing during an election. The people of Canada had seen and heard John Turner, in English and in French – with echoes provided by NDP leader Ed Broadbent – give voice to their worst fears about free trade with the Americans – that it would sell off our resources, emasculate our social programs, and eviscerate our national sovereignty. They had seen and heard Brian Mulroney feebly protest that it was, after all, only a trade agreement that could be abrogated if it did not work. If that was the best he could say in defence of the FTA, perhaps the critics were right after all and Canada should simply "say no."

To his great credit, Brian Mulroney is not a quitter. He realized that he had stepped into a swamp and that only he could get out of the mess. He rolled up his pant legs and went to work. He was not alone. Finally, after sitting on their hands through much of the public debate, the leadership of the business community, in Quebec and other provinces, from the biggest business to the smallest in virtually every sector, was galvanized into action. The Canadian Alliance for Jobs and Trade was established, under the co-chairmanship of Peter Lougheed and Donald Macdonald, with significant financial contributions from leading businesses directly and through such lobby groups as the Business Council on National Issues. It was seen as quite usual and proper for the leaders of organized labour to mobilize their considerable resources, but it was much more unusual, almost unseemly, for the business leadership to counter with a campaign of their own. The business campaign included national advertising, which played a role, although perhaps not so decisive as they and their adversaries subsequently claimed. More effective, in my observation, was the effort made by the chief executives of a number of large employers to help their workers relate the agreement to their own future prospects. This provided at least a partial counterbalance to the labour establishment's claims that the agreement would throw a million workers out on the street.

Meanwhile, the Turner/Broadbent onslaught was provoking a critical reaction. It was one thing for them to assert that the Free Trade Agreement would gut Canadian social programs. It was quite another for them to explain just how this would happen. What clauses in the agreement declare open

172

season on Canadian social programs? Which chapter would strip Granny of her pension? Where does it say that medicare is outlawed? The terrible twins had no answer to these questions. Broadbent at least had the honesty to admit that these were speculations, not direct results of the Free Trade Agreement. Turner blundered on.

As the architects of the agreement, Simon and I were also called on to play our very different roles. Simon went to war on the critics of the agreement, with a high-voltage, passionate, and often very personalized defence of the Free Trade Agreement and condemnation of its enemies. The prime minister and his handlers loved it. It made the PM at his most overblown seem balanced by comparison.

Although I was no longer on the public payroll, I was unwilling to take the gloves off in the same pugnacious fashion. I still believed that it was up to the Canadian people to judge whether the agreement was in their overall interest. It was up to me to help them understand the agreement so they could inform that judgment. I became a fixture on various call-in shows and radio and television debates.

Perhaps the most memorable came late in the campaign. Peter Mansbridge, anchorman for the CBC-TV national news, chaired a special Sunday edition devoted to free trade. I was invited to explain the agreement. On the other side of the table sat a former Saskatchewan farmer named David Orchard, who had found he could make a better living as an anti-free-trade crusader. He may not have been much of a farmer and had kept secret any past experience in international trade matters, but he was a highly skilled polemicist. He had a little black book, replete with page markers and highlighters, full of questions and answers that he had polished to a fine sheen.

Questions were put by a panel composed of talk-show hosts from across the country. With Mansbridge attempting to moderate, Orchard and I went at it. As the session wore on, I had to put more and more effort into controlling my indignation. Orchard had compiled every charge that had been levelled at the Free Trade Agreement and programmed himself to repeat them without any regard for the facts or the truth – at least as I saw them.

It became increasingly difficult not to play the same game – inventing facts and figures as they might suit the immediate purpose. For example, one of the central assertions was that the Free Trade Agreement would mean that the Canadian market would be flooded with American imports that would cost Canadian jobs. Meanwhile, Mulroney had promised the FTA would create "jobs, jobs, jobs." What was the truth? Mansbridge demanded to know.

Orchard quickly trotted out the definitive and scientific estimate by the Canadian Labour Congress that it would indeed cost one million Canadian jobs. When pressed, I stuck to my assessment that the main impact would be on preserving jobs by increasing productivity and limiting American protectionism. Most workers would be unaffected. Some workers in some firms in some industries would obviously lose their jobs over the coming years. Others would find new jobs. Free trade would play a role in this process. But I did not expect there to be a significant reduction or increase in unemployment as a direct result of free trade.

When I staggered home on the late-night plane to Ottawa, one of my fellow passengers asked me how it had gone. "I don't know," I answered. "I will have to see the tape. Then I will have to see the reviews." When I viewed the videotaped recording the next morning, I was pleasantly surprised. I believed that I had made the case forcefully but honestly. I hoped that Orchard's polemics were transparently empty of content. Then I started getting telephone calls. They came in two varieties.

One bunch of calls came from journalists and businessmen. I had never before, and have rarely since, been complimented by a journalist. Perhaps they thought I needed some consolation. They claimed to be impressed with the way I had held to the high ground in the face of great provocation and awarded the bout to me on points. Even more extraordinary was a call from someone I had never met who wanted to tell me that he had been opposed to free trade before the program but was now convinced that it was in Canada's best interest and that the charges levelled against it were unfounded.

The other calls were to tell me that the Prime Minister's Office and the Trade Negotiations Office were mortified. Their champion had gone down for the count. The only question was whether it was a deliberate dive. Some of my dear old friends at the trade office took the view that I had sold out – it was not clear for what or to whom. The most unfavourable comparisons were made between me and Simon – who had continued to fight the good fight with unmatched piss and vinegar.

I was probably fortunate that there was no opinion polling before and after our mini-debate. Such polls would probably have shown the same result as the leaders' debate – that my attempt at moderation would be seen as weakness in both me and the case I was making.

With the exception of Brian Mulroney and Simon Reisman, the supporters of free trade generally tended to get the worst of it in the public debates. Perhaps the most delightful example was the enormous popularity of

Marjorie Montgomery Bowker's "independent review of the free trade agreement" entitled *On Guard for Thee*. Mrs. Bowker was a retired juvenile court judge, living in Edmonton. While other Canadians were milling about in confusion over whom and what to believe on the issue, Mrs. Bowker took the time and trouble to work her way through this highly complex agreement and, even more important, to share her conclusions with others. On her own, with a typewriter and a photocopy machine, at a cost she reported at $4.48, she single-handedly outgunned the $20-million communications program of the federal government.

I suspect a significant part of the appeal of her book stemmed from the absolute certainty with which it is written, as one would expect from a judge's verdict. She told Canadians exactly what was in the agreement and exactly what it would do to Canadians, with no ifs, buts, or maybes. Unfortunately, she got much of it dead wrong, reflecting not only her misreading of the text of the agreement but her apparent ignorance of the underlying circumstances. She was not distracted by any awareness of the rules of the GATT, Canadian or American unfair trade laws, or the workings of the economy.

I took the opportunity to point this out in reviews of her book and responses in the print media. At a meeting in Toronto, I was again tasked with the gospel according to Bowker. I responded that her analysis was so wide of the mark there were only two possibilities – either she was deliberately misleading her readers or she had completely misread the text. In an attempt at humour, I suggested that I would prefer to believe the latter – that this self-proclaimed granny had misplaced her glasses. The *Toronto Star* seized on this as proof of arrogance and headlined my jest. I braced myself for an onslaught. In the event, all I received was a single letter from the member of a golden age society. She claimed that I had breached the Human Rights Code not once but thrice in that my remarks had disparaged women, the aged, and the handicapped (referring to the eyeglasses). Her letter, she warned, was but the first of thousands that were even then being drafted. I replied that in my family, "granny" was a term of respect, but that even grannies were under the obligation to tell the truth. I heard no more.[1]

In any event, the opinion of the electorate turned around in the closing

---

1. The ultimate irony came when the Order of Canada appointments were announced. No mention of Simon Reisman (who already held the second rank) or Derek Burney. But Mrs. Bowker had been named to the third or lowest rank of the order for her contributions. (It was rumoured that the Governor General himself had queried whether this could truly be the recommendation of the appointments committee.)

days of the campaign. Brian Mulroney was again returned to office with a majority – the first back-to-back Conservative majorities since Sir John A. Macdonald. The free trade bill was quickly passed through the House of Commons and handed on to the Senate for a speedy ratification. All of this was completed in time for the agreement to enter into force with a minimum of fanfare on schedule on January 1, 1989. It was somewhat anticlimactic for me personally. The negotiation and implementation of the Free Trade Agreement had been an important episode in my career. Now it was time for me to turn my attention to making a living in the private sector.

9

FTA Aftermath

One of the subjects Derek Burney and I had discussed on the party line to my summer cottage was my future in the public service. Of all the options before me, the most intriguing suggestion came from the prime minister himself. Through Burney, he proposed that I take a sabbatical to write the definitive book on the Free Trade Agreement. I would be given access to all the files and to any other resources I required, including appropriate research staff. Knowing me as he did, he knew there would be no suggestion that the result would reflect anything other than my own views. I was tempted, but only very briefly. Despite all the guarantees, it would be virtually impossible to write a truly independent book under those circumstances. Besides, I had other mountains to climb and was not prepared to spend a year looking backwards. In any event, it was much too soon to write an account of the negotiations, and it would be years before the results could be properly assessed. In the meantime, I did organize the trade office staff to fully document the negotiating record. You never knew when it might come in handy. Ironically, the project was not completed until after I had left the government and therefore no longer had access to these "confidential" papers.

The prime minister had not given up easily. Again through Derek, I was offered promotion to the rank of deputy minister at the head of the Employment and Immigration Department. I was genuinely flattered to be so highly regarded by the prime minister, particularly after the bruising I had received earlier at the hands of his entourage. I felt more than able to handle the assignment. But it was time to seek new challenges, and I therefore retired from the public service of the government of Canada at the ripe old age of forty-four to make my way in the private sector. Marg was delighted at our decision, which promised to give us the means to spend more time together.

Unlike that of most retiring public servants, my profile in the business community was high and favourable – probably undeservedly so by virtue of my close association with an initiative the business community strongly supported. I was offered executive positions with a number of Canadian corporations. After canvassing the options, however, I decided to set up my own consulting business. I had no interest in selling my services as a lobbyist, paid to influence government contracts. Instead, I hoped to make a living giving strategic advice to Canadian companies on how to take advantage of the free trade world.

I knew from the experience of others who had left the public service that the transition could be difficult. It meant leaving the helm of a large and powerful bureaucracy to function on the basis of my own wits – and my own money, which after more than twenty years at a government salary meant very little money indeed. To cushion the shock, I threw in my lot with a leading Toronto law firm, Lang Michener. Apart from its other merits, Lang Michener had the attraction of a powerhouse Ottawa office, which included a number of old friends. Foremost among these were Jean Chrétien, who served as counsel to the firm during his period in the political wilderness; his diminutive sidekick, Eddie Goldenberg, a partner in the firm; and Roger Tassé, the former deputy minister of justice who had played a central role in the constitutional negotiations. These represented an invaluable resource for a would-be public policy consultant. Some eyebrows were raised at my association, as a Mulroney protégé, with this collection of Liberals. I thought it served to underscore the non-partisan nature of my services, but I never could get the party loyalty label right – it was a standing joke that the Liberals were convinced I was a Conservative while the Tories suspected I was really a Grit.

I agreed to become a business partner of the firm and to set up and run a consulting enterprise on the firm's behalf. After some deliberation, we incorporated the firm as Strategico and advertised ourselves as "giving strategic advice to business on public policies." To my delight, my former secretary from the old DRIE days, Pat Colby, agreed to run the operation for me. My new office was fourteen floors below the Trade Negotiations Office and a fraction of the size of my former quarters. I had no clients, no agenda, and no work in progress. But, for the first time in my life, I was working for myself.

Salvage operation: Pat Carney
and Michael Wilson outside the
US Treasury Department.
(Canapress Photo Service/Tom Reed)

Éminence grise: Derek Burney arrives
at the Treasury as the real head of the
Canadian delegation.
(Canapress Photo Service/Barry Thumma)

Team Canada: From left: Allan Gotlieb, Stanley Hartt, Don Campbell, Derek Burney,
Pat Carney, Gordon Ritchie, Michael Wilson, and Simon Reisman pose for
the history books on October 3, 1987. *(Author's collection)*

Master strategist: James Baker announces the deal, flanked by Carney, Wilson, and Yeutter at the US Treasury on October 4, 1987.
(Canapress Photo Service/Scott Stewart)

Reisman was prepared to leave it to others to work out the final details of the text of the Free Trade Agreement.
(Courtesy of Aislin/The Gazette)

THE FINAL TEXT? NOT TO WORRY... WE'RE JUST CROSSING A FEW i's AND DOTTING THE t's...

AND ELIMINATING ALL THE z'eDS?

AISLIN St.
MONTREAL GAZETTE

Unsung heroes: Derek Burney, left, and Peter McPherson, right, look on as Reisman and Murphy announce the FTA text has been agreed, December 8, 1988.
(Canapress Photo Service/Terry McEvoy)

Tear up the FTA: Liberal leader John Turner promises to scrap the FTA if he wins the next election. *(Canapress Photo Service/Chuck Mitchell)*

Let's see him tear this up: Mulroney holds aloft one volume of the final FTA in the presence of Ritchie, Burney, and Reisman. *(Author's collection)*

Thumbs up: Mulroney salutes Reisman, Ritchie, and Burney from the floor of the House of Commons as he tables the agreement, December 11, 1987. *(Canapress Photo Service/Ron Poling)*

Third World country: Reisman denounces the American negotiating tactics as the bemused Ritchie looks on. *(Canapress Photo Service/Ron Poling)*

Fine print: Trade Minister John Crosbie concedes he has not read every word of the FTA, June 28, 1988. (*Canapress Photo Service/Ron Poling*)

The Americans showed great interest in Canadian culture. (*Toronto Star Syndicate*)

Legal advice: General counsel Konrad von Finckenstein is congratulated by Mulroney for his work on the FTA; Derek Burney looks on. *(Courtesy Konrad von Finckenstein)*

The deed is done: Prime Minister Mulroney signs the Free Trade Agreement with the United States on January 2, 1988. *(Canapress Photo Service/ Fred Chartrand)*

Quebec Premier Jacques Parizeau supported the FTA as a safety net for an independent Quebec. *(Courtesy of Roy Peterson/Vancouver Sun)*

Turnaround: As Liberal leader, Jean Chrétien returned the party to its historic support for freer trade and approved the NAFTA once his conditions were met. *(Canapress Photo Service/Chuck Mitchell)*

Death star: CRTC head Keith Spicer was furious with proposals by the panel chaired by Ritchie, which called for competitive licensing for direct-to-home satellite television broadcasting. *(Canapress Photo Service/Tom Hanson)*

Pyrrhic victory: Trade Minister Roy MacLaren hailed Canada's lumber victory in the FTA panels but was unhappy with the later agreement to restrict Canadian exports to the US. *(Canapress Photo Service/Chuck Mitchell)*

Timber: The Canadian team of experts in the lumber wars. From left: George Garndison, Bill Fox, John Reilly, Lance Morgan, Mike Apsey, Ritchie, Geoff Elliott. *(Author's collection)*

I was pleasantly surprised to find the group at Lang Michener even stronger than I had expected. Chrétien, Goldenberg, and Tassé were clearly the focus, but the Ottawa office included several other lawyers with public policy credentials, including Michel Bastarache, an outstanding constitutional lawyer, and Andrée Wylie and John Laurence, two experts in telecommunications policy. Best of all, the leadership of the Ottawa office was provided by two very different but equally exceptional individuals who were to become my very close friends and remain collaborators to this day – Kent Plumley and Paul Labarge.

The business also gave me the opportunity for a truly delightful association with a remarkable Canadian, Mitchell Sharp. A former civil servant, Sharp had served as a senior minister under both Pearson and Trudeau. More recently, he had acted as the commissioner for the Northern Pipeline Agency, overseeing Canadian interests in the proposed natural gas pipelines from Alaska. When he spoke out against free trade, he had been invited to step down. I had never enjoyed more than a fleeting acquaintance with Sharp, who had earned my father's respect and loyalty when Dad served as his deputy minister at External Affairs. But Sharp had long acted as mentor to Jean Chrétien, whom he had pegged from the start as a man with extraordinary potential. On the strength of these relationships, I was able to persuade Sharp to join Strategico as our "policy associate." Over the years that followed, his advice was invaluable and his friendship a continuing source of satisfaction. His mind was as energetic as his physical appearance was ageless.

Despite our best efforts, however, it became increasingly clear that my clientele would generally be very different from that of the law firm. Several hundred partners in half a dozen offices provided a full range of legal services. Their client list comprised thousands of individuals and corporations right across the country. All were billed according to an established system that required lawyers to allocate their time in six-minute increments. To my dismay, the firm's bureaucracy at times made the much-maligned government apparatus look efficient by comparison.

My business, on the other hand, proved much more eclectic. I was retained by the chief executives of a very small number of organizations to provide strategic advice tailored to their particular requirements. I preferred to make my arrangements on the basis of a handshake, followed if necessary by a two-page letter of agreement. I refused to operate a punch clock or to bill clients for faxes, phone calls, and photocopies. If they were happy with the value of my advice, they paid what seemed to me to be very large sums of money. If they were not satisfied, we had a clear understanding that either party could terminate the relationship at any point. In practice, my growing list of clients proved to be extraordinarily punctilious. To the stupefaction of my legal colleagues, I never faced a bad debt or a reluctance to pay my bill.

My best marketing tool proved to be word of mouth. The work was highly varied, ranging from sitting on an increasing number of corporate boards to providing highly technical advice on trade issues to Canadian export industries under attack by the Americans. Within eighteen months, it became clear that Strategico had outgrown the partnership with Lang Michener, particularly since the latter's Ottawa office had been decimated by the departure of the key players, among them Jean Chrétien, who had taken over as leader of the Liberal Party. The time had come to leave the shelter of the law firm and strike out on my own. It was bracing to realize that the undertakings required by my bank ensured that more than my job was riding on the success of Strategico, as my house and other assets were all pledged.

Fortunately, the business soon established its financial base. This gave me enormous freedom of action, to choose my clients and to keep my independence in public comments and continuing advice to governments. Sharp remained my associate. An economist from the trade office, Ian Currie, joined the team, which also included David Liston, a young lawyer from Lang Michener, who proved invaluable in the years ahead. A former colleague, Lise Lachapelle, later joined as my Montreal partner and ultimately president of Strategico until her departure to head the Canadian Pulp and Paper Association. Another TNO colleague, Diane Péladeau, took over the secretarial functions.

One of the first decisions I had taken was that I would not generally accept any Canadian government as a client. Over the preceding twenty-two years, the Canadian taxpayer had paid my salary as I got my education in public policies. If I was now asked for my opinion, by the government, by the opposition parties, or by provincial premiers, I believed it was only fair that I would not charge a second time for that advice. The lawyers even had a fancy term for this practice: *pro bono publico*, or for the public good. Whatever the title, this policy resulted in my giving advice not only to the Mulroney government but to the Liberal opposition of Jean Chrétien, the leader of the New Democratic Party, Audrey McLaughlin, and several provincial premiers including Bob Rae in Ontario and, through his senior ministers, Robert Bourassa in Quebec. It was great fun, as I was able to "speak my mind to power" – the classic definition of policy analysis. It was much better than becoming a paid gun for those in power, particularly since government does not pay very well, it pays late, and it is usually unable to make up its mind as to what it requires.

The one exception proved to be the negotiation of the successor to the FTA, the North American Free Trade Agreement, which included Mexico. I played no direct role in the negotiations but was commissioned to provide advice to the Canadian government and, with Ottawa's blessing, the Mexican government, in addition to the counsel I was called on to provide to my private clients.

Originally, the Americans planned to have a free trade agreement with Mexico in parallel with the FTA with Canada and, indeed, the much more modest free trade deal they had done with Israel. The Mexicans, under president Carlos Salinas, were eager to proceed. Then the Canadians kicked up a fuss at being left out of the party and managed to talk their way in. I was not a supporter of this strategy.

I could easily understand why George Bush would launch the negotiations with Mexico. After all, Mexico represented a substantial trading partner – American exports to Mexico were greater than total American exports to all the countries in Central and South America combined. There were substantial investment ties. More important, there were crucial strategic interests for the American superpower in stabilizing its southern border – through collaborating with a friendly government to increase Mexico's prosperity and thus reduce the desperate economic pressures forcing illegal migrants across that frontier. What I had more trouble accepting was that it was in Canada's interest to get involved.

I had always enjoyed my dealings with the Mexicans, with whom we shared a common experience of the American superpower – including their annexation, by war or trickery, of large swaths of our territory. I was all in favour of closer trade ties between our two countries, even to the extent of a free trade agreement. The fact remained that Mexico should have been very far down any serious list of Canadian trade and economic interests. At the time Brian Mulroney invited himself to the tea party with Carlos Salinas, Canada's exports to Mexico were under $1 billion – less than one-half of 1 percent of our exports to the United States. Our imports were greater at under $4 billion, but still only around 3 percent of our purchases from the US. Our investment interests were also very limited. Indeed it is probably no exaggeration to say that for most Canadians the main interest in Mexico was as a possible snowbird tourist destination.

Did that mean that the NAFTA negotiations were unimportant? Quite the contrary. The negotiations would give the Americans a heaven-sent opportunity to reopen key elements of their deal with Canada. I fully expected the Americans to come to the table with a long list of demands for "improvements" in the FTA. Perhaps it was misplaced pride of authorship, but I did not believe the new crop of negotiators should put back in play such sensitive issues as dispute settlement, unfair trade laws, intellectual property, automotive content rules, investment regulations, etc.

Initially, I expressed these views privately to John Crosbie and his officials. The response was disarming. I was encouraged to accept an invitation from the Mexican authorities to brief them on free trade negotiations with the Yanquis in March 1991, before the negotiations were formally launched. I accepted the offer with some trepidation. I was not sufficiently familiar with the Mexican situation and my Spanish was limited. My experience in dealing with the Americans was probably too fresh to draw objective lessons from it. Also, I was adamant that I would not under any circumstances discuss *Canadian* negotiating strategies and objectives with the Mexicans. Despite these limitations, the Mexicans pressed their invitation and I accepted.

The Strategico team assembled a set of thick black books laying out the elements of the Free Trade Agreement in a strategic framework. We sent those ahead to Mexico while I took a few days with my family skiing at the famous resort at Whistler, BC. I was struck by the fact that the elevation at the top of the mountain was almost exactly the same as that of Mexico City. But while the cold mountain air was as pure as any on the planet, the first and lasting impression of the great city of Mexico was the thick, almost gummy smog that permeated the atmosphere even inside the hotels. (My physical discomfort was increased by the fact that I had, as I later realized, cracked a couple of ribs in a fall on the ski slopes the day before I left, which made breathing painful.)

The Mexicans could not have been more gracious nor more efficient. They transported us from our hotel to a resort a couple of hours outside the city itself. There we were faced with a group of some twenty officials, whose intelligence and education was as impressive as their lack of free trade negotiating experience. Key to the new president's policies of *apertura* or opening of the economy was the recruitment of a team of highly trained and relatively young and apparently uncorrupted technocrats to bring about the new order.

I have never briefed an audience with a higher proportion of doctorates, all from the best American universities.

For the better part of three days, this group put me through the paces. I began by familiarizing them with the reasoning behind the structure of the agreement. They then worked back through the specific elements in careful detail. Even on the most arcane issues, the Mexicans asked exactly the right questions and probed for any soft spots in my answers. It was a gruelling experience but intellectually rewarding for both parties.

Perhaps my main contribution was in bringing home the nature of their adversary. I chose my words carefully. They might think, as some Canadians had believed, that they were embarking on a joint enterprise with the Americans, in which everyone stood to gain. That was not the way their American counterparts would see the situation. The Americans' mission was to extract every possible concession that could benefit American interests, and then to demand even more. As the negotiations drew to a close, the Americans would assume, correctly, that the Mexican government had made its own credibility hostage to the success of the negotiations and could not allow them to fail. They would then make even more difficult demands as a precondition to American agreement. Just when the Mexicans felt they had been wrung dry, their American counterparts would announce that the Congress would simply not be prepared to approve the deal without further concessions. My Mexican friends were deeply shocked and more than a little incredulous.

I assured them that this had been my experience over two decades of dealing with the Americans, and never more so than in the Canada-US free trade negotiations. Furthermore, our very success had made the Mexican situation more dangerous. Behind every point on which the Americans believed they had failed to get what they demanded and deserved, there stood an American negotiator whose professional pride, not to say pique, was squarely on the line. Rightly or, more often, wrongly, he felt bruised from his experience with the Canadians and was determined this time around to redress the balance. I went out on a limb and predicted the areas in which the Americans would push hardest at the very close of the negotiations.

On the way back to the city, the Mexican deputy chief negotiator, Jaime Zabludovsky, questioned me further on these points. It was obvious that he believed that I had overstated the case. The Americans realized that they had a huge stake in the Mexican government's success. They would be under firm instructions to focus on the bigger picture and not to seek every point of advantage. Perhaps you are right, I conceded. You can tell me afterwards if I was wrong. But you would be wise to adopt as your operating assumption that the Americans play tackle football, not soccer. Direct, crunching bodily contact is the name of their game. (After the negotiations were concluded, the Mexicans chided me: I had *understated* the vigour, not to say viciousness, with which the Americans negotiated.)

Back in Canada, I found myself in an ambiguous position. As one of the Canadians most identified with free trade, it was assumed that I would be in favour of the NAFTA initiative. Although I was no longer under contract with them, the Mexicans regarded me, rightly, as a friend. The media took it for granted that I would support the Mulroney government's approach. My old bosses shared that assumption. I found myself caught in the middle.

On the one hand, I was deeply offended by what I saw as the profound hypocrisy of the NAFTA opponents. They took the high moral ground. The political system in Mexico was far from perfect. Human rights were often trampled. Mexican standards of living were appallingly low. Wages were at subsistence levels. The environment was under continuous assault as Mexican workers and businesses tried to eke out a living under terrible conditions. To that point, I could only agree with their analysis.

But their conclusion was transparently self-serving cant. It had more to do with protecting the privileged position of their most powerful constituents – particularly among organized labour – than with helping the poor Mexican. They insisted that Canada should not be party to negotiations with the Salinas government to open up economic opportunities for Mexican exporters to Canada. But surely that was precisely the best, perhaps the only, way to address these problems: to give the Mexicans better access to our markets for their goods and services, in order to enable them to earn a better living for themselves and their families. To me, it made no sense to take the position that we should continue to limit their access to our markets and thus condemn them to continued poverty.

The last straw came when I took part in a televised debate in which a representative of the Canadian manufacturing industry advocated the NAFTA while the opposing case was made by a staffer to the Canadian Council of Bishops. I believed the latter to be a well-meaning individual. But I could not stand still as he dragged out this tired argument before an audience that included senior officials from the Mexican embassy in Ottawa. When he had finished his righteous peroration, I took the podium to apologize, personally and, I believed, on behalf of many of those present, to our Mexican friends for his patronizing and demeaning presentation. We had a long way to go in promoting human rights in our own country before we could criticize with impunity the record of another country. Nor had we the right to criticize the environmental record of a desperately poor country whose citizens were struggling to survive when we, despite the bounty of our natural resources, had such a shoddy record of our own. Above all, I apologized for the flagrant dishonesty of the argument that we should block the Mexicans from improving their own living standards – in their own best interest. The audience applauded these remarks.

On the other hand, I had deep misgivings about the changes I feared would be made to the Canada-US arrangements in these NAFTA negotiations. I, of all people, knew the FTA was far from perfect. But I saw no reason to believe that we would be able to improve it in these negotiations in the face of the aggressive American agenda. I saw no evidence that the Canadian negotiators had objectives of their own, beyond reaching an agreement that did not give away too much as the price of our admission. When the official heading the negotiating team was asked to state his objectives, he only confirmed my worst fears. He had clearly not thought through a Canadian agenda, and the few issues he identified were soon jettisoned in the negotiations. To be on the defensive, without clear negotiating objectives, is to invite disaster.

If our goal was to improve our trade with Mexico, I believed that was best done through a bilateral arrangement with that country. If our objective was to keep from getting pounded by the Americans, the best way was by staying out of the negotiations entirely. It was as if the Americans had invited the Mexicans to lunch. The Canadians felt left out and hovered over the table, soliciting an invitation. The Mexicans were reluctant to allow this intrusion but the Americans were persuaded to permit the Canadians to pull up a chair, provided they were prepared to pay a hefty cover charge.

By this time, the international trade portfolio had been combined with the industry portfolio under Mike Wilson, who had requested the dual role that put him squarely in charge of the NAFTA negotiations. At his request, I dropped my other commitments in the fall of 1991 to do a quick assessment of the options for revising the FTA deal on cars and parts. This required me to consult with the stakeholders in the industry. The presidents of the Big Three in Canada and the auto union, headed by Bob White, were all strongly in favour of much more restrictive rules to govern cross-border trade by non–Auto Pact producers. The presidents of the local arms of Toyota, Honda, and Hyundai naturally took the opposite view, demanding equal treatment with the Big Three. The industry associations and the provincial government of Ontario were all over the map. My confidential report was delivered within an impossible deadline and provided a number of new ideas, none of which were pursued by Wilson, on the advice of his officials. That was fine with me. I had done my job but the decisions were up to the government.

When the press sought me out on the broader issues of NAFTA, I stressed my support for closer ties with Mexico but shared my fears that the Americans would take the opportunity to reopen our agreement. Predictably, the negative comments got the greater attention. I also accepted invitations to appear before various parliamentary committees to elaborate on these views and answer the legislators' questions. It was not a happy experience and did not endear me to the minister.

Mike Wilson is a man of considerable personal charm and high integrity. He is perhaps not ruthless enough to be a true negotiator. His situation was made all the more difficult since his boss, Brian Mulroney, was politically committed to making a deal with his friend and comrade-in-arms in the Gulf War, George Bush. Wilson faced the Republican US special trade representative, Carla Hills, a tough but very narrow-minded Washington trade lawyer steeped in the American tradition of victory at almost any cost. Later, when he had to deal with Clinton's Democratic appointee, the former Hollywood lawyer Mickey Kantor, he was even more disadvantaged. He and his staff were closeted in the infamous Watergate Hotel for days on end as the Americans played their "thud and blunder" tactics to the hilt.

When the press reported my concerns with the overall NAFTA strategy, Wilson publicly dismissed them as exaggerated. I guess he was personally affronted that I would take any position other than that of complete support for the initiative or at least, like my friend Reisman, keep my mouth shut, whatever my private views. I was not prepared to play that game. Without giving undue comfort to the enemies of free trade, I believed I had an obligation to answer as honestly as I could those who looked to me for advice.

The conflict was made all the worse by the growing evidence that my concerns were well founded. The Americans made it abundantly clear that they had an attack agenda relative to Canada. They demanded patent protection for their pharmaceuticals – and Wilson agreed to give it to them in exchange for commitments to increased investment in Quebec. They demanded more restrictive rules on automotive imports to justify, after the fact, their deliberate twisting of the FTA rules against Honda and Toyota – and they got what they wanted, with the support of the Big Three, the auto workers, and the parts makers.

Most damaging, they demanded changes to the system that had put a damper on their abuse of American unfair trade laws to penalize successful importers from Canada. In November 1992, I was called on to analyze these proposals for the House of Commons committee studying the NAFTA. I pointed out that on the central issue of disciplines on unilateral application of American "fair trade" laws, the NAFTA reflects the American negotiating agenda, not Canadian objectives. Citing chapter and verse, I observed, "These changes reflect a considerable negotiating triumph for the American team who have obtained some, but not all, of their objectives without apparently making significant concessions in return."

When Jean Chrétien took over the reins from John Turner in 1990, he inherited a party in disarray. After the rout in 1984, Turner had managed a more creditable showing in 1988 by committing the party to an uncompromising anti-free-trade crusade. As a result, the Liberal members elected to the House of Commons had been closely identified with this extreme position – which some of them undoubtedly believed was the true path. This was the material with which the new leader would have to work, at least until the next election. I was reminded of the Duke of Wellington's comment to the effect that he did not know what impression his troops had on the enemy, but by God they scared the hell out of him.

Chrétien is a man of deep principles but, unlike his predecessor, does not wear them as badges on his shoulder, to be changed according to the circumstances. While his goals are fixed, he is highly pragmatic about the strategy for attaining them. He understood the vital importance of the American market for Canadian businesses. He had served, all too briefly, as Canada's trade minister and recognized the importance of access to markets. For all these reasons, Chrétien never shared the johnny-come-lately ideological fervour that Turner had instilled in his troops.

One of Chrétien's first, and shrewdest, moves as opposition leader was to entrust the trade agenda to Roy MacLaren. Dapper almost to the point of foppishness, MacLaren is a sophisticated internationalist. He had served in the Trade Commissioner Service at the beginning of his career and enjoyed his postings abroad in the 1960s. An amateur historian, he had written of little-known Canadian military adventures abroad, in Egypt and in Russia at the time of the revolution. He had been a highly successful businessman and a magazine publisher. He had served as a member of Parliament before the 1984 defeat and written a witty tome about his experiences. He had been re-elected in 1988. This long and distinguished experience had shaped his conviction that free trade could be in Canada's interest, as Chrétien knew when he named him to head the Liberal trade team.

Chrétien and MacLaren were not alone in their more liberal views of free trade. The runner-up for the leadership, Paul Martin, Jr., and a rising young star, John Manley, were among those who shared these convictions. It remained the case, however, that the great majority of the parliamentary caucus had been elected under an anti-free-trade banner, which had been borne stridently aloft by the left wing of the party, represented by Lloyd Axworthy, Herb Gray, and Sheila Copps. These self-proclaimed nationalists were particularly susceptible to demands that a Liberal government in the future should undertake to protect Canadians from the chill winds of the global economy by maintaining barriers against foreign imports and investments. It was a difficult challenge to reorient the party's thinking on the role of Canada in the world economy.

In 1990, when Chrétien turned to his old mentor for advice on how to achieve this redirection, Mitchell Sharp recalled the strategy Mike Pearson had followed with great success. He had convened a party conference in Kingston and invited many of the best thinkers of the day to present their views. The outcome was a fundamental shift in the direction of the party. At that time, the focus was on social policies and the shift was towards a more caring and sharing society. Times had changed and the issues were different, but the same procedure could work again.

The conference was held in November 1991 at the Château Aylmer, a modern hotel complex just across the river from Ottawa. It was by invitation only. Sharp, as the party statesman, and I, as an uncommitted outsider, went together. The meeting produced a mixed bag. Speakers reflected a wide range of views. That in itself was a departure for the Liberal Party, which had in recent years been the intellectual captive of an inward-looking ideology. Among the most important presentations were those made by Lester Thurow, an economics guru from MIT, and Peter Nicholson, a former federal official and provincial politician turned banker. The protectionists were represented in the hall but tended to drift into the corridors where they regaled the waiting media with their scathing condemnation of the "corporate agenda" of global economics. The closing statement was made by the leader himself. It had been toned down from earlier drafts to reflect his instinct that it would be unwise to nudge the party too quickly in new directions. Nonetheless, it squarely repositioned the Liberals as realists who understood the imperatives of the economic and political forces reshaping the environment in which Canadians had to make their way.

Meanwhile, MacLaren and his able young assistant, John Hancock, drew on my advice as they formulated positions on specific issues. Hancock frequently asked me to counsel him on this or that trade development, which I was pleased to do. MacLaren would invite me over to his office on Parliament Hill for a cup of tea. I would brief them on the issue, in line with my *pro bono* policy. MacLaren would then decide what position he would encourage the party to take.

A much more difficult issue was coming down the road – the Liberal position on ratification of the NAFTA. To assist them in defining the party's stand, MacLaren convened a private meeting with a number of caucus members. Three outsiders were invited: one made the case for rejecting the NAFTA and scrapping the FTA; another argued that the Liberals should simply go along with the NAFTA; I laid out my standard argument. I said there could be no thought of turning back the clock on the FTA. The issue was to ensure that the NAFTA did not give up ground in important areas, notably the bugaboo of American unfair trade laws. After hearing us out, the caucus excused us and undertook their own deliberations.

Before the 1993 election, Chrétien took another bold step. Against advice from all quarters, he committed his party to a Liberal plan for Canada under the title *Creating Opportunity*. This became universally known as the Liberal "Red Book" after the colour of its cover. It was assembled by a committee headed by Paul Martin, who as finance minister would later play a key role in its implementation, and Chaviva Hošek, who would serve as Chrétien's policy adviser in the Prime Minister's Office. This group engaged in a broad national consultation on a range of issues, of which free trade was one of the most contentious.

When their work was finished, I was asked to vet the draft paragraphs on trade to ensure that there were no factual errors. I was pleased with the position the Liberals were taking. Under the heading of "A Trade Policy That Works for Canada" they had singled out the flaws in the system for settling disputes, in particular over the American abuse of their trade laws. After a nod to the constituencies in Canada and the United States clamouring for side agreements on labour and environmental standards, the plan made a bold commitment:

> A Liberal government will renegotiate both the FTA and NAFTA to obtain:
> - a subsidies code;
> - an anti-dumping code;
> - a more effective dispute resolution mechanism; and
> - the same energy protection as Mexico.
>
> Abrogating trade agreements should be only a last resort if satisfactory changes cannot be negotiated.

I could not endorse the energy clause, but I recognized its origins in Chrétien's own experiences as Trudeau's minister of energy. I thought I recognized my own analysis behind some of the rest. But I was very hesitant to see the Liberals make an unqualified commitment to "renegotiate" the free trade deals. It would take two to tango, and the Americans could well refuse to dance. I passed these views on to the authors. In the final published platform, the language remained unchanged.

In the opening days of the campaign, Chrétien used the Red Book to great advantage. He was naturally helped by the Tories' instinct for self-immolation, led by Kim Campbell, whose refreshing naiveté was proving a serious political liability. Then John Turner entered the fray – on the side of the Conservatives.

When Chrétien became leader, Turner had largely disappeared from view. He continued to take his pay as a member of Parliament but was conspicuously absent from the House. The Liberals had long flattered themselves with the notion that internecine warfare was exclusively the practice of Tories. Former Liberal leaders would never be disloyal to their successors, tormenting them as John Diefenbaker had Robert Stanfield. This made it all the more distasteful when Turner went out of his way to savage Chrétien in the media at the height of the election. The party faithful were appalled at this breach of the etiquette of loyalty. There was much speculation about his motives.

The Turner statement hit the Canadian news media on the last Wednesday of September. He condemned the Liberals' position as unrealistic and irresponsible. This was interpreted to mean that there was no grounds for improving on the NAFTA regime, the successor to the system Turner had mercilessly attacked during his term as Liberal leader. It was one of the most extraordinary volte-faces in Canadian political history.

I was besieged with calls from reporters asking me to comment on Turner's remarkable conversion. Eddie Goldenberg and Chrétien's press aide, Peter Donolo, asked me to consider putting out a public statement of my own views. I could hardly refuse: my views were already on the record. On Sunday afternoon, six years to the day since the conclusion of the free trade negotiations in Washington, I made this statement:

> Jean Chrétien has been criticized for his determination to negotiate improvements in Canada's free trade agreements with the United States. As one of the architects of the original Canada-USA free trade agreement, I support his plan as both realistic and responsible. . . .
>
> Instead of holding the Americans to their commitment [to negotiate a new set of unfair trade rules], Canada was bullied into letting them off the hook in the NAFTA and abandoned this commitment to a new regime. Instead of advancing Canadian objectives, we took a dangerous step backwards.

My statement achieved its purpose. It largely defused the Turner attack. The predictable result was, however, to turn the fire on me. In its lead editorial, the *Globe and Mail* took a well-aimed potshot. After quoting my statement that the plan was both "realistic and responsible," the *Globe* observed:

> Not only does this place [Gordon Ritchie] squarely opposite former Liberal leader John Turner, who last week said it was neither, it effectively puts him in the position of attacking his own work. As one of the architects of the original Canada-US free trade agreement, he would appear uniquely unqualified to judge others' negotiating strategies, if he had done such a rotten job of it himself.
>
> Mr. Ritchie should not be so hard on himself.

I could not resist a rejoinder, which the *Globe* deigned to publish a full week later. I asked the editors of this mighty organ of public information:

> Perhaps you might explain why you considered it entirely appropriate for a new American president to reopen NAFTA negotiations on issues of interest to him, but now believe it would be wrong for a new

Canadian prime minister to insist on respecting the commitment in the existing free trade agreement to address our central objectives?

This provoked Lawrence Martin, who had just completed a book on Canadian-American relations, to drop me the following note:

> While researching "Pledge of Allegiance" I was frequently amazed at the strength of the neoconservatism, suggesting Canada surrender everything it had built to the market imperative and the American imperative. As your letter so correctly states, if they can stand up for themselves, why can't we?

It was all good fun and probably did not, in the end, sway a thousand votes across the country.

One of the consequences was, however, that when Jean Chrétien swept into power with a Liberal majority, his staff turned to me for advice on the first explosive issue he confronted: whether and under what conditions to ratify the NAFTA.

President Clinton faced a battle royal to get the NAFTA through the Congress. His special trade representative, Mickey Kantor, had taken up the file where the Bush administration had left off. There had been an ugly week of high-tension negotiations at the Watergate. Kantor's bullying tactics, particularly towards the Mexicans, had left everyone with a foul taste in their mouths. To placate some of his Democratic supporters, he had extracted side agreements, with little substantive content, on the issues of labour and environmental standards. But to achieve passage of the deal, Clinton depended heavily on the Republicans to support the NAFTA, which George Bush had negotiated. There was a dim awareness among the *cognoscenti* that the Liberal leader had expressed some serious reservations, but these had been dismissed with the comforting reminder that this was, after all, just politics.

Now Chrétien had won the election and would shortly be taking office. The Americans were desperate to discover his real intentions. The American embassy in Canada did its best, jumping official lines to contact the offices of the party leader who was not yet prime minister. To their dismay, they were assured that Chrétien's views were reflected in the Red Book. The pressure escalated. Mickey Kantor himself called the leader's office and found himself in negotiations with Eddie Goldenberg. It was a bizarre situation. Chrétien did not yet control the levers of power. He had no authority over the bureaucracy, which, until the formal transfer, was still under the direction of the prime minister, Kim Campbell. He had no staff, beyond the handful of loyalists in his office as opposition leader.

Goldenberg called me out of a board meeting to ask my advice. I did not believe it was possible or even necessary to reopen the actual agreements themselves. Side agreements had been good enough for Clinton. Surely it would be possible to agree on side letters that would meet Chrétien's minimum requirements, at least to resurrect the commitment to negotiate new rules for anti-dumping charges and countervailing duties. On energy, I really had nothing to suggest. Perhaps those who were concerned on this subject might be placated if progress was made on another front, through a more formal exchange to confirm that water was no part of the trade agreements. Chrétien alone could judge whether these improvements, meagre as they were, could justify ratifying the NAFTA. In any event, I did not believe that abrogating the original FTA was a serious option, given the massive restructuring of the Canadian economy that had occurred over the past half-dozen years as Canadian businesses positioned themselves to seize the new opportunities.

The strategy was accepted. Now it was necessary to execute it. I was able to give my personal assurance that the public servants responsible for this issue, the deputy and assistant deputy ministers of international trade, were thoroughly reliable. Steps were taken, with the knowledge and blessing of Prime Minister Campbell, to make the bridge. When Goldenberg continued his negotiations with the redoubtable Kantor, he was now able to rely on the expert assistance of the professional bureaucracy.

As is usually the case, the final outcome did not entirely satisfy anyone. The side letters on trade laws were drafted and signed by all three countries, only to have the resulting working parties face continued stonewalling from the Americans. The note on water was forthcoming but failed to quiet those who had made alarmism a career. Chrétien did proceed to ratify the NAFTA, to the indignation of those who had hoped he would abrogate the FTA.

The trade strategy of the Liberal government, led by Prime Minister Chrétien and Trade Minister MacLaren, was a highly practical amalgam of ideologically uncomfortable elements. To an unprecedented degree, Chrétien put his personal enterprise into helping Canadian firms sell their goods and services abroad. The centrepiece was the Team Canada program, which he personally led with impressive success. To meet the concerns of the left wing of the party, the government's rhetoric focused on the need to develop trade with other markets, leading to support for free trade initiatives with the Asia–Pacific region and with South America as well as for the work of the GATT and its successor, the World Trade Organization. On the other hand, the Liberals recognized that Canada's prosperity depended on access to the American market, and that, in turn, meant making the free trade agreements work to Canada's benefit.

10

THUGS AND BULLIES

During much of my government career, I had fought to defend Canadian interests against American protectionism. It was a simple and quite illuminating step to engage these issues from the perspective of Canadian companies trying to do business within the free trade framework.

Although in later years more conventional work as a business strategist and corporate director came to occupy an increasing proportion of my days, trade issues were my first love. Canadian firms and industries that ran into difficulty came to enlist my advice and assistance, which I was more than pleased to provide.

The list of companies and industries with which I worked is too long to include in this account. Each had its specific concerns. All had in common the objective of making the Free Trade Agreement work for Canadian interests. It was my good fortune that one of my very first clients became one of my best: the Canadian softwood lumber industry.

The softwood lumber industry was no stranger to American protectionism. Lumber trade disputes lay at the heart of the bitter controversy in the 1820s between the state of Maine and the colony of New Brunswick over ownership of the Aroostock Valley a few miles up the Saint John River from my father's hometown. Over the last twenty years, softwood lumber has been *the* major trade irritant between Canada and the United States. When trade analyst Daniel Schwanen of the C. D. Howe Institute attempted a detailed quantitative analysis of bilateral disputes, he soon found that the value of disputed lumber trade had to be excluded from the analysis "because it would dwarf all the others."

My involvement with the industry began with Adam Zimmerman, the intellectually brilliant chief of Noranda Forest, who had been badly burned in the softwood lumber disputes of the early 1980s. As president of one of the major Canadian exporters and chairman of the Canadian Forest Industries Council (CFIC), the industry association he had formed to fight the trade disputes, he had been front and centre. When the issue exploded in 1986, Zimmerman was held responsible, by the International Trade Department and by his industry, for much of the difficulty. He felt, not without some reason, that he had been betrayed by the government and, in particular, by the minister, Pat Carney. His relations with her were not helped when he publicly rebuked her, asserting, "You don't work for you, you work for us."

In the fall of 1988, Zimmerman approached me to give him some advice. His first question was whether the industry was best served by sticking together in CFIC despite the departure of the members from the Maritime provinces. After checking with the responsible government officials, I confirmed that CFIC was seen as a valuable instrument to coordinate government and industry activities.

Shortly thereafter, I received a visit from the coordinator of CFIC, Mike Apsey, who also served as the president of the British Columbia Council of Forest Industries. Apsey is a Bunyanesque figure who looks every bit the backwoods lumberjack. He is actually a highly educated and widely travelled professional, fluent in several languages. Trained as a forester, he served for many years as the provincial deputy minister for forests. He was a natural choice to head the provincial industry association. This is a position of real importance in a province where such a high proportion of the economy is dependent on the forest industry. The BC industry was by far the largest in the country. It naturally led the fight against American restrictions under the national umbrella of CFIC. Apsey retained me to advise CFIC on the best strategy for the industry to follow.

I had no inkling that my acceptance would lead me to become so deeply involved in the travails of that industry as it faced the brunt of American protectionism over most of the next decade. What follows is obviously coloured by that experience. I freely admit that I have an axe to grind. I believe this case dramatically demonstrates appalling bad faith by our American friends as well as the limits to what we achieved through the Free Trade Agreement.

The latest round of disputes dates back to 1982, when the American lumber industry was reeling under a number of self-inflicted wounds, including the fallout from the boom-and-bust management of the sector and the mounting environmental pressures to withhold forests from cutting. Industry pressure had become intense, focused on the senators from the western timber states led by Bob Packwood and Max Baucus. As a first step, the US Senate Finance Committee directed the International Trade Commission (ITC) to conduct an investigation under Section 332 of the Tariff Act. Normally, an industry that wants protection from imports would be required first to collect the information to make a case for a full investigation. Under Section 332, the government does the industry's dirty work, putting the importer through the wringer before a case is even formally begun. In this instance, the tactic at first appeared to have backfired, since the ITC report in 1982 most uncharacteristically gave Canadian imports a reasonably clean bill of health.

That naturally did not deter the protectionists. If there is one field where Washington lobbyists excel, it is in the use of loaded language to advance their cause. The law firm Dewey Ballantyne manufactured a front organization styled the Coalition for Fair Canadian Lumber Imports to mobilize the domestic industry to pay their legal bills. This mysterious group's identity was always kept a closely guarded secret – the Canadians were obliged to face a masked accuser. The coalition applied its own rather imaginative interpretation of the data the government had collected to file a petition with the Department of Commerce, alleging that subsidized lumber imports from Canada were wreaking havoc among American producers.

They had the misfortune of running into an honest man in the person of Gary Horlick, the official in charge of these investigations as the head of the Commerce Department's International Trade Administration. On May 25, 1983, he reached the following decision:

> In conclusion, based on information in the record, we determine that Canadian stumpage programs ... do not confer a subsidy within the meaning of the Act because they are not offered contingent upon export performance, because they are not provided to a "specific enterprise or industry, or group of enterprises or industries," and because they do not confer a domestic subsidy.

He therefore threw out the case. End of story? Not on your life.

The American industry and its allies in Washington merely turned up the political heat. They flooded Capitol Hill and the administration with demands that the government deal with imports of "subsidized Canadian lumber." They did not make much immediate headway at first. Canadian imports had, after all, just been acquitted on all these charges.

Then President Reagan asked Congress, specifically the Senate Finance Committee, to give him authority to negotiate the free trade deal with Canada. As recounted earlier, Packwood and Baucus orchestrated a ritual dance with their senatorial colleagues to threaten to refuse permission for the negotiations to proceed. In November 1985, sixty-four members of Congress wrote to the US secretary of state to demand that he resolve the lumber issue before the free trade negotiations began.

The formal position of the Mulroney government was categorical: we would not be prepared to pay a price for the talks to commence. In the trade office, we did have our suspicions that this message was losing some of its clarity in transmission. We also suspected that the White House was doing deals on the side, the usual pattern of business in the Washington game. It was only later that these suspicions were confirmed: President Reagan had indeed undertaken to deal with the lumber problem. As his special trade representative, Clayton Yeutter, scribbled on a note to one senator, "We'll get timber fixed." Indeed, the fix was in.

One month later, a new Commerce Department investigation was launched. The facts were the same as before. The law was unchanged. The political dynamic, however, had changed dramatically. This was brought home to me at one of our sessions in Washington. To this point, the trade office had been watching the unfolding of the lumber case with interest, but we had played no direct role. Then the ranking Commerce Department officer, Ann Hughes, asked Simon and me to meet with the US secretary of commerce, Malcolm Baldrige.

Mac Baldrige was widely admired for his straight-shooting. He was an avid cowboy who later came to an untimely end when his horse threw him to the ground at a rodeo. At the time we met him, his style and appearance bespoke a true western gentleman of great character and integrity. The Canadians had taken some comfort from the assurance that he would personally hold the ultimate responsibility to rule whether Canadian lumber imports were to be penalized at the end of the new investigation.

We had been well briefed before this meeting. The officials of our External Affairs Department assured us, on the basis of advice from their highly paid Washington lawyers, that Canadian lumber would again be acquitted. In Washington, things are never that simple, as Secretary Baldrige patiently explained to his Canadian visitors. The upshot of his message was that we should not focus unduly on the facts and the law. The political reality was this: he would have to determine that Canadian lumber should be penalized, or Congress would run amok and impose its own restrictions, which could be much more damaging to Canadian interests. He really had no option.

We were somewhat taken aback by his bald-faced assertion. This was, after all, the man who presided over what Joe Clark had repeatedly assured the Canadian House of Commons was a "quasi-judicial process." He was telling us: Heads you lose, tails and the American coalition wins.

We passed Baldrige's veiled threats on to the responsible authorities in Ottawa. It was not, after all, our file. We were after bigger game with the Free Trade Agreement. Contrary to later rumours, at no point did I nor, to the best of my knowledge, Simon press anyone to make any special concessions in order to facilitate our negotiations. Quite the contrary. This episode further strengthened our determination that any agreement to free cross-border trade must not run the risk of being gutted by the politically motivated decisions of the authorities in either country.

The Commerce Department moved to its predetermined conclusion. In a patently trumped-up preliminary ruling, it determined that Canada's provincial stumpage programs did constitute a subsidy of 15 percent (giving the American coalition exactly half the 30 percent they had demanded). On the divide-and-conquer principle, however, lumber shipped from the Maritime provinces was effectively exempted. The duties applied only to imports from British Columbia, Quebec, Alberta, and Ontario.

Messages continued to be sent to Ottawa that the Americans were ready to bargain on lumber. The pressure tactics worked. Faced with the prospect that their producers could be compelled to pay 15 percent to the US Treasury, the four major producing provinces soon concluded they would rather keep the money themselves. The federal government agreed to act as their agent and impose an export tax that it would pass on to the provincial governments on condition that it not be handed back to the lumber producers. The producers, who were fully ready and willing to fight the case to a successful conclusion in the American courts, were left high and dry. The dirty deal was enshrined in a 1986 Canada-US "memorandum of understanding" that added insult to injury by putting the American producers in the driver's seat to police the agreement through their agents in the administration.

This softwood lumber memorandum of understanding was, in my view, the most obscenely craven trade deal ever signed by the government of Canada. I deplored the reasons why the provincial and federal governments had caved in to the Americans, but I understood their position. Despite their brave words, the federal and provincial governments did not believe Canadian exporters could expect a fair shake from the American trade authorities. Even if the companies eventually won a case in the highest US courts after great effort and expense, the damage would have been done as huge sums of money would have been sucked out of Canadian pockets while the case was under way. Thus, they calculated, it was better to keep the money at home, in their provincial treasuries.

It was as if a mugger brandishing a gun had demanded that his victim hand over his wallet. "Here, let me take that for you," the victim's friend says, grabbing the wallet and running off. "It's all right," he shouts to the mugger. "I promise never to give it back to him." Substitute the administration for the mugger, the lumber exporter for his victim, and provincial governments for the poor sap's erstwhile friend, and you have the fable of the 1986 lumber deal.

This dismal episode only strengthened my personal resolve to make every effort to see that this kind of extortion would at least be less likely and less profitable in the future. Our efforts to get the Americans to clean up their act and set aside those unfair trade laws that had absolutely no place in a free trade agreement have already been described. We did, indeed, secure their agreement that they would negotiate a new and better set of rules in the future. To our disappointment but no one's great surprise, the Americans showed no interest in living up to their promise. Talks to put a new system in place went nowhere, and Michael Wilson's NAFTA took them off the hook. The Chrétien government shamed them into resuming the negotiations, but again the administration had no stomach to face the wrath of the protectionist lobbies. Eventually, the whole business predictably dissolved in futility.

This left us with the binational panel system. The best I could say of this system was that it would ultimately ensure that the Americans applied their own laws fairly, even if it left those laws intact. When questioned at the press conference following the announcement of the FTA, I went so far as to state my belief that if the FTA had been in place, the lumber case would have had a very different result. If the Americans cheated as they had in the lumber case, the binational panels would strike down their decisions. Knowing this, I claimed, the American authorities might well be less eager to do their clients' bidding in order to avoid public humiliation. In a triumph of hope over experience, I suggested that we should give the Americans the benefit of the doubt, unless and until they proved unworthy of this confidence.

We had faced the problem at the very end of the Washington FTA negotiations of what to do about the side deal on lumber. The bilateral agreement had been captured in the memorandum of understanding (commonly called the MOU) between the two countries. This left open the question: What happens now to the MOU? It was obviously inconsistent with any free trade agreement.

Given Pat Carney's high exposure on this issue as the trade minister elected from British Columbia, she took personal responsibility for the negotiations on this point. She drafted the provision in her own handwriting. The result was a deliberately ambiguous formula under which both sides agreed that the FTA "does not impair or prejudice the exercise of any rights or enforcement measures" arising out of the MOU. This left each side free to put its own spin on the issue back home. The Americans went a little overboard, reassuring Capitol Hill that this meant that the MOU was untouchable and they could keep duties on Canadian lumber imports for ever. In effect, we had merely postponed the fight to another day.

By the time I met with Adam Zimmerman and Mike Apsey, the MOU had been in place for a couple of years and had rubbed the Canadian industry raw. The fatal flaws in the arrangement had become painfully apparent. In the Maritimes, the lumber producers, led by the Irving interests, were gleeful that their competitors were being punished while they were allowed a free run into the markets of the eastern seaboard, exempt from the MOU. In Alberta and Ontario, the federal government played the thankless role of tax collector, tacking 15 percent onto the price of every shipment of lumber to the United States and passing the proceeds on to the provinces.

In British Columbia, the province decided to go one step farther. It imposed its own regime of higher costs on the harvesting of timber in its territory. It persuaded the US Commerce Department and its principals, the American coalition, that these measures would add more than the equivalent of 15 percent to the cost of every shipment to the United States. The federal government was therefore no longer required to collect the export tax. The icing on the cake was, of course, that the same higher costs would be imposed on *all* the wood harvested in the province, whether destined for the American, Canadian, or foreign market in the form of lumber or any other end product. The province thus reaped a bonanza estimated at perhaps

$800 million. To complaints from the industry and its powerful unions it could reply: Don't blame us. The dastardly Americans made us do it.

In Quebec, they settled for a hybrid. The province introduced some increases in costs. Quebec exporters were then subject to a smaller export duty. Thus there was no tax in the Maritimes, a small tax in Quebec, a 15-percent tax in Ontario and Alberta, and a cost increase equivalent to much more than 15 percent in British Columbia.

When Zimmerman and Apsey approached Strategico in 1988, I was more than delighted to sign on to help the lumber industry work its way out from under this preposterous arrangement and, in the process, demonstrate the value of the FTA. My client, the CFIC, represented the producers in the four main provinces, who in turn accounted for over 90 percent of total Canadian lumber exports to the US. Three-quarters of this production was located in British Columbia, which naturally led the charge and paid the largest share of the bills, including my fees. My job was to advise the industry leadership on the most effective overall strategy. I did not represent the industry but I firmly believed in the validity of the Canadian position.

The first step was obvious: to persuade the government of Canada to exercise its right to terminate the offensive lumber agreement. I believed the evidence was clear and overwhelming. My old American adversaries freely admitted in private that the 1986 decision that Canadian lumber was subsidized was strictly a negotiating tactic. Besides, even the Commerce Department had conceded in public testimony that the huge increase in BC stumpage charges meant that the "subsidy" was more than offset. If the American industry complained, the facts and the law said the Commerce Department should find in Canada's favour. But even if they cheated again, under political pressure, the FTA panels were now in position to set things straight.

The reasoning was impeccable. It was heavily buttressed with study after study demonstrating that there had never been and certainly was not now any unfair advantage bestowed on Canadian lumber producers. Unfortunately, even I had underestimated the ability of the American lumber producers and their legal gunslingers to turn the US government on its head.

The Canadian industry forcefully carried the case to its own government. In public and private arguments it built up support for its position. Among its strongest allies were the very officials who had been forced to do the dirty side deal, led by Derek Burney, who had played such an important role in our efforts to correct the problem with the FTA. Burney now served as Canada's ambassador to the United States. At various occasions over the next few months, Burney, Trade Minister Crosbie, and Prime Minister Mulroney himself put their American interlocutors on notice that Canada was fed up with the lumber understanding and the abusive behaviour of the Commerce Department lackeys under that arrangement. Canada had the right, which it was prepared to exercise, to terminate the understanding on one month's notice. These warnings were no secret. Indeed, Crosbie issued a press release on the subject following a meeting in Newfoundland with his American counterpart. Having given ample warning, the government formally advised the administration on September 3, 1991, that it would indeed terminate the understanding in thirty days' time.

Incredibly, the Bush administration, from the White House through to the Commerce Department and the US special trade representative, professed to be completely taken aback. They reacted like scalded cats. It soon became clear that there had been a communications breakdown of majestic proportions *within* the administration, as each of the officials the Canadians had alerted had kept the information to himself.

The embarrassment was quickly transformed into outrage. In my experience, the Americans are never more indignant than when they are dead wrong. In this case they outdid themselves. The flames were naturally fanned by the coalition's law firm, which saw a golden business development opportunity. They soon persuaded no fewer than sixty-six senators to write to the president demanding that he take sharp action against Canada for our "breach" of the MOU.

Two articles of faith became widespread in Washington and remain part of the received truth to this day: first, that Canadian lumber had been proven, time and again, to be heavily subsidized; and, second, that Canada had broken its obligations in unilaterally breaching the MOU. That both these assertions were demonstrably false did not in the least diminish their effectiveness with the politicians who were governed by one basic principle – Canadian lumbermen do not vote in their state.

The appointed date for termination came, on October 4, 1991. It passed unnoticed that this marked the fourth anniversary of the original Free Trade Agreement in Washington. The Americans went right over the top. I had feared that, despite the evidence that Canadian lumber was not subsidized, the Commerce Department would be reluctant to refuse to investigate a complaint from their domestic coalition. I had never dreamt that the administration would take the actions they now took.

In an unprecedented move, the Commerce Department itself initiated a countervailing duty complaint, without waiting for the American industry to take action, and thereby placed the officials in the position of adjudicating a complaint they had themselves brought against Canada. Then, without even waiting for a preliminary decision on the issue, the US special trade representative invoked the trade equivalent of chemical warfare, unilaterally slapping new duties on lumber from Canada under the infamous Section 301 of their Trade Act. This was an open declaration of trade war. As a result, imports from the four major producing provinces were immediately thrown into disarray. A 15-percent tax was levied at the border and the American industry clamoured for it to be raised even higher once the Commerce Department had completed its charade.

Predictably, the minions in the Commerce Department did their masters' bidding on cue. They did have a little problem: even applying the discredited methods used in the 1986 lumber case, they would be hard pressed to find that Canadian stumpage prices constituted a subsidy, given the increased charges imposed in Quebec and, above all, British Columbia. The Commerce Department wizards were equal to the task. They found that stumpage prices were still much too low. Amazingly, the subsidy gap was widest in the province that had raised its charges the most, British Columbia.

Even then, the Commerce Department bureaucrats needed another rabbit to get the desired applause from their industry masters. Their solution was as ingenuous as it was dishonest. They determined that the biggest problem was so serious that it had, until now, entirely escaped their attention.

On behalf of British Columbia, Canada restricts exports of raw timber, as do a number of western states with the blessing of the American government. The Canadian measure was ancient and had never been seriously challenged. Indeed, the FTA had permitted only three specific exceptions to the rules against export and import controls, of which two were:

a) controls by the United States of America on the export of logs of all species;
b) controls by Canada on the export of logs of all species...

Incredibly, these very controls on the Canadian side were now determined to be equivalent to a subsidy. Indeed, they were the main element in the Commerce Department's preliminary finding that lumber imports were subsidized to the tune of 14.48 percent. That amount was to be collected on all imports from the four major provinces. To no one's surprise, the independent International Trade Commission fell into line, finding that these imports injured the American industry.

I worked with the Canadian industry as it fought the case before the American authorities. The Canadians did a superb job of marshalling their considerable resources under the leadership of Jake Kerr. Kerr is the hard-driving chief executive and owner of one of BC's leading lumber producers, Lignum. He proved a brilliant general for this major campaign. He forced the various elements of the BC industry to work with one another and with the provincial government, not without ruffling feathers when that was required. He skilfully played the politics of the other provincial governments and industries as well as the federal government.

Jake also showed a keen appreciation of the workings of the American system, in part because of his earlier experiences at the University of California at Berkeley, once the hotbed of American experimentation. Jake had been involved in the 1982 lumber case, as had Mike Apsey and CFIC's principal Washington adviser, John Reilly.

Reilly is a Kennedy Democrat. He ran Bobby Kennedy's campaign for the party's presidential nomination in 1968 and Walter Mondale's campaign as the Democratic standard-bearer in the presidential race in 1984. The old pro and his charming wife, Margaret Warner, one of the stars of the PBS *NewsHour*, enjoyed considerable status in official Washington even under the Republican administrations of Reagan and Bush.

The industry's top-notch legal team was headed by Charlene Barshevsky, with her razor-sharp mind and voice to match. (Barshevsky was later named the US special trade representative in the Clinton administration, over objections that she had worked with Canadians in the past.) The legal team was supported by leading American economists, including Bill Nordhaus of Yale University. They used the most skilful Washington lobbyists and public relations experts. The industry group worked hand in glove with the lawyers hired by the Canadian government and by the four provincial governments. They made the most powerful and compelling case that could be made.

It was all pissing in the wind, and the wind was blowing squarely in the Canadians' faces. After this tremendous effort, the Commerce Department redid its scientific analysis to find that it had indeed miscalculated, but not by very much. The final subsidy rate was cut to 6.51 percent (note the precision), of which well over half was due to the BC log export controls.

In a deliberate move to split the common front of the producing provinces, Commerce found that Quebec lumber was also subsidized, by 0.01 percent. If Quebec were on its own, this would mean the case would have been dropped, as the subsidy was too small to matter. But Quebec was part of the broader case against the four major producing provinces. This meant that exporters from that province would have to pay the full national countervailing duty as a price for being a part of Canada. This deeply angered those Canadians, all the way up to the prime minister, who were fighting to keep the country together during a difficult period of constitutional disagreement.

My blood still boils when I think back on this part of the decision. In order to serve their domestic industry clients, the Commerce Department was prepared to take steps deliberately designed to pit Quebec against the rest of Canada. Such a cynical action could surely not have been taken without the knowledge and sanction of the top levels of the administration, including the secretary of commerce, the special trade representative, the secretary of state, and the White House itself. This was the single most dishonourable and contemptible action the Americans have taken in my thirty years of observation.

To make matters worse, the forces of protectionism in the United States had been on the rampage right across the board. Around this time, I published my third annual report on free trade under the title *FTA Year Three: Put to the Test*.

Among the long list of actions taken by an administration that proclaimed its devotion to free trade, the report highlighted the following:

- The US Customs Department had deliberately misapplied the FTA rules to penalize the Japanese companies Honda and Toyota for assembling cars in Canada.
- American private meat inspectors had been allowed, indeed encouraged, to hold up trailers at the border loaded with imports of Canadian beef in breach of both the FTA and a special agreement between the two ministers of agriculture.
- The administration continued to apply tariffs against imports of Canadian plywood and waferboard to pressure us to lower our building standards to favour their product.
- They had broken all the rules of the GATT as well as the FTA in their assault on imports of lumber from Canada.

The Canadian government had so far proved ineffectual to defend our interests under the Canada-US Free Trade Agreement.

206

In the one major case, involving pork, where we had put to the test the binational panels Canada had worked so hard to establish, we had won an overwhelming victory. The Americans had turned around and invoked the "extraordinary challenge" that I had persuaded the government to accept on grounds that it should never be used. In the end, Canada won the case as I had expected. But my report noted:

> The judgment day was unconscionably long in coming, as American stalling tactics postponed a final decision until nearly two years after the original final CVD [countervailing duty] determination, or a total of two and one half years after the case was first initiated.

In retrospect, the lumber producers should have been so lucky.

As I probably should have expected, the press had a field day. The front-page headlines blared: "US Abusing Free Trade: Ritchie" (*Ottawa Citizen*); "US Accused of Violating Free Trade Agreement" (*Globe and Mail*); "US Abuses Free Trade" (*Financial Post*); "Un artisan du libre-échange critique sévèrement l'attitude des E-U" (*Le Devoir*), etc. My personal favourite was the *Ottawa Sun*, which proclaimed "Yanks' free-trade 'hardball' irks feds" beside a provocative photograph of a SUNshine girl.

The federal government was in no position to disagree with my assessment. The *Ottawa Citizen* confronted the blunt-spoken industry minister, Harvie Andre, with my criticisms:

> Andre said he agrees with Gordon Ritchie, an architect of the pact, who warned that Washington is not honouring the "spirit or, in some cases, even the letter" of the deal....
>
> "They are playing hardball," Andre said in an interview. "They are becoming very isolationist and worried ... and that's not good for anybody."
>
> Despite the disputes, he said: "I still maintain we are better off with the free-trade agreement and the dispute resolving mechanism to deal with that."

Of course, I agreed completely. The Americans were behaving like thugs and bullies. We would see whether the FTA would help us to survive their wrath.

My modest foray into constructive criticism hardly shook the Americans out of their evil ways although it did provoke the bible of American conservatism, the *Wall Street Journal*, to invite me to lay out my analysis in an op-ed article that the *Journal* followed with a supporting editorial. The main result, as far as I was concerned, was that I was struck off the "A" list of special guests for dinner at the American embassy in Ottawa. This was a real sacrifice since I had long enjoyed the status of the knight in shining armour who was one of the few outspoken Canadian defenders of the FTA. I later learned that the last straw was when the ambassador read my comment: "It's wise to expect the worst of the Americans because then they will never let you down."

More seriously, I was painfully aware just how far, personally and professionally, I was out on a limb. I had strongly encouraged my clients to follow this route and terminate the MOU. I was hardly naive about the unfairness of the American system. But I had believed that they would keep their word and respect the letter and, indeed, the spirit of the commitments they had made to their free trade partner.

Finally, I believed that the FTA panel system was designed to ensure that if all else failed, and the Americans acted in the most dishonest fashion, the Canadian industry would ultimately have the opportunity to make and win its case before an honest arbiter. But I must admit that I was unprepared to have the binational panel system subjected to such a terrible test so early in its existence.

On leaving the government, I had become a member of the Canadian-American Committee, a gathering of business leaders from both sides of the border which had enjoyed a long and distinguished record of achievement. It had successfully advocated the Auto Pact. It was this committee that had sponsored the original analysis I had examined when I first studied free trade more than twenty years before. It had spoken out in favour of the Canada-US Free Trade Agreement. Now that its original objectives had been largely achieved, its meetings were somewhat less dynamic than in earlier times. Nonetheless, it provided a valuable forum for discussion of the economic issues between the two countries.

Its meetings alternated between Canada and the United States, between the capitals and the centres outside the government hubs. At a crucial meeting in Washington in March 1992, I was invited to take part in a discussion of trade issues with Jules Katz, the deputy US special trade representative. As noted earlier, Katz was on the short list to head the FTA negotiations and had now been recruited to head the negotiations that led to the NAFTA. I had great respect for Jules and was interested to see how far he would go to defend the official line.

Once we had cleared some NAFTA issues out of the way, Katz and I were immediately at loggerheads over the lumber dispute. I claimed that the record would soon clearly show that the American reaction to the termination of the MOU was totally unwarranted. Canada's decision had been perfectly within our rights. The American reaction was, I argued, contrary to their obligations under the GATT, the FTA, and their own law. I predicted that once the Canadians had their day in an honest court they would win on every count. The Section 301 duties would be struck down by the GATT, and the countervailing duties would be struck down under the FTA. The United States would be found to have treated its best friend and free trade partner in a way that it would never have abused its worst enemies. I closed by pointing out that these were all provable assertions. I invited Jules to revisit these issues with the committee once the final verdicts had been rendered.

Jules was furious. He flushed with what appeared to be genuine anger that a Canadian should have the gall to challenge America's decisions. He accused me of being "intemperate." None of what I had said was true. Canada should never have terminated the MOU, even if it was our technical right, because of the political sensitivity of the issue. The administration had every right, indeed a responsibility, to take counteraction. Its response had been measured and fully consistent with America's obligations. The Section 301 action was fully in accord with the GATT. The countervailing duty was entirely proper. The panels would have no choice but to support it.

Two years later, when the dust had settled, Jules was unfortunately not available for a repeat encounter. It was probably just as well. He would not have enjoyed the reminder of the positions he had taken with such passionate conviction as a government official. By then, the panel system had done its job, and Jules had been proved wrong on every count.

I will not bore the reader with a lengthy recapitulation of the intervening events. What happened was that a GATT panel found that the US was indeed wrong in its Section 301 action and, in an unprecedented move, ordered the Americans to refund any cash deposits they had collected. An FTA panel with an American majority refused repeatedly to accept the International Trade Commission's decision that American producers had been injured and heaped scorn on the commission's lack of supporting evidence or analysis. The decisive FTA panel, comprising three Canadians and two Americans, initially *unanimously* rejected the Commerce Department finding that Canadian lumber was subsidized.

Commerce responded by not only sticking to its claim but actually jacking up the subsidy margin, which it now found was nearly double its last calculation – Canadian imports should pay a tax of more than 11.5 percent. This time, the two Americans on the FTA panel ran for political cover and found that a case decided by US courts about another industry under another statute could be interpreted to justify the Commerce Department's decision – a truly remarkable about-face. When the panel majority refused to follow this flight of imagination, the department was ordered to reverse its decision and refund the duties it had improperly collected.

Then the administration, at the demand of the coalition, launched an "extraordinary challenge" of the FTA panel decision, claiming that two of the Canadian panellists were biased (because other partners in their law firms had previously done entirely unrelated business with the Canadian government) and that this panel had manifestly exceeded its authority, threatening the whole system. When the issue was placed before a panel of three retired judges, they split again on national lines, with the Canadian majority ruling that the panellists and the panel decision were not in conflict with the rules set down by the FTA. Even then, the coalition was not prepared to accept defeat and promptly launched a challenge of the constitutionality of the entire system established by the FTA. The administration meanwhile claimed that it was unable, under the law, to meet its unquestioned treaty obligation to return the duties it had improperly collected on lumber imports from Canada, now totalling over C$1 billion, although it did agree not to collect any more.

Readers who did not follow this case closely in the past will by now be incredulous. It is simply not plausible that the same American government which five years earlier ratified a free trade agreement with Canada would behave in this manner. Regrettably, that is exactly what they did when their political system came under extreme pressure from a highly effective and amply funded lobby.

The underlying reason is very simple. Canadian lumber supplies around one-third of the American market. That is more than enough to make it worthwhile for the domestic producers to do everything in their power to force up the price of those imports, and therefore the prices they receive themselves. It does not take an economic genius to do the arithmetic: if prices for lumber from Canada were raised by the amount of the duties collected, i.e., $1 billion, the American producers stood to gain as much as $2 billion on their share of the market. These higher prices also automatically raised the accounting value of the vast stands of timber these companies own.

210

Washington politicians may be cheap but Washington lawyers are terribly expensive. Even at those rates, however, you can buy an awful lot of legal and lobbying talent for that kind of money. Ultimately, the real price is paid by the American consumer, above all the homebuyer, for whom this illegal duty was estimated to have raised the cost of a house by an average of well over $1,000 apiece. Of course, $1,000 will not buy even one day of the time of a Washington lobbyist.

For the Canadian industry, the bottom line was also very simple: the system had worked. Finally, the industry had been able to make its case away from the Star Chamber atmosphere of the American trade authorities. Both in the GATT and in the FTA, the decisions had come down squarely in Canada's favour.

I would like to think that this was not a matter of luck nor of national bias. The luck of the draw decided which country enjoyed a majority on an FTA panel. The panel with the American majority had unanimously kicked back the International Trade Commission's decision that imports from Canada injured the domestic industry. The panel looking at the subsidy issue was also unanimous in its initial rejection of the Commerce Department's case. It was only later, when the political pressure was so intense that you could cut it with a knife, that the two American panellists recanted. If there had been another American on the panel, would he have sided with the two late converts or stuck to the original ruling? No one can say.

As for the extraordinary challenge before the committee of judges, again it was purely by chance that the majority was Canadian. The American judge's minority opinion was highly inflammatory. If there had been a second American judge and if – a very big if – that second American had sided with his colleague, the entire FTA panel system would have come crashing to the ground.

Canada would have been forced to consider very seriously whether the whole agreement should be abrogated. I, for one, would have argued that without the protections of the panel system we would be facing one-way free trade. The Americans could and, based on the lumber case, would put up barriers to imports of any sort from Canada whenever we were too successful for their tastes. Fortunately, none of these dire eventualities materialized. The system had actually worked.

By now the administration had changed, and the Democrats had retaken the White House but not the Hill. The Liberals were in power in Ottawa. None of this seemed to make any difference.

When the decisions came down in December 1993, there was no inclination to break out the champagne and glory publicly in our triumph. Relief that the system had worked was tempered by the realization that we had won an important series of battles but the foes remained implacable and very powerful. The American coalition was still waging war, and the new Democratic administration and Republican Congress were still their close allies. The coalition was threatening to bring down the entire FTA system. Their congressional lackeys were busy, as it turned out, rewriting the rules to ensure that this could never happen again. And the administration was still dragging its feet on repaying the monies it had collected improperly.

An experienced negotiator knows that there are few decisive victories. Instead, each struggle serves to position the parties for the next negotiation. The first step is to come to the table. Our price was met when the American industry dropped the constitutional challenge and the administration began the laborious process of reimbursing the duties. Incredibly in this era of supercomputers, this took many months as they sent out tens of thousands of cheques, one for every truckload of lumber that had crossed the border. By the time all the payments were completed, the total reportedly came to around C\$2 billion, to cover the original duties plus the interest that had accumulated. This was by several orders of magnitude the largest reimbursement ever made under any international trade arrangement.

Our position was stronger as a result of the FTA decisions, but it was vital that we not overplay our hand. Although he found it personally offensive, the Canadian trade minister, Roy MacLaren, agreed to bilateral consultations to try to find a better way to manage lumber issues in the future.

The breakthrough came at a meeting in July 1995 at Kelowna, British Columbia. The discussions took place in a downtown hotel. I played no direct part in the meetings themselves, which involved a cast of dozens from Canadian and American governments and industries. I was holed up with the other industry advisers in a spacious suite with a magnificent view over Lake Okanagan. (During a break in the proceedings, I drove with a colleague across the lake and up the other shore to the site of the Big Horn Ranch, where my mother was born as her parents tried, unsuccessfully, to make a go of raising cattle on the rocky, rattlesnake-infested slopes.)

My task was to advise the Canadian industry. With the support of Washington adviser John Reilly, I proposed that we cut to the heart of the matter. It was not enough to demonstrate that the Americans' continuing assertions that Canadian lumber was subsidized were wrong-headed and even self-contradictory. The entire exercise, including all three lumber cases, was only a means to an end.

The real issue was that Canadian lumber exporters were successful in capturing a huge and growing share of the American market. That share had nearly doubled, from well under 20 percent in the early 1970s to more than one-third of the entire American market for lumber by the mid-1990s, as imports from Canada supplied the shortfall in the domestic market and thus kept lumber prices from going through the roof. What if we were to let our American tormentors know that we understood their real concerns and were prepared to contemplate some arrangement that restrained our share of their market in return for guaranteed immunity from further trade harassment?

This would call the American bluff. If they truly believed that the problem was the unfairness of our subsidies, they would refuse even to discuss a proposal that would allow these unfair imports continued free access to their market. If they pursued the proposal, it would demonstrate that their real objective was to restrict the volume of import competition from Canada, however fair that trade. The American producers would be laughing all the way to the bank, and our own exporters would do just fine.

There were shock waves when this idea was floated by Jake Kerr and his industry colleagues. It was met by protests from all sides. Most vocal then and later was the Canadian government, where Trade Minister MacLaren was most unhappy at the thought of caving in to American pressures to go in the opposite direction from free trade. Quebec's trade minister, Bernard Landry, publicly condemned this terrible departure from free trade principles.

I shared their distaste. But I was even more appalled at the prospect of continuing harassment by the Americans, especially since the coalition had bullied Congress into sneaking in changes to their unfair trade laws to nullify arguments that had been pivotal to our defence in the last case. Sure, once they had put us through the wringer again in the next rigged case, we could protest to the new World Trade Organization that these changes were contrary to the rules. Meanwhile, Canadian lumber exports would be paying heavy penalties for several more years with no guarantee that these enormous sums would be repaid the next time around.

By April of the following year, the deal was done. It had taken nearly nine months of extremely difficult negotiations. Kerr had done a superb job of leading the Canadian industry side. Yet another trade minister, Art Eggleton, the former mayor of Toronto, closed the deal for the federal government.

After all this work, it strangely resembled the outlandish proposal we had floated in the Okanagan. For the next five years, it provided that:

- Canadian lumber exports would be immune from any trade action by the US government – no more countervailing duties or anti-dumping charges, nor even any more Section 301 actions;
- exports from the four major producing provinces would enter the US market free of any duties up to a level of 14.7 billion board-feet – well above our historic average and around 90 percent of the record highs reached the previous year; and
- exports above that level would face a sliding scale of charges.

For the Canadian lumber industry, it was an acceptable arrangement that could not have been negotiated if our earlier FTA victories had not put us in a stronger bargaining position.

As a precedent, it stank. We had built an entire free trade arrangement on the premise that we would allow market forces to determine where production was located within North America. The Americans had demonstrated that, when it really counted, they were not prepared to accept the consequences of high and rising imports of sensitive commodities. Both sides had faced the inevitable and done a deal that made a mockery of our free trade principles. But it did keep Canadians at work harvesting timber and manufacturing and shipping softwood lumber to the US at record levels.

Having stood on the sidelines while Canadian lumber interests were being savaged, American consumers awakened, much too late, to the impact of their government's decision to do the American producers' bidding. As the president of the American National Association of Home Builders said in the June 1997 issue of the trade publication *The Merchant Magazine*, "The only people benefiting from the Canada-U.S. lumber agreement are the timber barons. The duty on lumber from Canada is essentially a tax on home ownership that is costing home buyers billions of dollars a year."

11

Culture Clash

The members of the Ritchie family are all voracious readers, from my parents to my children. I average three books a week (except at the very height of the trade negotiations), including the latest Canadian works on current affairs as well as the best fiction offerings past and present. We have a modest collection of original Canadian paintings. We all enjoy the theatre, and my siblings have inherited our mother's histrionic aptitudes: both my sister, Heather, and my brother, Donald, attended the National Theatre School in Montreal before going on the stage professionally. My brother continues as an actor to this day, with extensive experience on stage and screen; my sister eventually left the profession to become a lawyer, where her performing skills come in handy. Some of us displayed snatches of musical aptitude, although my third-form teacher in the United Kingdom gently noted on the report card that "Gordon appears to be temporarily tone deaf."

None of this prepared me for the critical role that Canadian culture would play in the free trade negotiations and beyond, as the Americans pulled out all the stops to clear the way for their "entertainment industry" to capture our market. In the course of the negotiations, I became committed to the view that it is essential to our national survival that we keep open the channels that permit Canadians to talk to other Canadians, in Canadian accents in both official languages. The succession of confrontations in a number of sectors were complex and painful but served only to strengthen this belief.

One of the sectoral groups established in preparation for the talks was formally responsible for advising the Canadian negotiators on cultural trade issues. It was chaired by a dynamic Quebec film producer, Marie Josée Raymond. Her Rose Films had made one of the very first commercial triumphs of the Quebec film industry. Entitled *Deux femmes en or*, it contained an epic scene in which two liberated housewives pursue their mailman up the street as he hops naked through the snowbanks, unsuccessfully trying to pull on his pants.

The sectoral group was quite unique, not to say bizarre. Appointed on the recommendation of the erratic federal minister Marcel Masse, it included every "cultural" interest from Luc Plamondon, the writer of successful rock musicals, to the former goaltender for the Montreal Canadiens Ken Dryden, who must have wondered what on earth he was doing there. Predictably, this group did not provide the solid support we obtained from other industries. Under Raymond's leadership, they threw a succession of tantrums.

Finally I met with the group at a Montreal hotel. Wooing them in both French and English, I eventually brought them to the central issue: Did they want to be in or out? There was really no middle ground. If they wanted guaranteed free access to the American market for their products and services, including Canadian performing artists seeking to travel to the major US cities to ply their craft, they would have to be prepared to allow the Americans to come north to compete.

The answer united this disparate group: Not on your life. They would rather protect the part of the Canadian market that remained to them, even if it meant forgoing opportunities to export. Without a dissenting voice, they demanded that we safeguard the status quo, in which they were subsidized by the state, given preferential advantages through Canadian content rules, and protected from foreign competition.

I did not particularly like their answer. It certainly made my job as negotiator more difficult. But I could understand their logic. My only concern was to ensure that they were not deluding themselves. They really could not count on having their cake and eating it, too. If we somehow stonewalled the Americans on their demand for access to Canada, we had to expect a rough ride in their market. Thinking of my siblings, I asked: "Do you understand, for example, what that means in terms of actors and musicians? If we reserve the right to refuse American artists entry to Canada to perform, we will have no complaint if they close the border to our artists." They professed to understand and agree.

The advisory group was a curious amalgam of artists and business interests. The latter tended to be overwhelmed by the rhetorical outbursts of the performing talents. The business interests had to find other ways to get their messages across. One evening Simon and I were invited by Pierre Juneau, the president of the Canadian Broadcasting Corporation, to dine with him and a few friends at the Rideau Club in Ottawa. This has been the dining place for the Ottawa establishment since the days of Sir John A. Macdonald, the club's first president. Since fire had razed the original building, facing directly onto Parliament Hill, the club had moved to elegant new premises atop the tower adjoining the trade offices.

Styled the Canadian Culture/Communications Industries Committee, Juneau's group had prepared a well-reasoned brief under the title "Free Trade & Cultural Identity: Will We Have Access to Our Own Markets?" The group included two highly charismatic figures with whom I would be closely associated in the future – Philippe de Gaspé Beaubien, of Télémédia, and Harold Greenberg, the larger-than-life CEO of Astral, builders of the pay-television movie network. Others included the heads of the leading Canadian television, broadcasting, film production, and sound recording companies.

With the help of consultants they had marshalled a devastating account of the existing situation. Canadians were already pushed back to the margins of their own market: only one-third of Canadian television viewing time was spent watching Canadian programs, and for drama the figure fell to a pitiful 6 percent; only one-quarter of the books sold in Canada originated here; fewer than one-quarter of all newsstand periodicals were Canadian; less than one-quarter of movie distribution revenue went to Canadian-controlled companies; and the eight largest sound recording companies were foreign-owned. This despite the much-vaunted measures to protect and promote the Canadian "cultural industries."

As businesspeople, this group believed that a free trade agreement with the United States could be in the overall economic interests of Canada. They were convinced, however, that if these free trade rules were applied to their industries, the result would be to strip away the last vestiges of Canadian cultural expression. They urged us to find some way to keep the existing measures, however inadequate, in place. They cited an opinion poll that found that "almost half of Canadians feel that including these [cultural] industries in the negotiations would threaten Canadian cultural identity," and most of those would be prepared for us to make concessions costing jobs in other sectors if required.

Simon's and my initial reactions were very cautious. This was, after all, remarkably similar to the self-serving pitch we were getting from uncompetitive firms in other sectors – we want free trade for everybody else but not for ourselves. The culture crowd prettied up the argument with more flair, but beneath that elegant finery was the same old tart.

The more I reflected on the issue, however, the more I became convinced that there was a serious structural problem. As the cultural group's report pointed out, at that time a one-hour episode of a TV drama such as *Dallas* cost about $1 million. It paid for itself in the US and could then be sold into Canada for as little as 3 percent of its cost. How could a Canadian television producer compete with those prices and maintain a quality that would be acceptable to millions of viewers? In any other field this would be called dumping.

In its starkest terms, the Canadian cultural producer is forced to choose: sell to the American mass market by completely de-Canadianizing the work, or try to speak to a Canadian reality – and go broke in the process. This was not and is not a choice any self-respecting country should impose upon its creative talents. This has nothing to do with "elitism" versus consumer choice, as the chief propagandist for the movie cartel, Jack Valenti, would have you believe. It has everything to do with the intrinsic inability of the market to produce results compatible with fundamental national interests.

That did not mean that our existing protective measures were hugely successful. They were not. The indirect financial incentives had proven woefully inefficient. The trickle-down theory seemed to be that by increasing the wealth of Canadian investors in the cultural sectors we would increase the opportunity for the creation of Canadian works. A study we commissioned by a former Finance Department expert found that while this system had significantly increased the bottom-line profits at a number of leading companies, its contribution to increased Canadian product was much less clear. As my brother acidly commented, it had produced more jobs for grips and gaffers but little in the way of leading parts for actors.

For me, the issue had been epitomized at one of our very first negotiating sessions at Mont Tremblant. Following that memorable softball game, I joined CBC-TV newsman Mike Duffy in the bar with some highly attractive young women and men who were on a film shoot in the area. As a result of the various government programs of protection and financial support for the making of films in Canada, these young people had jobs. But their jobs were the lowest-paid, acting for scale while American imports were flown in to take the lead roles. It was a film without redeeming merit, pretending to be situated in an American national park – a sort of *Meatballs* in the woods, as one of the actors described it. In the real world, this was what our policies were achieving.

More direct intervention had achieved somewhat better results. Instruments included the regulation of Canadian content on the airwaves by the Canadian Radio-television and Telecommunications Commission and the direct subsidization of postal rates for Canadian magazines. I believed the most effective were the state enterprises themselves – the National Film Board, which had put Canada on the map around the world, and, of course, the CBC. The state broadcaster was our most important instrument of cultural expression, and our most costly by a very wide margin. Ambiguities in purpose, linguistic divisions, and above all managerial ineptitude had made the CBC an easy and very popular target for public demands for funding cutbacks or privatization. It remained to be seen whether the result would be a more effective CBC or its ultimate demise.

Admittedly, this put me in an intellectually awkward position. I had the most serious reservations about the wisdom of our measures to protect and promote our cultural industries – not that they were too restrictive but, quite the contrary, that they were not effective enough. Personally, I would favour putting substantially more public monies directly into the hands of creative Canadians – the writers, composers, filmmakers, artists, actors, and other performers. Second in line should be the state enterprises that provided a vehicle for their expression. The private enterprises in the cultural industries should come a distant third. My views were not relevant, however, as it was my task to attempt to protect the measures we had in place from the insatiable demands of the Americans.

Two disasters befalling successive communications ministers illustrate the gravity of the problem: Marcel Masse's Baie Comeau book publishing policy and the stillborn Canadian film distribution policy of Flora MacDonald.

Although the Mulroney government had replaced FIRA, the new promotional agency, Investment Canada, still had the authority to review acquisitions by foreigners of Canadian companies, including indirect acquisitions. In the cultural industries, the policy was simply to disallow any such purchases.

Just at this point, several transactions occurred which had serious political repercussions. In one case, control of a Canadian publishing house was acquired by the American media giant Gulf+Western. Gulf+Western was a particularly bloody-minded operation that adopted a strategy of aggressive confrontation with government. Through Paramount Publishing it had acquired control of a small Canadian publishing subsidary, Ginn Publishing Canada. Gulf+Western saw red when it was advised that it would have to divest the Canadian subsidiary. The issue quickly became explosive, and the shock waves reached into the free trade negotiations.

Marcel Masse has always had a highly developed sense of his own importance, extreme even for a politician. As communications minister, he had set out to become the messiah of the cultural mafia in Canada. He had made extravagant promises on which he knew he would be unable to deliver. On most, he was able to leave his successor holding the bag. On book publishing, he had no choice but to take some action.

The problem was that the policy was unworkable. It required the government to direct Investment Canada to order the American purchaser to sell the Canadian subsidiary to Canadian buyers. But what if there were no buyers or, worse, if the few Canadians that showed an interest were obvious bottom-feeders, seeking to use the situation to get an extraordinary bargain? In a brilliant move, Masse bootlegged his proposed solution into a meeting of the cabinet Priorities and Planning Committee, at its special annual meeting, which took place in Mulroney's home riding. Masse christened the policy the "Baie Comeau policy" in a transparent and successful effort to smooth the way for its acceptance by the leader.

The policy required the government to stand by as the purchaser of last resort. If there were no Canadian takers, the government would buy the subsidiary at a "fair market value." This bizarre scheme then left the government of Canada paying over $10 million to acquire a small publishing subsidiary that had been cut off from its normal channels of supply and distribution.

We protected this ludicrous policy in the free trade negotiations. It had its own little clause that stipulated:

> In the event that Canada requires the divestiture of a business enterprise located in Canada in a cultural industry ... [the government of] Canada shall offer to purchase the business enterprise from the investor of the United States at fair open market value, as determined by an independent, impartial assessment.

Predictably, some years later, the Chrétien government was stuck with the problem of what to do with this orphan operation. Under the terms of the original agreement, when Canada changed its publishing policy, the government was required to sell Ginn back to Paramount for the original purchase price of $10 million. There was loud public outcry, largely orchestrated by Canadian interests who had no doubt hoped to pick up Ginn for a song. The flap nearly cost the minister of the day, Michel Dupuy, his job.

When Paramount in turn was acquired by another American giant, Viacom, I was conscripted to serve the cabinet as its unpaid troubleshooter on this file. Happily, the negotiations between Investment Canada and the American company were successful in extracting commitments to significant benefits for Canada in film development and other fields.

Film production and distribution was another extremely sensitive issue during the free trade negotiations. Masse was succeeded as communications minister by Flora MacDonald, a delightful woman who, as a party stalwart, ran unsuccessfully for the Conservative leadership in 1976. She was used to betrayal – in political jargon, the "Flora effect" refers to those convention delegates who pledge their support for a candidate in far greater numbers than the ballots that somehow find their way into the box. On this occasion, I believe she was betrayed by bad advice.

Her advisers, principally the curious cast of characters in the Communications Department and their industry clients, sold her a bill of goods. The proposal was another trickle-down variant. The plan was to make Canadian film distributors rich in the hope that this would somehow lead to more investment in film production. The scheme was as simple as it was self-serving: licences would be required to import and distribute films; the owners of films could get special licences to bring in their own products; all other films – most of the business – could be brought in only by distributors holding general licences; and those general licences would go only to Canadians.

During this period, the TNO was required to review any proposals that would bear on the free trade negotiations. Obviously, this film policy had the potential to drive the Americans up the wall. I sat down with MacDonald to review the plan. I had serious reservations about whether it would be effective, but that was obviously her call to make. My only advice was that if she decided to go ahead, she should go public as soon as possible. That would give us the opportunity to protect the policy by "grandfathering" it in the Free Trade Agreement, despite American objections. She made her announcement in the House of Commons. It attracted the predictable firestorm of objections from the Americans, spurred on by Jack Valenti, the head of the motion picture lobby.

Why the fuss, when over 95 percent of the screen time in Canadian cinemas is already devoted to foreign, overwhelmingly American, films? The majors' film cartel relies on its domination of foreign markets, beyond the easy reach of American anti-trust police, using this control to keep the independent producers in line. The majors' control of the Canadian market serves this purpose well: it enables them to force the independents to make more favourable deals back home in order to have access to this market; and it enables them to sell the Canadian distribution rights as part of a package, bundled up with the American rights. This was the pernicious system MacDonald was trying to break.

Unfortunately, the proposals came crashing down of their own weight. The fact was that they were unworkable. When a watered-down version was proposed and then also allowed to fall by the wayside, there was bitter criticism. Later, it became an article of faith in the cultural community that the free trade negotiators had forced MacDonald to back down on the original film policy. Nothing could be farther from the truth.

Under the terms of the Free Trade Agreement, as finally drafted, the original film policy and its successors were grandfathered. To avoid placing the Americans in an unduly embarrassing situation, the language was carefully crafted. After making all sorts of commitments not to treat the Americans unfairly with respect to the provision of services and the regulation of investment, we effectively repealed those commitments for any "non-conforming provision of any existing measure." We went farther and stipulated in the chapter on investment that this included "any published policy." This was the point of getting the film policy into the public domain well before the agreement was signed.

It was one thing to find some way to preserve Canada's right to maintain these policies on the distribution of films or the ownership of book publishers. It was quite another to provide blanket exemption from the free trade rules for the sweep of our cultural industries.

The Americans had great difficulty in even understanding Canadian sensitivities on these issues. At the height of the negotiations, in February 1987, Yeutter lectured the Canadians at a conference on free trade: "I'm prepared to have America's culture on the table and take the risk of having it damaged by Canadian influence after a free trade agreement. I hope that Canada is prepared to run that risk, too." With friends like this, I wondered, who needs enemies?

Simon, with his instinctive aversion to nationalism and protectionism, had some sympathy for the American arguments. He and I did not see eye to eye on the issue. It was a standing joke among the negotiators on both sides that when the question came up at one of the periodic dinner meetings we had with Murphy and Merkin, the result was an angry shouting match – between Simon and me, as Murphy and Merkin watched in bewilderment. But whatever his personal sympathies, Simon was a true professional: having taken his mandate, he did his best to deliver. Besides, he had made a personal commitment to Flora MacDonald that he would safeguard her beloved cultural industry protections.

Despite the most forceful American bullying, I believe we not only held the line but even advanced it a little with what came to be known as the "cultural exemption." There was virtually unanimous support for this among the Canadians, including Derek Burney and the prime minister.

We first insisted on defining these industries as "cultural" and made the definition very broad indeed. It included all facets of the publishing of books, magazines, or newspapers; the production and distribution of films or videos; the production and distribution of audio or video music recordings and of sheet music; and radio, television, and cable television broadcasting, including satellite programming and broadcast networks. As a sop to the Americans, we did concede that it would be going too far to include the printing industry in our cultural carve-out. After all, our printers were doing a land-office business in the American market, selling everything from broadsheets to lottery tickets. Everything else was covered.

Then we exempted these industries from the rules of the agreement. The Americans insisted, fairly enough, on maintaining their right to retaliate against us if we acted against their interest. But we insisted on limiting the scope of that retaliation to what we called "equivalent commercial effect." This to avoid a repeat of what had happened when we had introduced an earlier protective measure and they had slapped a tax on conventions outside the United States, which had a much greater negative impact on the Canadian economy by several orders of magnitude. Finally, we insisted on impartial arbitration to enforce these rules.

The cultural community is professionally paranoid. There were loud denunciations of our failure to get the Americans to agree that they would give us free and unrestricted access to their market for these cultural products and services while we could do whatever we wanted to them with complete impunity. Sensible people realized that this was simply unrealistic. I went to great pains to explain exactly what we had achieved and what it would mean in the future.

"Do you mean they can punish us for acting in our national interest?

That can't be true?" I would patiently explain that they had always had that right and had not hesitated to use it in the past. The only difference now was that they had agreed to some limits on what they could do and when they could do it.

The so-called exemption was meaningless, the critics then charged. It meant just what it said, I would explain. These industries were not subject to any of the disciplines of the agreement. Obviously, they also did not stand to reap any of the benefits of the agreement in improving their ability to break into the American market.

Reality shock was not long in coming to this sheltered community. Not long after the Free Trade Agreement came into effect, with its provisions to allow designated occupations to cross the border much more easily, the Americans announced they were clamping down on visas for Canadian performers and athletes. The Canadians erupted with indignation. They couldn't get away with this. After all, we had a free trade agreement. They blissfully forgot that this was exactly the problem I had warned them about some three years earlier. Only after much diplomatic effort and congressional lobbying was it possible to reduce the impact of these new restrictions.

By that time, I had left the government and set up shop advising a number of Canadian firms, including Southam, the principal national newspaper chain. I also served on several corporate boards, including Philippe de Gaspé Beaubien's company, Télémédia, the publishers of such magazines as the Canadian *TV Guide*, *Canadian Living*, and *Homemaker's*. At Beaubien's request and that of John Fisher, the president of Southam, I joined a reactivated Canadian Culture/Communications Industries Committee. It was chaired by Harold Greenberg of Astral and involved a stellar cast from all walks of the culture business. Our purpose was simple: to keep the government on the right track in the ongoing negotiations leading to the NAFTA and the World Trade Organization (WTO).

The government did not need a great deal of persuasion. It stuck to its guns in the NAFTA, maintaining the cultural exemption intact. The WTO proved a much more difficult setting involving more than a hundred countries, thus greatly restricting Canada's bargaining room. The Americans were not about to accept an exemption, let alone give permission, for the protection and promotion of what they still called the entertainment industries. The Europeans talked a supportive game but were, as usual, wobbly when it came time to cut the deal.

The predictable result was to carry forward the old GATT rules into the new regime. After all, these rules had not given us undue problems in the past. This proved to be a mistake. The ultimate proof of the value of the cultural exemption came when the Americans, in continuing to attack our cultural industries, found the door slammed shut by the FTA and had to use, instead, the multilateral mechanisms of the WTO, which had been touted by the anti-free-trade nationalists as the protector of Canadian interests. The case threatened the very survival of Canadian magazines.

The "C-58" system for magazines, named after a measure introduced in 1965, was built around the support of Canadian magazines and the prohibition of imports of split-run editions into Canada. A split-run edition is one in which the publisher tacks a few token pages onto the national edition and then sells it as a regional issue. This enables the publisher to turn to regional advertisers and offer them a deal based on the fact that his editorial costs are already laid off on the national edition.

In the mid-1960s, on the advice of a royal commission, Canada took action to counter the threat that this practice would kill the fledgling magazine industry. Under the Income Tax Act, advertisers were allowed to deduct the cost of an advertisement only if it was placed in a magazine that was at least 75-percent Canadian-owned and in which the editorial content was at least 80-percent distinct from the contents of other editions. Although this helped Canadian magazines to get off the ground, the importance of the tax deduction was steadily eroded over the years. An exception was made for two magazines that were long established in the Canadian market, *Time* and *Reader's Digest*. In the mid-1970s, following yet another royal commission, the exception was withdrawn, although *Reader's Digest* found a way to continue to operate as Canadian.

More important was a provision of the customs tariff that flatly prohibited the entry of split-run editions and issues in which more than 5 percent of the ad space was primarily directed at Canadians. For thirty years, this provided an important protection for the Canadian industry. Behind it, literally hundreds of Canadian magazines were able to get established. By 1992, the Canadian periodical industry produced nearly 1,500 titles and was approaching a billion dollars in revenues.

A third device, our postal rate subsidies, figured prominently in the final crunch in Washington in October 1987. Curiously, the press missed the issue entirely, despite the fact that it was in their own backyard. I have never seen this episode reported in the press or electronic media.

Canada operated a highly discriminatory system of rates at which the post office delivered magazines: our magazines were carried at a rate of 5 cents per copy; most American magazines were carried at a rate of 32 cents; the only exceptions, as I recall, were *Reader's Digest* and *Watchtower*, the Jehovah's Witnesses publication, which had been grandfathered in the original legislation and paid just 6 cents per copy. These lower rates for Canadian magazines were made possible by a subsidy, which at the time of the negotiations amounted to over $200 million.

Right to the end of the Washington talks, the Americans had pushed very aggressively to strip away the protections enjoyed by our cultural industries. One of the few points we did concede was on postal rates. They trumpeted their success to the American magazines that stood to benefit, and to their allies in the Congress. We had agreed that Canada would "phase out discriminatory postal rates for magazines of significant circulation." They interpreted this to mean that we would have no choice but to lower the rate for a publication such as, say, *Sports Illustrated*, from 32 cents down to 6 cents, saving them nearly two bits a copy.

The American negotiators had miscalculated. We were able to meet our commitment simply by raising the postal rate on certain Canadian magazines from 5 cents by a penny to the *Reader's Digest* rate. This put a few more dollars into the post office but did absolutely nothing for the American magazines lined up to flood the Canadian market. They were apoplectic when they realized what had happened, and they were furious with their negotiators for having been duped by the cunning Canadians. When it came time to write up the final text of the agreement, the Americans pressed us to enshrine the deal they had reported back home. We refused to budge off the letter of what had been agreed in Washington. Rather than face the anger and derision back home, the Americans preferred to drop the matter entirely. They would take their chances in the GATT.

It was nearly a decade later that they finally took action. The trigger was the decision by *Sports Illustrated* to vault the border prohibition and print a split-run edition in Canada via satellite transmission to the printing plant. This caused consternation in the Canadian industry. For example, Télémédia had just launched a French-language sports magazine, which would now face intensified competition for advertising dollars from the American giant. As it turned out, the Télémédia venture flopped without any help from the Americans.

More to the point, others could follow once *Sports Illustrated* had breached the wall against split-runs. The government hastily convened a task force to examine the issue, co-chaired by lawyers J. Patrick O'Callaghan and Roger Tassé, a former deputy minister of justice. Studies they commissioned indicated that the threat was very real. At least 20 and perhaps as many as 120 foreign magazines aimed at consumers could follow *Sports Illustrated* through the door.

The result would be devastating for the Canadian industry. The consumer periodical industry, which was already teetering on the edge of profitability, could face the loss of nearly 40 percent of its current advertising revenue to the new entrants. Few publications could withstand the shock. If the average magazine lost just half that amount, it would fall below break-even and begin to lose money. This would inevitably lead to the closing of many if not most of the Canadian consumer periodicals. The smaller and much more numerous Canadian trade magazines would be clobbered even worse.

The task force reaffirmed its view that "the best way to encourage the viability of the Canadian magazine industry is to foster conditions in which magazines with original editorial content can be profitably published, distributed and sold in Canada." It recommended that the government maintain the existing framework of instruments under the income tax and tariff codes and through postal subsidies. This should be buttressed by a special new excise tax on split-run magazines distributed in Canada, thus closing off the technological end run. The tax was to be set at 80 percent of the amount charged for all the advertising appearing in that issue. Wisely, the task force recommended that *Sports Illustrated* be grandfathered to avoid any appearance of retroactivity.

The task force was keenly aware of Canada's international obligations but believed they had been met. They made the case that the new tax on advertising in magazines lacking original content did not violate the GATT requirement that foreign goods be treated the same as domestic production. The government essentially followed the task force's advice and implemented the new tax in 1995. Stupidly, they did not grandfather *Sports Illustrated*. Someone obviously did not understand the risks of bluffing with a weak hand.

The Americans were provoked into calling Canada's bluff. It was bad enough that Canada was reaffirming its odious past practices. The new measure was, they believed, nothing less than retroactive confiscation of the business that *Sports Illustrated* had begun to develop with its new edition. They took the case to the newly established dispute settlement machinery of the World Trade Organization. They challenged not only the new tax but the original split-run prohibition and the postal subsidies to boot.

I was not directly involved in the case but was occasionally consulted by my contacts in the government and briefed by the managers at Télémédia. To my astonishment, the industry was apparently being advised that the Canadian case was strong. They were told the odds were that we would win our case before the WTO.

I did not share this optimism. When Canadian Heritage (successor to the old Department of Communications) asked for my opinion, I gave it freely. I warned them that this was not a cultural crusade but a narrowly technical matter that would be decided by technicians in the WTO. It was entirely possible that the specific measure Canada had adopted might be found to break the rules. I was prepared to give odds that we would lose the case. That would not mean the end of the world. We should be able to find other techniques that would achieve our legitimate cultural objectives without running into the same problems. These could include direct subsidies and other measures that did not distort trade interests quite so blatantly.

If we could not find some way to satisfy the WTO, the one option I did not believe this or any other government could consider would be to hang the Canadian magazine industry out to dry. If worst came to worst, we should ensure that the American authorities understood that we were not prepared to open our doors to an invasion that would kill off what remained of our magazine industry. We should be prepared to offer some reasonable compensation for what was, after all, pretty small potatoes in an overall trade of $1 billion per day. Failing that, we should face their retaliation, but strictly limited to the equivalent commercial value of the interests affected. Bottom line: we would continue to promote and protect our Canadian magazine industry but would endeavour to do it in the least objectionable manner under the rules of international trade.

When the preliminary decision was reported in early 1997, it confirmed my worst fears. The WTO panel had been at pains to stipulate:

> Before concluding, in order to avoid any misunderstandings as to the scope and implications of the findings . . . we would like to stress that the ability of any Member [country] to take measures to protect its cultural identity was not at issue in the present case. The only task entrusted to this Panel was to examine whether the treatment accorded to imported periodicals under specific measures identified in the complainant's claim is compatible with the rules of GATT 1994.

It then determined that the split-run tariff was incompatible. So was the excise tax. But it was permissible for the government to fund Canadian magazines through the postal subsidies.

If they had asked my advice, I would have strongly urged the Canadian ministers involved to take the lowest possible profile on the issue to minimize the damage. Naturally, the opposite posture was adopted: the sky was falling on all of Canada's cultural industries. Press conferences were urgently called, speeches were given, and emergency summits convened to discuss the response to this great American victory. With every headline, the American win took on added importance. What had been a preliminary decision, subject to appeal, on a narrow technical evaluation of a couple of specific instruments became the trumpets of Joshua threatening to bring down the walls of Jericho.

Incredibly, the Canadian ministers then engaged in a public debate. The heritage minister, the volatile and passionate Sheila Copps, took up a fighting stance, rallying her troops against the American invaders. The trade minister, Art Eggleton, took this opportunity to raise some fundamental policy questions about our cultural protectionism in a speech before the Canadian Club.

At a parliamentary committee hearing a few days later, I was asked for my views on the issue. Taking the trade minister's speech as the context, I pointed out that the ideal situation would be, as Eggleton proposed, to have the special nature of the cultural industries adequately reflected in the international trade rules, but it was highly unlikely the Americans would agree, judging by our experience in the free trade and WTO negotiations. Next best was to exempt these industries from the international rules, as we had done in the FTA but failed to do in the WTO negotiations; but the worst situation was the trap we had now walked into, where we were committed to WTO rules that make no exception for the cultural industries.

The government should take this opportunity, I suggested, first to define clearly and narrowly our cultural interests. Then we should take whatever steps were necessary to promote and protect those interests. I did observe that this was a very strange time to be cutting funding to the state organizations – such as the CBC and the National Film Board – and the postal and other subsidies provided to the private-sector enterprises. These remain my views.

In May 1997, the government announced that it would appeal the part of the WTO decision that struck down the excise tax. The Americans challenged the part of the decision that allowed us to continue the postal subsidies. The decision of the appellate body was timed for three weeks after the federal election. It confirmed the American win and took the matter one step further, ruling against the postal subsidies. Canada was given fifteen months to toe the line.

Meanwhile, Canadian television broadcasting policy had continued to be based on the central importance of the cablecasters as the government's chosen policy instrument. For 90 percent of the Canadian population, living near the American border, it was simply impractical for the regulators to impose their will on "off air" television reception. Cable, on the other hand, was perfect for the regulators, who could use this vehicle to control Canadian content and meet other objectives. The result was an incestuous relationship between the regulator – the Canadian Radio-television and Telecommunications Commission (CRTC) – and the regulated cable companies. The implicit deal was this: We will give you a "licence to print money" (in the immortal words of Lord Thomson of Fleet), provided you spend some of that money on good purposes we designate, such as Canadian programs. For many years, it was apparently successful.

Then technology smashed this cosy regulatory scheme. The trigger was the arrival over the horizon of the so-called death stars – high-powered broadcast satellites capable, thanks to the marvels of digital compression, of carrying 500 television channels or more. Stars launched by American giants such as Hughes and positioned to serve the US market could also cover much of Canada with their "footprint" – the mapping of the area that could receive a clear signal. The American market exploded as these direct-to-home (DTH) satellite broadcasters, led by Hughes subsidiary DirecTV, blanketed the country with hundreds of thousands of pizza-size dishes on the homes of subscribers. Canadian subscribers soon followed suit as suppliers offered them the equipment and an American billing address.

The CRTC reacted like the proverbial ostrich. For years, it dismissed the technology as immature. When faced with the inevitable, the CRTC vicechairman for broadcasting was widely reported to have met in a closed room with a number of the industry leaders during a pause in a cable television industry convention in May 1994. Shortly thereafter, a consortium was announced, dominated by the cable and telephone companies, proposing to launch its own truly Canadian DTH service using Telesat's bird. The new service was to be called ExpressVu. The cartel would be alive and well and extended into the heavens. It was undoubtedly a coincidence that the giant Canadian conglomerate Bell Canada Enterprises was a major shareholder of both Telesat and ExpressVu.

Then the Hughes subsidiary entered into a joint venture with the Canadian conglomerate Power Corporation to form a new satellite television service named, rather unimaginatively, PowerDirecTV. The CRTC studied the matter and decided that companies meeting certain criteria – strangely similar to the configuration of the original "Canadian" consortium – would not need to obtain a licence. All others would have to face a formal licensing process before the CRTC, and there were some not too subtle hints that the process could be arduous.

PowerDirecTV cried foul. It pointed out that one of the key CRTC criteria was an interpretation of government policy to require that the broadcasts be transmitted solely by Canadian satellite. This went far beyond the government's stated policy and far beyond previous interpretations by the regulator. Coincidentally, this was the criterion that made it particularly uneconomic for PowerDirecTV to slip through the exemption. PowerDirecTV appealed the issue to the government. The American government weighed in on the dispute. The Canadian DTH regime was included in the annual administration round-up of offensive measures around the world. Hughes and its parent company, General Motors, were dismayed by the obvious attempt to cut them out of any role in a market they had been instrumental in developing.

André Bureau, the president of Astral, chose this moment to lead the cultural wolf pack in a savage personal attack on the integrity of the prime minister. He accused the PM of favouritism and nepotism, since Chrétien's son-in-law was André Desmarais, of the family that controlled Power's holding company. Power's share of the fledgling venture was hardly the major investment interest of this giant conglomerate. Indeed, stock market analysts concluded that the success or failure of the DTH venture would have little or no impact on the value of Power's shares.

It took the media a while to make the connection. Astral was a major beneficiary of the troublesome CRTC decision. The company had originally been given the monopoly on the lucrative central and eastern Canadian market for pay and pay-per-view cable television, and in this latest CRTC plan it would retain the monopoly from the heavens. This manna had been conferred by the vice-chairman of the CRTC, who had been recruited by none other than the Astral president back when Bureau was himself the chairman of the regulatory body. Meanwhile, the head of the ExpressVu consortium was the recently retired deputy minister of communications, who had gone straight from that government post. I have heard of throwing stones in glass houses, but this was more like tossing hand grenades in a crystal palace.

These outlandish charges made the issue too hot politically to handle by normal means. On November 29, 1994, the ministers of industry and of heritage asked me to chair a panel to advise the government on the appropriate policy to adopt. My fellow panellists were outstanding: Roger Tassé and Robert Rabinovitch, the former deputy minister of communications, now a senior officer with the Bronfman holding company, Claridge. We were given six months and up to $250,000 to do the job.

To general surprise, we wrapped up our work on April 6, two months ahead of schedule and well below budget – a precedent that has obviously not guided subsequent panels and commissions. This was thanks in no small part to the efficiency of our panel secretary, Matthew Fraser, a former author and journalist who had come to us from the office of the chairman of the CRTC. We received written briefs from all interested parties and then allowed a second round of submissions to assist us in our deliberations. In a brief report we proposed refocusing of government policies towards DTH satellite television broadcasting and, in the process, pointed the way towards fundamental changes in broadcasting policies more generally.

We released our report at a press conference that, to my astonishment, was covered live by CBC Newsworld. Essentially, we called on the CRTC to do its job and to do it better. We reaffirmed Canada's cultural policies and strongly endorsed the principles of the CRTC's Canadian content regulations and the agency's role in making compliance a condition of broadcast licence. The problem was that the commission had ducked its responsibilities in the satellite TV case. Instead of granting conditional licences, it had quite improperly exempted the service from licence requirements. In the process, it had created a de facto monopoly in DTH television just when consumers were turning to this new technology to provide an alternative to the local cable television monopoly. (The biggest cable monopolist, Rogers, had succeeded in upsetting just about everyone with a heavy-handed scheme, endorsed by the CRTC, to push subscribers into paying for a set of new services through a so-called negative option plan – you get it and pay for it unless you take the trouble to decline it formally.)

We therefore proposed that the CRTC rescind the offending exemption and proceed immediately with a proper licensing process. We suggested the principles that might govern such a licensing hearing, including some important innovations to strengthen support for Canadian film development while opening up more choices for consumers. I very much hoped that the CRTC would have the courage to act on these recommendations on its own initiative.

If not, we recommended that the government use its power to direct the CRTC to get into line.

We were not moved by the objections of the American government. These issues were for Canadians to decide. True, the CRTC had wrapped its monopoly plan in the Canadian flag. This was not the real issue, which was how Canadian authorities should regulate competition to best serve televiewers while advancing our cultural objectives. The proposal we had made, if properly implemented, should set to rest any American concerns that they were being unfairly treated.

The report was generally well received by the media and by expert commentators. This did not stop Jan Brown, the photogenic MP who was then the culture critic for the Reform Party, from following our announcement with her own press conference, obviously scripted before our report was released, to rehash the old charges. Predictably, there was a fusillade of protest from several of the interested parties, who had been accustomed to having things entirely their own way on their home turf at the CRTC.

The real battle was fought out before the responsible committees of Parliament, in the House of Commons where the Liberals enjoyed a majority and in the Senate where the Conservatives held sway as a hangover from the Mulroney years. To my dismay, I found myself pitted in combat against the CRTC chairman, Keith Spicer. Spicer was the media's darling. A man of many facets, he had himself enjoyed a distinguished career in both print and electronic media. He had also served in some of the most high-profile assignments in the country, as the original official languages commissioner, then head of a task force on national unity. With his flamboyant style and passionate eloquence in both French and English, he was a powerful and persuasive adversary. His term was about to expire with no prospect for renewal, so he really had nothing to lose by picking a fight.

To accommodate their star witness, who was about to leave for holidays in France, the two parliamentary committees allowed Spicer to make back-to-back appearances before them in a single day. Spicer swirled into those meetings, clad in his trademark cape, surrounded by a retinue worthy of a prince – his commission vice-chairmen, his lawyers, and his press aides. He put on quite a show before the glaring television lights. Spicer pulled no punches. In a carefully crafted statement, bearing the trademark Spicer command of language, he excoriated the government for its temerity in following the advice of its misguided panel of advisers. He called down the heavens on his tormentors.

I had enjoyed many dealings with Spicer over the years. I was an unabashed admirer of the work he had done to help implant our language policies and frankly envious of his greater gifts of communication in both French and English. In this instance, however, I was convinced he had been taken for a ride. As chairman of the CRTC, he had picked his targets, generally the highest-public-profile issues such as the control of violence on television.

I preferred to think that the sorry business of the DTH satellite broadcasting exemption had been engineered by his vice-chairman, Fernand Belisle. Belisle was much too savvy to stand front and centre when the decision came under attack. Instead, he had apparently persuaded Spicer that the government was challenging his – the chairman's – prerogatives. Did Spicer want to go down in history as the man who had surrendered the independence of the CRTC? This certainly had engaged Spicer's attention, and he put his communications skills to work.

It was a steep order to meet Spicer on his own terms, particularly before a Senate committee predisposed to find an issue on which to hammer the Liberal government in revenge for past unpleasantness. (Readers will recall the job the Liberal senators had done in stonewalling the Free Trade Agreement.) I arranged to follow Spicer before both committees a few days later. Quite deliberately, I arrived accompanied only by Tassé, as Rabinovitch was out of town. The only television cameras were those of the parliamentary network. My presentation was as cold-blooded as Spicer's had been inflammatory. On the substance, however, I gave no ground.

The first, phony issue was that of nepotism. Jan Brown had been "unavoidably detained on other business." Her Reform colleague was at pains to distance himself from her claims. He put the question, he said, to enable me to refute it. I was able to testify that at no time did the prime minister, his staff, or anyone else exert or attempt to exert any influence whatsoever on the independent deliberations of the panel.

The real fight centred on two issues. The first was the status of ExpressVu. Spicer had rather pompously rejected our observation that the CRTC had given them a monopoly, saying, "This accusation is demonstrably false since any applicant not meeting the exemption criteria could still apply for a licence under our normal open procedures."

I invited the parliamentarians to judge for themselves. The CRTC plan would offer other competitors the opportunity to embark on an arduous and uncertain licensing process for the dubious privilege of going up against the company that had been given a deliberate head start. "Only the CRTC is surprised," I commented, "that no one has come forward to take up this generous offer, eight months after the exemption order took effect. To call this anything other than a de facto monopoly is, I submit, to invent yet another official language."

In both committees, the members were openly amused by this puncturing of Spicer's balloon. If it walks like a duck and quacks like a duck, no one should object to finding it in their *canard à l'orange*.

Spicer also backed ExpressVu's claim that its imminent launch would be put in limbo by the lengthy licensing proceeding we had recommended. I was convinced this was utter nonsense – that the CRTC could, if it wished, issue the licences long before ExpressVu was ready to actually launch its services. Nonetheless, in the interests of complete fairness, I encouraged the government to permit the launch as soon as it was ready. This called their bluff. Two years later, ExpressVu was still on the ground and still encouraging the revisionist myth that it had been held back by the government. It reminded me a little of Chiang Kai-Shek and his oft-repeated claim that he was ready to retake China if only the Americans would stop holding him back.

The really serious brawl came over what I considered a complete red herring: the independence of the CRTC. The question had been carefully studied by our legal advisers, under the watchful eye of one of Canada's outstanding experts in public law, my fellow panellist Tassé. They were in no doubt that while the CRTC had been created to ensure independence in the awarding of licences, it remained the right and responsibility of the government to provide the overall policy direction.

Spicer took the rather astonishing view that the CRTC was under no obligation to take policy direction from the government. He tried to translate the broad support for an independent licensing process into CRTC control over policy itself. I reminded the committee of the traditions of parliamentary government:

> The elected Government also has its role. It must set overall policy as definitively as possible. Where there is confusion or misinterpretation or evolution of policy the Government must set the CRTC straight, through a Policy Direction if necessary. This is the business we are on today.
>
> There is no requirement that the CRTC be regarded, or regard itself, as infallible. The Policy Review Panel was forced to agree with

the overwhelming bulk of submissions we received and with the overwhelming weight of editorial opinion that in this specific case, the DTH exemption order, the CRTC got it wrong.

The result of this battle could not have been more decisive. The Senate committee joined with the House committee in adopting the government directive based on the panel's recommendations. This meant complete rejection of Spicer's claim of unwarranted interference with the independence of the CRTC. It meant rejection of any claim of unfairness in the treatment of ExpressVu or favouritism towards PowerDirecTV. This was testimony to the strength of our arguments in the face of Spicer's impassioned attack.

We were able to win the battle but the war continued. After threatening court action, the CRTC finally conceded that it was subject to the direction of Parliament. It grudgingly implemented the directive but did so in such a way as to subvert the policy objectives. It attached conditions to the PowerDirecTV licence that made it commercially unworkable. As a result, we were deprived of the one service that could have been up and running quickly and, in the process, shut down the "grey market" of Canadians subscribing directly to DirecTV. The joint venture dissolved, leaving the field clear for the chosen instrument, ExpressVu.

Meanwhile, the Canadian landscape was dotted with a growing number of receiving dishes capturing the signals directly from the American satellites. Ironically, the biggest winner was DirecTV: instead of holding 20 percent of the joint venture to provide a high-cost licensed Canadian broadcast service, this company was "forced" to accept 100 percent of the same market for an all-American service. It would be hard to blame them for their choice. In a weak effort to stem the tide, the industry minister flooded the market with pamphlets telling Canadian consumers that they really should not install the "grey market" dishes from the United States. What other option did they have?

The biggest losers were Canadian film and television producers and the consumers who wanted greater access to these Canadian cultural products. We had fought to enable that consumer to purchase from a licensed Canadian system, with the assurance that this would include Canadian content and that a portion of the charges would go to develop Canadian products. As a result of the CRTC's bungling ineptitude, or worse, that consumer was now migrating in large numbers to American services, unlicensed in Canada, containing no Canadian content and contributing nothing to Canadian production and development.

There can be no question that this represents a tragic failure of Canadian policy. There may be disagreement over the authorship of this disaster, and there may still be some who believe the CRTC was correct in its chosen course. There may also be disagreement over the magnitude of the débâcle, although I would rate the damage as very serious. We have blown an opportunity to harness a powerful new instrument for enriching Canadian cultural expression and have instead unleashed an unrelenting flood of American cultural preferences on hundreds of thousands of Canadian homes. This may have a profound influence on the tastes and attitudes of a growing number of Canadians, when they choose not only films to watch but toothpaste to buy and politicians to elect.

Furthermore, by its heavy-handed behaviour, the CRTC had created a totally unnecessary and potentially destructive confrontation with the Americans. The US administration had good reason to complain that the CRTC decision had, de facto, undercut the commercial interests of DirecTV. But for the moment the company was not pressing the issue, since, as I have pointed out, they were making much more offering an unlicensed, wholly American service.

Matters came to a head when the sole Canadian satellite operator, Telesat, whose interests the CRTC had so zealously been safeguarding, ran into serious problems with its Anik satellites. The problem was attributed to fluke electromagnetic phenomena that crippled one bird and killed another. Suddenly the problem was not how to force broadcasters to use Telesat, as the CRTC had attempted, but how to muster enough capability to carry existing services. The ExpressVu consortium, whose monopoly was based on its use of the Telesat satellites, was plunged into limbo.

At that point, Telesat somehow convinced the industry minister, John Manley, to confirm that the company held the sole rights to a couple of highly attractive satellite slots. Manley is the very antithesis of the cynical politician, tall, with boyish good looks and an engaging smile. He is a man of unimpeachable integrity and lively intelligence who has grown steadily in competence and confidence as he has matured in the role of a senior cabinet minister. In this instance, however, I believe he made a serious mistake in accepting Telesat's demands.

Telesat promptly turned around and did a deal that would have in effect leased those slots to American satellite operators. Those American operators would then be free to beam their signals back to their home market. All hell broke loose.

The American competition was furious. In the most recent allocations, comparable American slots had been auctioned for close to $1 billion, payable to the US government. There were no more American-controlled slots that were remotely as attractive as the two that Telesat had just been handed for a pittance. These companies demanded that the US Federal Communications Commission take a hard look at the transaction and its implications for the American system.

The Canadian competition was also apoplectic. This was, after all, the same company that had wrapped itself in the Canadian flag in the first place. Companies such as Shaw Communications, a highly successful and entrepreneurial company from western Canada, demanded to know why they were not given a shot at these choice slots. Others wanted to know why Telesat had been handed these extraordinarily valuable privileges. After all, it was no longer a government-owned monopoly. It was owned and controlled by a consortium of the Canadian telephone companies, led by BCE's Bell Canada.

The American government stepped into the fray. On advice from the US special trade representative, the FCC determined that these Canadian slots could not be used to beam programming into the US. This effectively shut down the original deal. Telesat continued to scramble to restore its business.

At the same time, difficult and protracted negotiations under the World Trade Organization produced a breakthrough deal on telecommunications. It opened the American market to Canadian telecommunications services. The ink was no sooner dry than the Americans announced they were explicitly exempting direct satellite television and satellite digital and audio services. The American market would be opened only for those countries which gave American companies "substantially full market access and national treatment." They made no bones about their target – Canada. The result could be a highly unpleasant continuing dispute in which the Canadian position will be extremely difficult to defend. The beat goes on.

12

BREAK-UP

Free trade was not the only issue preoccupying Canadians in the mid-1980s. At the same time as we were trying to establish a solid basis for a closer relationship between Canada and the United States, the political leadership was also struggling with the question of Quebec's proper place within, or outside, the Canadian Constitution. The two became intimately intertwined: the same political elites were involved, led by Brian Mulroney, Robert Bourassa, David Peterson, and Jacques Parizeau. As PQ leader and later premier, Parizeau used the Free Trade Agreement as a safety net to embolden Quebeckers to take what René Lévesque had called "le beau risque."

French was not my mother tongue. Indeed the language was rarely spoken in my parents' household. If you draw a line across New Brunswick from northwest to southeast, you would find very little French spoken below that line, and that was surely the case in Andover, my father's birthplace. As for my mother, the hillsides of the Okanagan are not a major centre for the language of Molière. As a result of my years in Washington, particularly as a high school student, I received less French instruction than most of my Ottawa classmates. Despite this, my sympathies for many years lay with French-speaking Québécois.

I painfully recall one evening in the early 1960s when I accompanied my father to a lecture at Carleton University. It was a talk by André Laurendeau, the editor of the great Montreal newspaper *Le Devoir*, on the subject of his famous predecessor, the paper's founder, Henri Bourassa. It was an eye-opener for me, made all the more shocking when a couple in the seats ahead of us began to mock Laurendeau's accent. It was really quite incredible – here was a man of stature giving a lecture in his second language, being ridiculed by these fools. The incident certainly sensitized me to the need for the subsequent Royal Commission on Bilingualism and Biculturalism, which Laurendeau co-chaired with Carleton president Davidson Dunton.

Nonetheless, more than a decade later, despite my intellectual awareness of the situation, I remained very much a unilingual Canadian. One of the incentives for joining the public service in 1968 was the hope that I could be trained in the French language during what I expected to be a brief sojourn with the government, but I was largely unsuccessful in persuading my superiors to release me to study French. My main education came from spending my coffee breaks with a close colleague who was very nearly as unilingually French as I was unilingually English. I also studied the editorials of *Le Devoir*, putting dots beneath the words I did not understand. For the first few months, these dots were nearly solid lines, but eventually I was able to get the gist, which I found surprisingly nationalist. Finally I was also permitted to put in three weeks at a language school at the far end of Ottawa, on the understanding that I would then report to the office and do my regular day's work.

Meanwhile, events were moving very quickly and dramatically in Quebec. In the fall of 1970 the drama reached a peak when gunmen from one cell of the Front de libération du Québec (FLQ) kidnapped a British diplomat, James Richard Cross, while another cell kidnapped and later brutally murdered the provincial labour minister, Pierre Laporte. This was brought home to me very directly through my father who, as head of the External Affairs Department, was responsible for the safety of the diplomat. As the tension heightened and armed men patrolled the streets of Ottawa, I was shocked and angry and frustrated that I had no idea what was happening. I resolved to do something about my ignorance.

In 1972 I arranged on short notice to be sent on educational leave to the École nationale d'administration publique in Quebec City. This school had been established as an autonomous unit of the Université du Québec by the Union Nationale government a few years earlier. It enabled me to combine postgraduate studies in public policy with an intensive immersion in the French language in the glorious setting of one of the most beautiful and liveable cities in North America. The following eighteen months were among the most enjoyable of my life.

There was one extraordinary side benefit that I had not anticipated. The school was small, with a handful of professors and two classes of twenty-five students. Among those students and professors was an impressive representation of the separatist "government in waiting." This was the period when the Parti Québécois under its charismatic leader, René Lévesque, was a powerful political force in the province but lacked representation in the legislature, the Assemblée nationale. Among my associates at the school were many who were to become influential figures in the party when it came to power in 1976 – the master strategist and intergovernmental affairs minister, Claude Morin, my tutor; his protégée, Louise Beaudoin, who later became a senior minister in the Parizeau and Bouchard governments; and officials such as André Beaudoin (no relation), who served as chief of staff to Camille Laurin, the author of the PQ's language and cultural policies, before becoming an assistant deputy minister for education.

As I was the only anglophone at the school, it was an extraordinary learning experience. I became fluent in French, developed a taste for Québécois music and literature, and deepened my theoretical understanding of public administration. More important, I gained some appreciation of the revolution that was under way in that province.

When I returned to Ottawa, I found there was little interest in making use of my language fluency or network of contacts. Indeed, there may have been some suspicion that I had become too close to the separatists, almost a fellow traveller. These suspicions could only have been heightened when I attended a conference of first ministers which, as a minor point of the agenda, was reviewing and approving a set of papers I had written on the redirection of federal industrial policies and programs. Claude Morin was there as Premier Lévesque's minister of intergovernmental affairs. As we embraced in greeting, I could see Marc Lalonde, Trudeau's long-time collaborator and chief hawk, giving me a penetrating stare.

I had no direct involvement in the referendum of 1980. Like millions of other Canadians, I found myself excluded from a decision that would literally determine whether my country would live or die. The vote appeared to have been won by the separatists until the final few days – an ironic twist on the outcome of later referendums. When Trudeau imposed his constitutional package, I did not approve of his importation of an American-style charter of rights and his heavy-handed flouting of constitutional conventions.

In view of the subsequent demonization of Trudeau and his "humiliation" of Quebec, I should observe that I did accept, like the overwhelming majority of Canadians including Quebeckers, that patriation of the

Constitution was desirable and could be done only over the opposition of the separatist government. That the new Constitution was unanimously supported by the Quebec MPs in the federal Parliament and unanimously condemned by the MPPs in the Assemblée nationale came as no surprise, since the changes would shift some power away from the province and towards the citizenry through the courts.

Over the succeeding years, I maintained my contacts in Quebec. As I moved up the ladder to head the Department of Regional Industrial Expansion, various jobs required me to work closely with my Quebec counterparts, adding new acquaintances to old friendships in the provincial government service and the political and business leadership.

Earlier chapters have touched on the role played by Quebec and the other provinces in the Free Trade Agreement. The close relationship between Brian Mulroney and Robert Bourassa was undoubtedly a factor in our success. The relationship dated back many years and went beyond the usual bonds among the select circle of Quebec's political elite.

Bourassa designated as his chief adviser on the trade negotiations the enormously respected former federal trade official and my old boss, Jake Warren, who had retired from the vice-chairmanship of the Bank of Montreal. In the private meetings that I attended with Mulroney and the ten provincial premiers, Bourassa proved a valuable ally. He did have his sticking points. He insisted that trade in agriculture could not be on the table in these negotiations, and in the end he was instrumental in protecting the system to shelter Canadian poultry and dairy producers, concentrated in Quebec. Generally, however, we could count on him to nudge along the bad boy, David Peterson of Ontario. Their private conversations must have been fascinating, as Bourassa depended on Peterson's support for the Meech Lake constitutional amendments. Bourassa's brilliant deputy minister, Diane Wilhelmy, played a key role in keeping both files moving in the direction Quebec was seeking. In the free trade election, Quebeckers voted overwhelmingly for Brian Mulroney and returned him with enough seats for a substantial majority.

Bourassa could have given lessons to Machiavelli. For several decades he had pre-empted much of the middle ground in Quebec politics, portraying himself as a federalist but then defining the term to be virtually indistinguishable from Lévesque's sovereignty-association. Under his leadership, the provincial Liberal Party produced a position on the issue that defined an acceptable federal arrangement as one that transferred virtually all powers to

Quebec, leaving Ottawa with the national debt and the responsibility to continue fiscal transfers to the province.

It is much too early to anticipate the verdict of history on the man. It will depend very much on the eventual outcome since, as the adage goes, history is written by the winners. The separatist version will undoubtedly follow Jean-François Lisée in describing Bourassa as a "trickster" and a "shipwrecker" for his success in postponing the day of independence. If the history is written by federalists, I believe Bourassa will be regarded as the man who, more than any other single person, brought the country to the point of breaking up.

To be fair, if Mulroney and Bourassa had pulled off their gamble on the Meech Lake constitutional accords, I believe the flap would have subsided and the country could have moved on to other questions. But they failed in their terrible "roll of the dice." A provincial commission was established with great fanfare to examine the options for Quebec. It was co-chaired by my next-door neighbour from Quebec City, Jean Campeau, whom I knew to be a separatist. The commission conjured up a two-track scenario in which either the rest of Canada made Quebec an offer it could not refuse, or a referendum put Quebec on the path to unilateral independence. To his shame, politicologue Léon Dion (father of a future federal minister of constitutional affairs, Stéphane Dion) coined the obscene phrase to the effect that the rest of Canada would negotiate only with "a knife to their throats." Bourassa bought the proposal and set the train in motion in 1990.

Down one track, prodigious efforts were made to stitch together the constitutional package that eventually foundered in its own referendum, the so-called Charlottetown Accord. Down the other, the Assemblée nationale undertook an assessment of the implications for Quebec of the breakup scenario. The Toronto-based think tank the C. D. Howe Institute, under the leadership of the former investment banker Tom Kierans, put substantial resources into an examination of the issues with some professional objectivity. They asked me to do the lead study on the implications of a breakup for trade relations between Quebec and the rest of the world. The study, published in 1991, was entitled "Putting Humpty Dumpty Together Again." It was an attempt to shift the debate onto more solid ground, away from the misleading rhetoric that was flooding in from both sides.

On the one hand, the federalist forces fell far too easily into the trap of arguing that separation would cut off Quebec from the rest of the world. The other provinces, the US, and other countries would lose interest in trading with Quebec, and the result would be the loss of all those jobs dependent on outside markets. This proposition was transparent nonsense and served only to discredit the opposition to separation.

On the other hand, the separatists maintained that now that free trade was achieved, nothing would change with independence. Parizeau and his acolytes pretended to believe that an independent Quebec would automatically be entitled to continue to enjoy an economic union with the rest of Canada and a free trade area with the United States and Mexico. After all, they pointed out, for other countries and the rest of Canada to break off relations in a fit of pique would be to cut off their nose to spite their face.

I understood the vicissitudes of politics but was disappointed that so many Quebeckers appeared to be swallowing these falsehoods. Polls taken later found that an incredible number of Quebeckers believed that the main impact of independence would be that they would no longer have to send taxes to Ottawa but would keep their current services. They would somehow remain citizens of Canada, retain their Canadian passports, use the Canadian dollar, and have free access to the Canadian market for their goods and services.

The research project was premised on Quebec separation. Given that starting point, my analysis was based on the best of all possible situations, where Quebec becomes independent through a process that is accepted by all the other players as entirely legitimate. No one reacts with rancour or bitterness, let alone economic sanctions or physical violence. This was a huge assumption, and I conceded it was almost certainly unrealistic. It assumed that there was no manipulation of the referendum question or result and that the resulting independence was achieved in full harmonious agreement.

Even in that case, the issue was not *whether* there would be continued trade but *on what basis* that trade would flow. Would the free trade agreement maintain the status quo after separation? I went over the basic economic analysis, which demonstrated that:

- the maximum economic benefits for producers and consumers could be achieved only through a complete economic union of the sort that we now enjoyed in Canada, despite some problems;
- failing this, the second-best alternative would be some kind of true free trade arrangement along the lines of the NAFTA, which would require careful negotiation and would mean the loss of significant economic benefits to the partners;
- failing this, the partners could always fall back on the multilateral

trading framework of the GATT, which would be relatively easy to negotiate but would impose substantial costs on the Quebec economy relative to the present arrangements.

As to the suggestion that everything would go on as before, I discarded that as patently absurd, as Parizeau knew very well. It was clearly established that there was no automatic right of accession. Everything would have to be negotiated.

I tried to put myself in the position of the Quebec negotiator. What was achievable and what was not? It was obvious to me that it would be utterly impossible to negotiate to reinstate the full economic union between Quebec and the rest of Canada. That would mean a unified policy for monetary matters, including exchange rates, and trade, including tariffs. Who would set that policy? To Quebeckers it might seem obvious that these policies would be set by consensus between the two equal parties. This was delusional. If over the years Canadians had not been prepared to accept that Quebec had status equal to the rest of the country combined – the other nine provinces with three times the population and five times the economic clout – it was hardly likely they would agree to such an arrangement after separation.

Alternatively, Quebec could simply go along with the policies set by the Canadian government. This would mean a substantial *loss* of independence for Quebeckers. Decisions affecting their currency, interest rates, tariffs, and quotas would be made by a body in which they had no influence – a far cry from the present, when Quebeckers occupy many of the senior portfolios, have a substantial role in the House of Commons, and, in the view of many western Canadians, have much too dominant an influence over national affairs.

The best I could hope to achieve as a negotiator would be some kind of free trade arrangement. That would mean customs and immigration posts at the frontier, just as there are today between Canada and the US. It would mean trade disputes, as Ontario firms charged Quebec competitors with unfairly subsidized or dumped shipments into what would be a foreign country. If it could be negotiated, however, such a free trade arrangement could keep down the losses to Quebeckers. Other Canadians would also pay a price, particularly in Ontario, but the evidence was clear that the bulk of the costs would be borne by Quebec producers and consumers.

The negotiations would be difficult, particularly when it came to those areas in which, despite the propaganda, Quebec interests have been strongly favoured within a united Canada. I reviewed a number of those areas, from a double allotment of dairy quotas to subsidies for building ships and planes. But negotiations would, in my judgment, be possible on terms that would reduce the costs.

I was also optimistic that it would be possible for Quebec to remain part of the North American Free Trade Agreement with the US and Mexico. Again, the negotiations would not be easy. I identified a long agenda of items on which the Americans would be demanding concessions from Quebec. They might also attempt to use the opportunity to reopen some issues with Canada. Provided that Canada and Quebec could get their act together, I nonetheless believed we could work out an arrangement that would keep our loss of income to a minimum. As for the GATT, I was highly confident that it would be possible for Quebec to become a member in good standing.

The truth was this: under the best possible circumstances of an entirely amicable separation, Quebeckers would face some loss of jobs and incomes. Even this would require very skilful negotiations to establish a free trade agreement with the rest of Canada and the NAFTA partners. Obviously, if the separation were less than amicable, if the path to independence were strewn with questionable practices, the negotiations would be that much more difficult and the results less palatable.

None of this should have come as a surprise to anyone who followed these matters. Predictably, it generated an angry reaction from the separatists. With their strange bedfellows, Bourassa's provincial Liberals, they staged a confrontation on their home ground before the Assemblée nationale. A special committee of the Assemblée set aside an entire day in January 1992 to examine the issue of trade arrangements for an independent Quebec. The morning session was given over to Bernard Landry, who appeared before the committee to present the separatists' best case. Landry is a professional economist whom I had known and liked for many years. He had been a credible ally in the free trade debate, when he and I shared many a platform together. He was also a senior officer of the separatist Parti Québécois, which he would later serve as deputy prime minister under Bouchard. To my disappointment, he stuck very close to the propaganda line the separatists were then pushing. Stripped of the rhetorical devices, it amounted to saying that trade was a good thing, therefore the rest of Canada would continue to trade with Quebec, and Quebec would be entitled to remain a part of the NAFTA. A full complement of Parti Québécois deputies had turned out, and the questioning by the Liberals was less than aggressive.

My turn came in the afternoon. It was not the first time I had testified before the Assemblée in the ornate committee room that looked as if it had been plucked from a European palace, with its royal colours and gilt trappings. In the past, I had been impressed by the relatively informal and businesslike manner in which these committees went about their work. This was, of course, a somewhat different occasion.

I laid out my argument very much as I had done in a French version of the earlier study for the C. D. Howe Institute. Again, I emphasized I was tackling the issue as if I were their trade negotiator following an amicable separation. I put some rough estimates on the costs of the various alternatives to the typical Quebec family. These were significant but not overwhelming, and I recognized that the debate would turn on much more important issues. Then the floor was opened to questions.

At that point, the designated hitter for the separatists, Jacques Léonard, weighed in with a diatribe that had clearly been prepackaged. He condemned me for fear-mongering and lectured me that it would do the rest of Canada no good to act out of spite towards an independent Quebec. When he finished, I asked whether he had read the text I had circulated or listened to anything I had said. Clearly, his notes had been written in advance. He had attributed to me the exact opposite of what I had actually said. If he had listened, he would have discovered that I had based my analysis on the best possible scenario, one that I frankly regarded as excessively favourable. It was discouraging to see such an important issue treated in this close-minded fashion. As I should have anticipated, the committee churned its way to its predetermined outcome with a report that added nothing to the debate.

During much of this period, Bourassa's health was threatened by the skin cancer that would eventually kill him. When he stepped down, his successor, Daniel Johnson, Jr., quickly proved unequal to the task. Johnson initially presented himself as a genuine federalist who believed in Canada. That is, he was until he came under attack, at which point he fell apart completely.

The result was the return to power in 1994 of the Parti Québécois under Jacques Parizeau. As recounted earlier, his decision to go for the leadership had put paid to the bizarre plan to recruit him to work on the free trade negotiations. Knowing him, I was not in the least surprised that he moved so aggressively to focus the entire government's activities on winning the upcoming referendum.

I was dismayed at the extent to which Parizeau and Landry so directly linked their case to the Free Trade Agreement. On this score, it was a reprise of the battles we had waged a few years earlier. I made what contribution I could to the discussion, including a few speeches and articles as an independent expert on the subject. But I was clearly not one of the family, the *vieille souche*, and as such was not welcome to participate directly in the debate. At least I was not charged with electoral offences, as were many other Canadians who had a misplaced belief in the right of democratic discourse in a free society.

It was therefore very much as an outside observer that I watched in horror as the 1995 referendum unfolded. In my judgment, the much-maligned Prime Minister Chrétien went into the campaign with the appropriate strategy and was heading for a substantial victory. Two things then occurred which knocked the strategy out of the box, both turning on leadership. First, Parizeau stepped aside to allow Lucien Bouchard, the saviour returned from the dead, to lead the separatist forces on an emotional rampage. Second, Daniel Johnson proved to be without courage or conviction, turning his fire against his own allies. Under those circumstances, it is too easy to criticize the federal forces under Chrétien for not being able to turn their campaign around, with Johnson paddling hysterically in the other direction, shouting imprecations as he went.

Many Quebeckers have been conditioned by the separatists and their media allies to discount any comments or analysis from outside the province. Americans, on the other hand, are treated as oracles speaking the gospel truth. There was therefore quite a stir when a rookie congressman from California, Tom Campbell, initiated a day of congressional hearings on September 25, 1996, into the impact of Quebec independence on American interests.

The trigger was an article by Charles Doran in *Foreign Affairs* that argued rather pretentiously that in the event of an untidy separation, the Americans would be called on to act as policeman and arbiter of the dispute. Doran heads the ambitious Canadian Studies Program at Johns Hopkins University. He is one of those Americans who have made a career out of studying Canadians and interpreting them to an American audience. Doran was called to testify at Campbell's hearings. (I have always found it interesting that the Americans instinctively prefer to have foreign affairs analyzed by one of their own. The Canadian news media, led by the CBC, tend to the opposite bias, preferring to pay foreign experts rather than interview at least equally qualified Canadian specialists who are freely available.)

CBC Newsworld alerted me that they proposed to carry the hearings live. I was somewhat amused, explaining that this was purely a sideshow initiated by a rookie legislator bucking for stripes. The administration would be absent, as would any congressman of any stature. The CBC risked inflating the importance of the event. They not only decided to go ahead but invited another American analyst who would be testifying at the hearing, Joseph Jockel, to appear on the nightly program *Face Off*, which pitted the left-wing activist Judy Rebick against journalist Claire Hoy as the unrepentant right-winger. They asked me to take part and I reluctantly agreed.

Jockel is quite a character, thin as a rail, with piercing eyes atop a trademark bow tie. His career had been based on the strategic analysis of the Soviet Union, a topic that suddenly dropped off the radar screen with the fall of that empire. He therefore turned to an equally exotic specialty, Canadian affairs. It proved a good business development decision.

As it happened, we flew in on the same plane and joined forces to make our way downtown for the broadcast the night before the hearings. After a few wrong turns, we somehow found our way to the right studio in the labyrinth of the CBC headquarters in Toronto, an incredible indictment of the planning skills of that organization. The format dictated that we sit on opposite sides of the table. To our considerable amusement, I found myself on the same side as Rebick, whom I rather liked but with whom I had very rarely agreed on anything.

For obvious reasons, Jockel maintained that the congressional hearings on the following day were an important occasion. I demurred. It would be surprising if five people of any influence in Washington even knew they were occurring. Experience suggested the audience would be almost entirely Canadian. The Americans had legitimate serious concerns. Successive presidents had made clear the benefits of a strong and united Canada. But apart from some well-documented meddling by the American consul general in Quebec during the Lévesque years, they had very wisely kept out of what was strictly a domestic matter for Canadians to resolve.

Jockel attempted with proper academic seriousness to allay concerns about the message that would come from the hearings. He noted that he and every other witness would be confirming what the Americans took to be self-evident – that an independent Quebec would face tough negotiations to gain entry to NAFTA. The Americans would have a very aggressive agenda of demands for concessions from Quebec. They would even attempt to reopen some of the existing arrangements with the rest of Canada. I concurred and identified cultural industries and the dispute settlement machinery as two obvious American targets.

The most heated exchange came over the suggestion by Doran, supported by Jockel, that the Americans would play peacemaker if things got nasty. This was really too much. The Americans could teach us absolutely nothing about the amicable resolution of disputes, I suggested. If the substantial majority of Quebeckers in a serious referendum determined they would prefer to go their own way, the rest of Canada would obviously have to be ready and willing to negotiate appropriate arrangements. Neither side would need any interference from our southern neighbour – indeed, I ventured to say that the one thing guaranteed to unite the country would be meddling by the Americans.

That spirit of accommodation would not apply to a unilateral declaration of independence following a manipulated result in a referendum such as we had just passed through. Jockel agreed that a unilateral declaration of independence would be a very different situation. He maintained that the Americans would be faced with a real dilemma, particularly if the French persuaded the European Union to recognize Quebec's independent status. He used an interesting American analogy. "The next day, a Quebec representative would appear at the State Department to say: 'It's 1776 and here we are to assert our right to independence as a sovereign country.' The Canadian ambassador would show up to counter: 'It's 1860, and a state has just unilaterally tried to split the union.'"

Under questioning, Jockel asserted that it was "probable" that separation would occur, although he did not concur with Doran that this would necessarily lead to the "fragmentation" of the rest of Canada. "I am impressed that you Americans have such a clear crystal ball," I interrupted.

"That's what makes us Americans," Jockel admitted, in a self-deprecating attempt to deflect irritation at his pretension to have the inside track on the future.

"What makes us Canadians is that we sit still and listen to this guff," I replied.

As we shared a taxi to the airport after the broadcast, I pointed out that my real concern was not with what Jockel and his fellow witnesses said, with all the appropriate nuances and qualifications, but how these remarks would be interpreted in Canada, particularly Quebec. As it turned out, my fears were unfounded. The hearings were a comic farce. The chairman, Dan Burton, began by dealing with some matters relating to his pet project, the bill he had concocted with Senator Jesse Helms to punish foreign investors in Cuba. When this was resolved, the seats beside him on the dais emptied as his congressional colleagues left to attend to pressing business elsewhere. As a courtesy, Burton stayed long enough to permit Congressman Campbell to read a statement. He then decamped himself, leaving the empty chair to Campbell. I squirmed with embarrassment as Jockel and his fellow academics were then paraded to strut their tired old stuff before the rookie congressman.

Although my crystal ball is admittedly cloudy, I would wager a substantial sum on the following predictions. If Bouchard goes into the next provincial election against Johnson, the separatists will win in a walk. There will then be another referendum with a question no more balanced than the last. Finally, the debate will turn almost entirely on other, non-economic issues, and free trade will be the farthest thing from the minds of most Quebeckers. That will be fine with me, as I would hate to see an economically sensible free trade initiative misused to pry the country apart.

The separatists are not the only ones to argue that there is a reduced role, if any, for the federal government in this era of free trade in a global economy. It is certainly the case that some of the traditional functions of governments are obsolete – restricting imports, subsidizing industries, and generally micro-managing the industrial economy. These activities have failed to generate the promised benefits and have significantly contributed to the mountain of debt under which the federal and provincial governments now labour. Getting governments out of these lines of work is no great loss. In other fields, it makes a lot of sense to push the administration of programs down as close to the local level as is feasible rather than attempting to run everything through a cumbersome central bureaucracy. But that is very different from having the federal government abdicate responsibility for overall economic management and the setting and achievement of high standards in health, education, and welfare.

Specifically, I believe the world of free trade imposes even greater responsibilities on the national government to achieve the most effective mix of policies. Our federal government should have unchallenged authority to manage our trade relations with other countries and to ensure the preservation of the economic union within Canada. We all lose when provincial governments maintain barriers to trade within Canada or meddle in international trade negotiations or trade promotion. The provincial premiers are members of Team Canada but the undisputed captain must be the prime minister of Canada.

The federal government must also ensure the effective coordination of trade with other economic policies. This has not always been the case. Sometimes it has clearly been the fault of the federal government, as when poorly timed monetary policies cost Canada dearly in the first few years of free trade. In other instances, the provincial governments must share the blame, as when Michael Wilson's feeble attempt to slow the growth of public debt was more than offset by the profligacy of provincial governments, led by Bob Rae's Ontario. In these times of intense international competition we cannot afford to have such government policies working at cross purposes. The federal government must have the power to lead and must then be held accountable for taking the economy in the right direction.

Our international competitiveness also depends on achieving high standards in other fields more effectively administered by the provinces. Education is perhaps the most important. Provincial politicians have been more than willing to see the federal government pass on monies it has collected from the taxpayer. They have been much less willing to accept the most basic principles of accountability: the definition of clear goals and objectives; the measurement of progress towards these goals through national testing; and the requirement that these funds be spent and spent efficiently on education and not diverted to other purposes. There are different techniques by which this coordination can be achieved, but the federal government must be accorded its role of national leadership even where administration falls to provincial or local authorities.

It would be a tragic error for us to weaken and even paralyze the national government at precisely the time when globalization requires that it lead the country most effectively.

13

Taking Stock

Canadians will be required to make some very difficult strategic choices as we enter the third millennium. It would be tragic if the shape of this debate continued to be dictated by the entertainment requirements of modern media, television in particular, which feeds on the confrontation of close-minded ideologies in an increasingly noisy dialogue of the deaf. On the one hand are the proponents of the newly ascendant corporate capitalist agenda, clamouring for governments to reduce themselves to nothingness to make way for the triumphant rule of the unfettered marketplace. On the other are the Marxist-nationalist and anti-American dogmas that have become the tired old cant of those who seem to believe they hold a monopoly on caring about Canadian society. Neither of these factions speaks for me nor, I suspect, do they truly reflect the views of most Canadians.

Ideologies are wonderfully energy-saving devices: the answers are all pre-programmed and no painful thinking is required. If the facts do not quite fit, they can be manipulated. If the logic breaks down, it can simply be discarded. It takes some intellectual effort to put an issue in its historical context and then allow the facts as they become available to influence our conclusions. This nuanced analysis may make for better public policy but it comes across as boring television drama.

Nowhere is this more true than in the ongoing debate over free trade. The media love to portray it as a gladiatorial struggle between two contending armies of believers, and anyone caught in the middle will be trampled underfoot. Free trade is either the source of all our economic prosperity, or the cause of all the evils in our society.

I have resisted attempts to assign me to one or the other of these camps. Others could make the ideological case for or against free trade. My role was to provide facts and analysis on which people could form their own judgment. When I have been cast in an adversarial role, I have been profoundly uncomfortable. I firmly believe there is a solid middle ground. The free market can be used as a powerful instrument for economic progress, but it must not be seen as an end in itself. There are circumstances where governments must intervene to shape the operations of the market or to correct the problems the market has created. It takes careful study to determine when and how these interventions are warranted.

This applies with particular force to Canadian trade strategy, which can be seen to have gone through three distinct phases over the past fifty years. First was the period after World War II, lasting approximately twenty years, in which Canada emerged as a successful industrial economy. Then came nearly two decades after Centennial Year, during which the world changed dramatically in ways Canadian policy-makers were painfully slow to recognize. The third stage, beginning with the free trade negotiations in 1987, will carry us into the next century.

Canada came out of World War II much stronger than when it entered, in absolute and, above all, relative terms. Europe was in ruins. Japan had been destroyed. The colonial empires were collapsing. By contrast, Canadians had a great deal going for them. While we had taken heavy casualties on distant battlefields, our population was healthy, relatively well educated, and highly motivated to work. We lived in relative security next to the United States, which represented half the world's economic activity and a fabulous market for half our total exports of goods and services. Our productive capability was impressive, based on the application of capital and technology to our natural riches. This wealth of economically accessible natural resources was largely unmatched among the industrial powers. Our industrial base had expanded exponentially in the mobilization for war, as entire new industries were created. Much of the needed capital and technology was imported from our ally the United States, but much was home-grown. A generation of outstanding business leaders had been forged in the war effort, working closely with, or inside, the government service. This legacy gave Canada a powerful momentum over the next two decades.

By the time I joined the government service in 1967, many Canadians had naturally come to believe they were almost entitled, by the accident of birth, to live richer lives than previous generations in Canada and immeasurably better lives than most of the current population of the globe. The focus shifted to the redistribution of this wealth in what Trudeau styled the "just society." There was a notable failure to nurture, or even to appreciate, those special factors that had led to our unprecedented wealth.

The next twenty years saw Canada's advantage slip away, partly through forces beyond our control. Europe and Japan rebuilt their shattered economies and came roaring back to superpower status, fiercely competitive in the production and trade of sophisticated goods and services. Many of their former occupied territories emerged as powerful competitors in their own right. With greatly increased global mobility of capital and technology, the possibilities became almost unlimited. Huge reserves of metals and other minerals now became economic to mine. Remote forests became accessible to the new technologies. The energy reserves of the Middle East were developed to an extent unimaginable a few years earlier, and the producing areas gained corresponding political clout. Previously backward countries built greatly increased manufacturing capability on, first, their huge masses of unskilled labour and, later, the increasing education and training of that labour force.

Meanwhile, Canadians and their elected governments were headed in what seemed at times to be the opposite direction. Although I opposed many of these policies at the time, anyone who occupied a senior government position during this period must share in the responsibility. We were in large measure the authors of our own declining fortunes. As our near monopoly of natural resources was being undermined by new competitors, we failed to sustain our renewable resources. We depleted our mineral resources, without insisting on adding value within Canada. We based national policies, most notably the National Energy Program, on reallocating the economic rents we expected to reap from these resources, just as these rents were evaporating. We tried in trade negotiations to use our bargaining leverage to force the upgrading of our resources within Canada, only to be brutally reminded that there were now alternative sources for these raw materials.

An even greater tragedy was the failure of our education system at precisely the time when other nations, the industrial powers but also the new commercial tigers of Asia, were investing in the quality of their human resources. The problem was not the lack of money, as Canadian governments were among the highest spenders on education in the world. It was where the money was spent, largely on the infrastructure, including inflated payrolls. The infatuation, against all evidence of research or experience, with "child-centred learning" – a euphemism for abandoning performance standards for students and teachers – was perhaps the most costly single error of Canadian economic history. The result is a workforce that is sadly lacking in basic literacy and numeracy and thus unable to earn through labour productivity anything approaching the higher incomes they have been led to expect.

In combination with human and natural resources, it takes capital and technology to develop an economy. Despite relatively high rates of savings by Canadians, massive amounts of capital had to be imported, principally from the United States, to fill the gap between our expectations and our own capacity. During the Liberal years from the early 1960s to the early 1980s, the country was badly split on the issue. In the economically disadvantaged Atlantic region and Quebec, almost any investment was welcomed, even at the cost of outrageous government subsidies. In the west, led by Alberta, the voracious capital requirements of the resource industries created an appetite for American dollars. The main impact of foreign capital was to be found in southwestern Ontario, where it provoked a backlash against the resulting foreign influence and aroused economic nationalists from Walter Gordon to Herb Gray. The resulting policies were ambivalent at best, and often at cross purposes. Whenever the nationalists imposed policies to discourage foreign capital, through such instruments as FIRA or the NEP, American investors were quick to demonstrate that while Canada remained a preferred location for direct investment, it was not the only competitor for American capital, which could now find profitable homes around the globe.

Nor could high technology bail us out of our problems. Just as Canadians were becoming increasingly dependent on the fruits of technology, we were losing ground in technology development. Despite some notable exceptions, an increasing proportion of our technology must now be imported, overwhelmingly from the United States.

This combination of increased competition from abroad with misguided economic development policies at home was clearly taking its toll by the early 1980s – arrested productivity, slow growth, high unemployment, and a mountain of public debt. To our dismay, we were forced to recognize that the world does not owe us a high standard of living after all. It would take decades to regain a competitive edge through upgrading our human capital and sustainable development of our natural resources. Meanwhile, we could build on the one outstanding strategic advantage we continued to enjoy: our access to the world's largest market next door in the United States. That, for me, was the ultimate purpose and test of the Canada-US Free Trade Agreement – to raise Canadian living standards by improving and securing our access to the American market.

The self-proclaimed nationalists would hearken back to the good old days of the postwar period when Canadians enjoyed the benefits of the extraordinary advantages described above. Regrettably, the approach they propose not only would not bring back those glorious times, it would further undermine our prosperity. These so-called new industrial policies prove, on close inspection, to be remarkably similar to discredited protectionist strategies that backfired in the past. Raising tariffs and quotas against imports would only provoke the closing, in retaliation, of the export markets on which we depend. That would indeed reduce the share of our production going to the American market, at enormous cost to Canadian workers and consumers. Discrimination against foreign investors would succeed mainly in discouraging much-needed investment in Canada and justify countermeasures by other countries against our large and profitable investments abroad. The extensive use of subsidies to induce companies to produce at otherwise uneconomic locations has succeeded only in increasing the public debt and attracting countervailing duties applied by other countries against our exports. The use of financial bribery and regulatory coercion is also proposed to induce companies to buy more in Canada or in particular regions, to export more or to do more research and development. Again, these measures have generally succeeded only in costing the Canadian taxpayer more and provoking foreign retaliation.

These new/old industrial policies are at the centre of the current debate over Canada's participation in the Multilateral Agreement on Investment (MAI) under negotiation in the OECD. The critics are incensed that we would renounce our ability to use such invaluable industrial policy instruments as locational subsidies, export requirements, local purchase requirements, and above all discrimination against foreign investors. Given the abject failure of such measures in the past, one would think we should be more than willing to surrender our capacity to damage our interests in the future. Indeed, we have already renounced most of these instruments relative to the Americans – by far the biggest investors in Canada – in the NAFTA. The NAFTA went far beyond the original Free Trade Agreement in protecting the right of foreign investors to equal treatment.

The negotiation of an MAI has already aroused a public furor, complete with front-page stories and full-page advertisements during the 1997 federal election. The fuss was a bit premature since no deal is expected before May 1998 and, although the detailed negotiations are obviously taking place behind closed doors, reports suggest that the most controversial issues for Canada remain to be addressed. These include the treatment of provincial governments, special arrangements within regional economic groupings such as the NAFTA, and of course the exemption of the cultural industries, without which no Canadian government should be prepared to sign any agreement. I suppose it would be uncharitable to suggest that the well-publicized protests by nationalist groups may have more to do with their fundraising and membership drives than with any real concern over the substantive issues.

Has the Free Trade Agreement been good for Canada? For ten years, I have been reluctant to give a categorical answer to this question. As I told Paul Martin at our meeting in Montreal in 1988, I never doubted that it was the best agreement that could be negotiated under the circumstances. It made compelling strategic sense. But the FTA was much too complex to be fully evaluated until the hard results were in from several years of operation. This was not a comforting or politically easy answer, but it was the best I could give.

Even now, on the tenth anniversary of the agreement, I do not find it easy to present a definitive assessment. One of the problems is that it is impossible to separate the impact of the Free Trade Agreement from the workings of a number of other factors before and since. When I made this point in the first few years of the agreement, when Canada was wallowing in recession, it was interpreted as a cop-out. Now that our trade statistics are so dramatically positive, perhaps the argument will be better appreciated. The simple reality is that the functioning of the economy depends on myriad individual decisions by workers, consumers, and companies, who are in turn affected by many factors. The influence of the Free Trade Agreement is swamped in the flood of other developments.

Above all, a trade agreement is obviously about exports and imports. Here the results are nothing short of extraordinary. In 1988, the last year before free trade, Canadian exports to the US totalled just over $102 billion. Eight years later, in 1996, the last full year for which the numbers are available, these exports had more than doubled to nearly $218 billion.

To put this performance in perspective, the data through 1996 can be looked at in any number of ways, all of which reveal an export performance totally unprecedented in Canadian history. Specifically:

- These gains have come across the board, with the greatest gains in those industries where the biggest barriers were broken down by the FTA, particularly in the high-technology and high-value-added sectors. From lumber to woollen suits to telephone switches, our exports have made great inroads into the American market.
- Exports to other countries have also grown, but not nearly as rapidly (by around $15 billion, or 44 percent), as we have had much less success selling to markets elsewhere in the world where we do not enjoy free trade.
- As a result, the share of our total exports going to the US has increased from 74.5 percent in 1988 to over 81 percent in 1996, increasing our "dependence" on the American market, a problem any other country would love to have.
- Imports have also increased, nearly doubling to $176 billion to represent nearly 76 percent of our total imports in 1996, showing that free trade is indeed a game in which both players win, as Canada is now by far America's biggest and best export market.
- Our merchandise trade balance with the United States, the difference between our exports and imports, has ballooned to more than $41 billion, nearly triple the amount before the FTA, as we now sell to the US around $5 worth of goods for every $4 we buy from them.
- Economists estimate that each $1 billion of our exports represents 10,000 to 15,000 jobs in Canada. Even using the most conservative figures, the increase in our trade surplus with the US alone since the FTA came into effect must have added at least 275,000 and possibly as many as 400,000 net new jobs for Canadians. In 1996, roughly one in four Canadian workers owed their jobs to exports to the US.

These are the straightforward, easily verifiable facts of the matter. Obviously, the doom and gloom predictions so confidently offered by the free trade critics have not come to pass. Far from being swamped, our companies have massively increased their exports, by much more than our imports. How do these discredited soothsayers react? Incredibly, some of the most rabid ideologues have not even bothered to change their scripted notes. During a CBC television show in July 1997, I was astounded to hear my old nemesis David Orchard prattling on about the terrible losses of output and jobs because of free trade. When it was pointed out by other guests that our trade had in fact enjoyed an unprecedented expansion, Orchard mumbled that this was because of the low dollar, conveniently ignoring the fact that at that time the Canadian dollar stood at nearly 73 cents US, or more than 4 cents *above* the low reached in 1986 when we began the negotiations. I must admit that it angers me that this kind of rhetoric continues. Facts do matter, and populists who consistently get their facts wrong are called demagogues.

The other claim made by the critics in 1988 was that the FTA would not put an end to American protectionism, as the dispute settlement procedures would prove useless. In the real world, we make choices among realistic alternatives. We were not able to conclude a perfect free trade agreement which eliminated unfair trade laws and provided for the completely equitable resolution of disputes. The choice was between no agreement at all, and the agreement as it stands. I am convinced that we made the right choice.

That does not mean there will be no more trade disputes between Canada and the US in the future. As total trade in both directions now tops $1 billion per day – nearly $400 billion per year – there are bound to be frictions. Barring a revolutionary change in human behaviour and the American political constitution, there will continue to be pressure to restrict or penalize Canadian goods and services that prove too successful in capturing a share of the giant American market. Some of these demands will be resisted, but many will be accommodated by a lackey Congress and a weak administration. The tools are readily at hand. They include America's unfair trade laws, which I do not foresee the protectionists surrendering any time soon.

These problems will be intensified once the North American economy falls into recession, as it must inevitably do in the next few years following the unbroken if sluggish expansion we have enjoyed. The most damaging impact will be largely invisible. The threat of trade restrictions will dissuade some investors – Canadian and foreign alike – from choosing Canada as the location for that new plant or next expansion to serve the North American market.

The real question is whether we are better able to stand up for our interests in those disputes under the Free Trade Agreement than we were before. I would much rather make the Canadian case before a binational panel under the NAFTA than rely on the objectivity of the American Commerce

Department or the good will of the US Congress. In the overwhelming majority of cases that have come before the free trade panels, the American actions have been struck down or significantly modified. The panels have found that the imports from Canada were not unfairly traded or the American producers were not injured or, at the very least, that any penalties should be greatly reduced.

Even when we win our case, we should not be surprised if the Americans are not prepared to admit defeat. The citizens of the superpower are accustomed to winning, particularly on home ground with their own referees. As we cannot overpower them, we must find other ways to protect our interests. Fate has put us in the ring with the elephant. We do our best to persuade him to agree to play by a set of rules – the FTA or the WTO – but we should not be surprised if he sometimes bends or breaks them in order to win. We have to be quick, smart, realistic, and tough-minded. The classic case was the lumber dispute, where the Americans continued to press after losing on every count in the binational panels. In the end, we did reach an arrangement that restricted Canadian exports, but on terms that were much more favourable than we could possibly have negotiated if we had not won the FTA case.

The basic lesson is not very different from what virtually every young boy learns in dealing with the schoolyard bully. If the ruffian is determined to have his fun at your expense, there is a strategic choice to be made. The easiest path is to give him what he wants. In the very tough schools I attended, this invariably encouraged him to demand more and more. If that is the approach we take under the NAFTA, the dispute resolution machinery will not save us from ourselves.

The alternative is to stand up for our interests, even at the expense of the occasional bloody nose. In the long run, this is the strategy I would strongly commend to Canadian trade ministers. In any given dispute, the Americans, if they are bloody-minded, can do more damage to Canada than we can inflict on them. But over time, whether because of an innate American sense of fair play or because thugs do not like to pick on victims that fight back, this approach is more likely to serve our interests.

Where will the specific disputes between Canada and the United States arise in the next few years? As each new dispute comes along, I am struck by the sense of sameness. The Americans will threaten various trade actions, including the usual run of complaints that Canadian commodities are dumped at fire-sale prices into the American market with the benefit of generous government subsidies. Targets will range from fish to steel. Indeed, I would not be surprised if lumber again becomes a difficult issue down the road.

Agriculture will obviously be highly contentious, from pigs to potatoes. The Americans are not at all pleased that the panels under the Free Trade Agreement have confirmed Canada's right to maintain our prohibitive tariffs on imports of dairy and poultry from the US. They will continue to threaten and bluster. Under the WTO agreement, the tariffs are to be modestly reduced over the first six years and then are open for review. At that point, we can expect that the Americans will renew their attack more aggressively than before.

American wheat farmers will also keep up the pressure against imports from Canada. In recent years, those imports have increased, in part because of supply shortages in the US which are, in turn, linked to high-cost subsidies to promote American wheat exports to other countries, as trade or disguised as aid. To American eyes, if imports are increasing, it must be because those cunning Canadians have found some way to cheat the system. One of the long-standing targets is the Canadian Wheat Board, which holds a monopoly on the export marketing of Canadian grain. The Americans have nothing comparable, as their marketing is done by private companies. They have repeatedly charged that the board is hiding subsidies of some sort. Two free trade panels have already examined these charges and dismissed them as unfounded. That will not stop the Americans from taking another run.

At the other end of the spectrum, the Americans will not give up their attempts to batter down the remaining walls against their "entertainment industries," and I very much fear that we will continue to be our own worst enemies. We must manage future assaults much more skilfully than we have handled them in the past in the areas of magazines, satellite television, film distribution, and book publishing. The tragic consequence of previous mistakes is that the arteries of communication among Canadians are becoming terribly constricted under American pressure.

The export statistics are impressive, but they too must be seen in a broader context. They probably could have been significantly better. Incredibly, the same government that negotiated free trade chose that moment to engage in an extraordinarily aggressive tightening of monetary policy. Interest rates were forced up into the high double digits, discouraging consumption and, above all, business investment. The cost of a Canadian dollar in American currency rose from its historic low of under 70 cents when the negotiations were launched in 1986 to a high of nearly 90 cents in 1991, before eventually falling back below 75 cents by 1995. I believe that this drive to push Canadian inflation rates down below American rates, if not to zero, was bad monetary policy, although others, including former Bank of Canada governor John Crow, will disagree. (When, at his invitation, I put my views to the bank's board in March 1990, Crow caustically observed that he really could not run monetary policy just to make me look good.)

This tight monetary policy crippled the ability of Canadian locations to compete at the crucial moment when firms were deciding where to put the plants to serve the combined Canadian-American market. This meant that we may not have captured the full benefits of the new investment resulting from free trade, and this may have slowed the growth of our manufacturing productivity.

Why does this matter? Simply put, capital investment gives our workers the tools to produce the goods and services that in turn improve our standard of living. If investment is weak, jobs will also suffer, as we have seen over the past few years of painfully slow growth in our employed workforce. If productivity is lagging, then overall living standards must also fall behind. Although one of our most important free trade objectives was to narrow the gap of more than 25 percent in productivity between Canada and the United States, this shortfall has actually widened to more than 30 percent in 1995. Only the most doctrinaire critic would claim that these problems are in any way the result of free trade. But supporters of the agreement must admit that the FTA has not done what we had hoped to remedy these difficulties.

Nor has it resolved the fundamental structural problem of the distribution of benefits and costs in this transition to a more competitive global economy. Unquestionably, the overall gains from free trade have massively outweighed the adjustment costs. But for a policy to be unequivocally successful, it is essential that some of these winnings actually be used to compensate those who stand to lose from the adjustment – a basic theorem of welfare economics. To some extent, this has happened automatically through our system of progressive taxation and our extensive safety net of benefits for the old, the sick, and the unemployed. Regrettably, the need for this adjustment assistance has come at precisely the time when past fiscal excesses have required governments at all levels to retrench their expenditures, including those underpinning the social safety net. Witness the successive changes in the unemployment insurance compensation program.

Particularly troublesome is the apparent widening of the gap beween the fortunes of the young versus the old, the highly skilled versus the uneducated.

This shows up most dramatically in the employment numbers. The past few years have seen the creation of hundreds of thousands of jobs in Canada, as employment has increased faster than in any industrial country other than the United States. But the job opportunities have been restricted to those with at least some postsecondary education, as jobs for those with no more than a high school diploma have been declining. Furthermore, the disparity in wages between youngsters newly entering the labour force and those older, more established workers has widened sharply. This reality is brought painfully home to the parents of university students and recent graduates who face very difficult employment prospects here in Canada.

It would be a grave mistake for the promoters of free trade to refuse to recognize these very difficult policy challenges. These problems will not disappear quickly. Indeed, they may be worsened through globalization. Failure to address them will provoke a backlash against exactly the openness to change that will be required in the third millennium.

Where do we go from here with the free trade agenda? Obviously, we are now linked with Mexico through the North American Free Trade Agreement. Although the NAFTA is not such an unequivocal success as the Canada-US arrangement, it is hard to imagine that it would be dismantled. It is possible that mounting protectionist pressures in the United States, fearful of the products of "cheap labour" from Mexico, could eat away at some of the elements of the agreement. On balance, however, I suspect the impact will be to slow the much-ballyhooed move to free trade down the hemisphere to Tierra del Fuego.

Chile may well join the club. Canada already has a side arrangement with that country, and it would not take much adjustment to bring Chile into full conformity with the NAFTA. Not that it matters much to us. We have already achieved most if not all of the limited benefits from closer trade and investment links with Chile.

As for the rest, I am doubtful that there will be free trade in the Americas any time soon. It is one thing to incorporate tiny Chile, with its market-based economy. It is quite another to free trade with the South American superpower, Brazil, with its very different economic structures. For the foreseeable future, I expect the political rhetoric to outrun the negotiating realities. American presidents will promise but fail to deliver. As for the Canadian government, the Liberals can be counted on to pay lip service to increasing the number of players in the NAFTA in a vain attempt to offset the inescapable preponderance of the Americans.

This will also fit with Canadian interests in promoting closer relations among the members of the Asia-Pacific Economic Cooperation group. This is the fastest-growing area of the world economy. It is extremely competitive but potentially very lucrative for those who succeed. Team Canada is well positioned to promote our export and investment interests in the area, which includes the enormous markets of mainland China.

The focus of trade negotiations will shift instead, I believe, to the multilateral arena. The World Trade Organization has moved well beyond issues of trade in goods as significant agreements have already been made on basic telecommunications, information technologies, and financial services.

A serious challenge in the future can be expected from those deeply concerned to protect the environment and preserve biodiversity, who see free traders and the international bureaucracy as mortal enemies. Only a knave or a fool would refuse to accept the overwhelming evidence that we are overstressing the natural world in order to feed not only our basic needs but our most frivolous wants. Sustainable development is more than a theoretical objective, it is a practical necessity. I am very troubled by the signs that environmental issues are being neglected, most dramatically in the failure to live up to commitments to deal with global warming.

The damnable thing is that it is so easy for the noblest motives to be subverted in the meanest actions. The environmental movement itself is not beyond reproach. Its leadership and some of its members make a living out of their unrelenting opposition to government and commercial initiatives. They have no incentive to make the compromises or strike the balances required in matters of public policy in a democratic society. When environmentalists talk of "zero tolerance," they make me very nervous.

Canada has also frequently been a victim of this "new protectionism" masquerading as ecological purity. To take one small example, in February 1997, I participated in a televised debate for the Australian Broadcasting Corporation on the subject of that country's prohibition of imports of fresh salmon from Canada. The Australian quarantine authorities had initially concluded that these imports posed no significant threat to the health of the local salmon industry. Following a public outcry from the salmon farmers in Tasmania, the authorities reconsidered their scientific judgment and this time determined that the embargo should be maintained to protect the purity of the local ecosystem. Canada and the United States proposed to take the issue to the WTO.

The Australian government view was presented by the minister for primary industries, who was keenly aware of the need for an exporting nation like Australia to play by the international rules. He stoutly defended the claim that the decision had been made on strictly scientific grounds, although he had some difficulty explaining the about-face. He came under heavy fire from the other participant, an environmentalist who condemned the Australian government for pandering to the "free trade juggernaut that is flooding the world." He claimed that the international bureaucrats in the WTO would go out of their way to strike down the Australian rules in the interests of opening up markets at any cost. I could not help observing how much it felt like home, with the same arguments being used by much the same cast of characters. But if the embargo was soundly based, the Australians had nothing to fear from a WTO examination since, in my experience, the much-maligned trade authorities were deferential to domestic regulators except in the worst cases of abuse.

There is grounds for honest criticism and sharp debate over the environmental practices of resource-based industries in Canada and other countries. For the moment, the best compromise appears to be that embodied in the so-called environmental side deal under the NAFTA. Rather than focus on specific protectionist responses to alleged environmental abuses, the side agreement applies to the total system. It is designed to restrain any tendencies for jurisdictions to lower their environmental requirements to compete for investment. An agency has been established to monitor the situation and report on systemic failures. It remains to be seen how all this will work in practice. If it succeeds, it is a small price for free traders to pay to point the environmental movement in more constructive directions, but it is unlikely that the extremists will ever be satisfied. Perhaps the most ludicrous illustration of the problem came when a collection of Canadian environmental and anti-free-trade organizations came together to bring a legal challenge under the NAFTA against the former Liberal government's failure to pass draconian legislation to protect endangered species before the last election. Ironically, in the cabinet shuffle of June 1997, the former minister of the environment, Sergio Marchi, was given a new assignment as minister of international trade.

The same issues arise in even more inflammatory form in the debate over the use of trade as a weapon in the struggle for human rights around the globe. In our anguish over savage abuses of human rights, we naturally reach in desperation for any tools to help the cause. We are reluctant to use military means, if only because they would require us to put our own lives at risk and very probably do most damage to those we are trying to help. In the Gulf

War, the Baghdad elites suffered much less than the simple citizenry of Iraq, not to mention the Kurds.

It sounds awfully high-minded to call instead for the use of trade sanctions or embargoes against the offending authorities. This argument has been used to keep China from full membership in the World Trade Organization, or to curb imports of the products of child labour from the Third World. Supporters of trade liberalization and its international institutions are immediately suspect. Anyone who has the temerity to challenge the logic of these crusades is liable to be pilloried for being soft on the bad guys.

Despite this, I seriously question whether trade embargoes are always and everywhere the best instrument for Canadians to use in advancing human rights internationally. In May 1994, I was asked to address this issue at the annual meeting of the Canadian Jewish Congress. The CJC is widely recognized as one of the most progressive forces in Canadian society. There is probably no group in Canada more committed to civil liberties, nor any other group that has done more to back that commitment with its active support. I welcomed the opportunity to meet with some of the CJC leadership to discuss these difficult questions in an intelligent and informal atmosphere. Instead, I found myself on centre stage in the cavernous Railway Committee Room on Parliament Hill. In honour of the seventy-fifth anniversary of the congress, they had pulled out all the stops. The room was filled with people, including a sparkling representation of the political, business, and religious leadership of the country, selected for their passionate commitment to the issue. The klieg lights were on and the television cameras were running.

My argument was simple. Our objectives were the same: to promote respect for human rights around the globe. The question was over the best means to achieve this. Using trade as a weapon was very tempting. But it was founded on false reasoning.

Why do we trade with other countries? Not to do them any favour. Trade is not aid, as the developing world has come to understand, to its dismay. The basis of trade is *mutual* advantage: both parties are better off following the exchange.

What if we refuse to import from another country because we do not approve of its politics? Our consumers will lose the benefits from the wider range of choices and the better values of the imported products. So be it. The other country will be obliged to find another customer. Usually, that should be no problem, unless the rest of the world has agreed to refuse all imports from that country. In that case, there will be a price for the offending country to pay: the workers will lose their jobs producing those items, the investors will lose some profits, and the state authorities will have to find other sources of revenue, through legitimate taxation or through corruption. The price, in other words, will be paid most heavily and directly by the weakest in that country.

If we refuse to export to another country, we are forgoing the benefits we might obtain from increased output, profits, and jobs. Unless we hold a monopoly on the items of trade – and I invited them to find an example where Canada holds such a monopoly – the other country could always strike a deal to import the products from elsewhere. Unless, of course, the entire rest of the world refuses to trade with the pariah country and it unable to achieve self-sufficiency on its own. In that case, the authorities will have to impose a rationing system. Guess whose rations will be cut the most? Not the privileged elite but the ordinary people.

In the nature of things, the supporters of such trade embargoes for the most righteous motives would find themselves in bed with other, less disinterested parties who stood to gain directly from such action. Thus import embargoes would be strongly supported by those who feared the competition from abroad. It is harder to get support for truly enforceable export embargoes precisely because there is money to be made by transshipment through other countries.

To have any hope of success, trade sanctions must be universally supported and enforced. We could all point to South Africa as an example where, with Canadian leadership, sanctions were imposed by most countries and very probably contributed to the transition to democracy. Of course, this was an exceptional case and took decades to achieve results. There were many more cases of failure – failure to get agreement to sanctions, failure to enforce them, and failure ultimately to achieve any positive results.

As soon as the floor was opened for questions, it was apparent that most of the audience did not share my conclusions. To drive home my point, I invited them to contemplate the economic embargo the US had applied against Cuba for more than thirty years. What had it achieved? It had made several American sugar refiners and tobacco manufacturers very rich by eliminating their Cuban competition. Their gratitude had been reflected in their support for politicians such as Jesse Helms. It had been a continuing irritant in relations with the other countries of the Americas, led by Canada, which continued to maintain links with Cuba. Most important, the last time I checked, it had not brought Fidel Castro to his knees. Indeed, I suggested, if he was on his knees it was to offer up this morning prayer: "Thank you, Lord, for the American embargo without which I would no longer be in power."

The futility of these measures was underlined two years later during the American presidential election year of 1996. A well-financed, Miami-based group of anti-Castro "freedom fighters" succeeded in provoking an international incident with their overflights of Cuban airspace, up to and including flights over Havana to drop propaganda leaflets. Playing their part in the script, the Cuban air force shot down two of these unarmed planes shortly before the Democratic primary in Florida. Well-orchestrated outrage over this incident gave the anti-Castro forces the opportunity they had been seeking.

Their instrument was Jesse Helms, an ancient senator from North Carolina, deep in the pockets of the sugar and tobacco lobbies and entrenched in the chair of the powerful Foreign Relations Committee of the US Senate. He had for months been promoting, unsuccessfully, a piece of legislation, bizarre even by American standards, which would make outlaws of any foreign investors using property that had been confiscated by the Cuban state. Since the revolution, nearly forty years before, had supplanted the unbelievably corrupt Batista regime which, with its cronies, owned virtually everything of value in the country, this bill covered a lot of ground. It would apply to Americans and to foreigners alike. The latter would be subject to property suits, in American courts, and the executives of these foreign corporations and their families could be barred from the United States. This proposed legislation, breathtaking in the way it rode roughshod over the principles of international law, had been regarded until then as another of those silly things "Ol' Jesse" had to do to keep his patrons happy and generous.

The public outcry over the shooting down of two civilian aircraft combined with the upcoming Florida primary to transform the bill into the centrepiece of the American human rights agenda. President Bill Clinton quickly jumped on the bandwagon, committed his administration to support the bill, won the subsequent primary, and added Florida to his landslide in the November presidential election. The bill, known as Helms-Burton after its Senate and House sponsors, became the law of the land – and reached out to other lands, including Canada. Indeed, one of the main victims was a Canadian company, Sherritt International, and its executives, led by its chief, Ian Delaney, who was prohibited from entering the United States.

When this issue exploded, I was drafted by various broadcasting and print media to explain the problem to Canadians. On one open-line television program, I was barraged with viewers demanding that Canada respond in kind.

In a one-hour broadcast, most believed and sympathized with the Cuban view that the doomed planes were bandits and outlaws infringing on sovereign airspace. Not one caller accepted the American claim that they were acting for high moral reasons. None believed that the administration, let alone the Congress, was motivated by concern for the civil rights of ordinary Cubans. They were outraged over the arrogance of an American government that wrapped its dastardly deeds in the cloak of moral authority.

To reporters from the American network ABC, I suggested that the offending legislation was equivalent to Canada encouraging the descendants of the United Empire Loyalists to lay claim to the properties brutally confiscated, without compensation, in the American Revolution. This would include large chunks of Manhattan real estate. They were so taken with the idea that they used the New York skyline as the backdrop for the clip on that evening's news. A little later, two enterprising members of Parliament went one better and introduced a private member's bill to that effect. Another Canadian claimed, through his ancestors, to own a parcel of downtown Washington now occupied in part by the Capitol.

I very much fear that we are in for more of this aggressive use of trade and investment sanctions to achieve political purposes. The Americans have extended similar regimes to other countries, notably Iraq and Libya. The list could well be lengthened. Canadian enthusiasts for sanctions will have to face facts. Without the support of the Americans, such trade embargoes are doomed to failure. On the other hand, the Americans will demand support for embargoes that most Canadians regard as unnecessary and unwise.

The real question is this: Do we want to feel good, through proclaiming sanctions? Or do we want to do good, by opening up these countries to the outside world? My advice would be to sever the issues entirely and keep trade and investment on a commercial basis. If, in the process, this helps to open up the country and thereby strengthens the hand of the reformers, all the better.

The most important issue we will face over the next few years is nothing less than the survival of Canada. As has been true for much of our history, the threat comes from both directions: from within, as we wrestle with the future status of Quebec; and from without, as we struggle to maintain an identity distinct from the Americans. On both counts, we are in serious trouble, and some would argue that free trade has made our problems worse.

An earlier chapter has addressed the implications of free trade for the future of Quebec. How is this issue likely to play out? My personal views would not make me popular in either camp. There is no constitutional provision to permit the separation of Quebec from Canada. Nor can the concept of self-determination for colonial peoples be extrapolated to the situation of Quebeckers, who enjoy extraordinary provincial autonomy and full national representation. But to the dismay of some federalist friends, I would unhesitatingly accept the outcome of a clear expression of opinion by Quebeckers on their future, even if it went against the continuation of the union – provided, that is, the verdict was definitive. That means a substantial majority overall and in all regions of the province voting to separate from Canada in a fair and democratic plebiscite. (None of those conditions was met in the 1995 referendum, and I find it difficult to believe that an honest plebiscite would produce the required majorities.)

There would, of course, be serious consequences for the rest of Canada. I do not believe the rest of the country would shatter into fragments, but there would be heavy costs. These would be very significant for the residents of Ontario and of the Atlantic provinces. There would be much less impact on western Canada, which may explain why there is such reluctance in the west to put the Constitution through contortions to satisfy the latest round of Quebec demands. But on balance, the rest of the country would, I believe, find enough common ground to make the effort to keep Canada together.

At that point, the most important economic challenge would be to determine the arrangements to govern the *partenariat* with a separate Quebec. I would be among those fighting to keep the relationship as close as possible. It would not be possible to reinstate the Canadian economic union nor to make our monetary and commercial policies subject to Quebec's veto. We could, however, reasonably attempt to negotiate a free trade agreement and together tie that in with the NAFTA. The result would be painful and costly for many on both sides of the Canada-Quebec border who would face customs and immigration officers at the crossing points. But if it were quickly negotiated, it would reduce the risk of catastrophic financial and economic collapse.

As a diminished country, Canada would also become more vulnerable to the other threat, assimilation by the American superpower. Canadians face the prospect of suffering the problems of a dysfunctional American society, without benefit of the vote. Even if Canada holds together, the risks are very substantial.

Have these risks increased with free trade? Perhaps. Certainly to the extent that our society has become increasingly dependent on the two-way economic relationship, it must be more vulnerable to American influence.

This concern was put to me with great force by a number of thoughtful Canadians whose views I very much respect. My friend and former associate Mitchell Sharp made his opposition to free trade known, even though it cost him his cherished job as commissioner for the northern pipeline. My father was usually too discreet to speak out on the issue but clearly believed I was playing a very risky game of getting too close to the Americans, whom he knew perhaps better than any other Canadian diplomat.

The argument is very difficult to deal with, because it involves a highly subjective determination not only of where we are with free trade but where we would have been in its absence. There is no question that Canadian society has grown closer to the American model over the past ten years. Our increasing wealth has not been evenly shared and the disparities of income have become more pronounced, particularly between those with jobs and those without, between the old and the young. Our cities have become more violent and the cancer of the drug trade more pervasive. Our politics has generally moved farther to the right at the national and provincial levels. Governments at all levels have reduced their spending, even on such vital areas as health and education.

I deplore these trends, but it is much too facile to attribute them to increased American influence because of the Free Trade Agreement. Many of these problems arise from mistakes entirely of our own making. The Americans, after all, did not force us to overspend massively in the 1970s and 1980s to the point where we are now obliged to slash government expenditures to get back on a sustainable fiscal track. After a twenty-year binge, we can expect a few more years of hangover. Other problems are much more fundamental than any commercial agreement. In particular, the total domination of our film, video, and television media by the American industry puts our very national survival in jeopardy. The solution is not to be found in the Free Trade Agreement, which after all exempted the cultural industries, but in aggressive policies to promote the Canadian substance of these media.

That is not to say, with Brian Mulroney in his televised debate in 1988, that the FTA is only a trade agreement. It clearly is much more, reaching into the very core of government regulation of our society. Mishandled, it can do great damage to our interests. I am particularly concerned when I hear government officials talk of harmonizing with American rules and regulations as if this were a desirable objective. To the contrary, we ensured in the negotiation of the Free Trade Agreement that we did not accept any obligation to make Canada regulations identical to American rules. In many instances, *vive la différence*. It is essential that we not become mesmerized by the rhetoric of the ideological free traders.

If these arrangements are properly managed, I believe we can extract considerable benefit from them. To the extent that it makes us less vulnerable to the nastier caprices of American protectionism or the weaknesses of an uncompetitive protected industrial sector in Canada, the FTA can be used to enhance rather than diminish true Canadian sovereignty. It can be used to increase our economic prosperity and thus our capacity to share that wealth among the less fortunate in our society. Free trade can be used as a powerful instrument to advance Canada's political, social, and economic interests in a challenging and competitive world.

EPILOGUE

At the height of the free trade debate, one of my TNO colleagues passed me a tape of Peter Gzowski's *Morningside* CBC Radio program, with advice that I should listen to it. Gzowski read a letter he had received from a listener commenting on the previous week's program on obscure American political figures, notably Millard Fillmore, who served briefly as president of the United States. The letter-writer quoted an observation that Fillmore stood as "the dim and forgotten president." He went on to point out that Fillmore had played an important role in the original reciprocity agreement between Canada and the United States. He solemnly warned: "Those who hope their place in history will be assured by their role in the Free Trade Agreement should remember the fate of Millard Fillmore." Gzowski then took great pleasure in pointing out that the letter's author, A. Edgar Ritchie, was the father of the FTA negotiator. It was a sobering comment during this heady period.

What has been the fate of the key players in the free trade negotiations? On the American side, the inspiration for the free trade initiative came first from President Ronald Reagan, whose place in history, fortunately for him, does not depend on his role in the subsequent agreement. There is a pointed saying in French: "Il a le défaut de ses qualités." Reagan's extraordinary strength was his ability to lead the American public to accept radical concepts, of which free trade was only one relatively minor example. His weakness was his total detachment from the actual implementation of these concepts. Free trade with Canada was no exception. This lofty detachment would come to

274

haunt him in the Iran-Contra affair, in which he pleaded total ignorance of the mischief that was going on around him. Following his retirement, it was his cruel fate to be afflicted with Alzheimer's disease.

The man who made things happen, including the Free Trade Agreement, was James Baker. As Reagan's surrogate and chief operating officer, he made an absolutely pivotal contribution to the success of the negotiations. He subsequently served as US secretary of state in the administration of George Bush, whose 1988 presidential campaign he masterminded. Even his skills were unable to do the trick in the following election, however, when Bush went down to defeat by Bill Clinton. Baker then retired from public life but wrote his memoirs of the politics of international diplomacy. The Free Trade Agreement barely figured in this account.

Two American officials played important but largely unheralded roles in the negotiations. Peter McPherson was Baker's deputy secretary at the Treasury Department. In the crunch in Washington and then in the final agreement on the text of the FTA, he served as Baker's lieutenant. He quickly mastered the complex brief and provided highly capable leadership to the floundering American team. McPherson subsequently served as the head of the US Agency for International Development.

His chief resource in the negotiation of the agreement text was Ambassador Alan Holmer, who then oversaw the preparation of the American implementing legislation. To all intents and purposes, Holmer was the senior US negotiator for the closing of the FTA file, nominally reporting to Clayton Yeutter, the US special trade representative. He brought some coherence to the preparatory work and translated it into the language of international agreements and international law. Subsequently Holmer returned to the practice of law in the Washington trade bar, where he has enjoyed considerable success.

The Canadian media spotlight shone brightest on Ambassador Peter Murphy as the designated American chief negotiator for the FTA. As reported earlier, Murphy was largely shunted aside when the big hitters, led by Baker, moved in to close the deal in Washington. He also played very much the second fiddle to Holmer in working out the text of the agreement and was largely invisible in the legislative implementation process. Once that was completed, Peter signed on as a consultant with a Washington lobbying firm. It was not a happy experience for one whose strengths were not in salesmanship or communications, and the relationship ended in his abrupt departure. Our paths crossed occasionally, usually at meetings in Washington, when we would share some reminiscences of the free trade wars. His health problems worsened and he endured a prolonged bout with cancer; the chemotherapy cost him his trademark carrot-top of bright red hair. Peter Murphy died tragically young, at age forty-six in October 1994.

Murphy's associates at the USSTR were more successful in private practice. Following the FTA, deputy chief negotiator Bill Merkin became a trade consultant with a largely Canadian clientele. After playing a key role in the NAFTA negotiations, Chip Roh went to the trade bar with a large Washington firm. Both kept a much higher profile in Canada than back home. The designated bad cop from the Commerce Department, Jean Anderson, also joined the trade bar as a partner in one of the most prestigious firms in the United States, from which she did excellent work with a number of Canadian firms, including some of my clients and the Canadian embassy.

When the negotiations began, I fully expected that close friendships would be forged among the main participants. That had always been Simon's and my experience in dealing with Americans in the past. Even when the official line was confrontation, warm professional and personal relationships would be established. In this instance, although we were together for days at a time for better than two years, little of this camaraderie developed between the negotiating teams. The bitter chemistry between the chief negotiators poisoned the overall atmosphere, although there were some exceptions at a more junior level, where subject experts or lawyers made links across the national boundary. Over the past decade I have encountered most of the Americans involved in the negotiations and our discussions were always most cordial. But there was never any urge to organize a grand reunion to celebrate the historic enterprise.

Of the wondrous cast of characters on the Canadian side, I would single out five individuals as having been absolutely indispensable to the successful completion of the Free Trade Agreement. First among these is, of course, the Right Honourable Brian Mulroney, former prime minister of Canada. It was his decision, for whatever reasons, to launch the free trade negotiations, and it was his political leadership that brought the negotiations to a successful conclusion and ensured the FTA's implementation following his electoral triumph in 1988. After his retirement from politics five years later, Mulroney was cast as the convenient scapegoat for the country's problems. At the same time, however, he earned an enviable reputation as a director of some of the leading Canadian and American companies, including Archer-Daniels-Midland

and Barrick Gold Corporation. He may have won a measure of public sympathy when the government of Canada was forced to reach an out-of-court settlement in the highly publicized libel suit over allegations about Mulroney's personal role in the Airbus affair. I have not encountered him since he left office.

After the extraordinary public profile enjoyed by Canada's chief trade negotiator, Ambassador Simon Reisman, during the FTA saga, his later activities could not help but seem anticlimactic. Simon returned to the private sector, where he set up a business consulting firm and served as director of a number of leading Canadian companies. As chairman of Ranger Oil, he steered that company through a very difficult period following the untimely death of its chief executive officer. As he reached his late seventies, he remained very active in public affairs and private business while enjoying more time with his wife and family. Simon and I work in the same building and regularly have lunch together with a few old friends.

Derek Burney's contribution did not end with the conclusion of the Free Trade Agreement. After serving as Prime Minister Mulroney's chief of staff through the 1988 election, Burney went to Washington as Canadian ambassador. The rapport he had established with American Secretary of State Baker stood him and Canada in very good stead, as did his relationship with President George Bush. Burney retired from the public service in 1993 to become a top executive with the Canadian telecommunications giant Bell Canada Enterprises. As chairman, president, and CEO of Bell Canada International, Burney was directly involved in the stream of global deal-making in that fast-moving industry.

Canada's ambassador to Washington during the FTA negotiations was Allan Gotlieb. He had been appointed to that post by the Trudeau government in 1981. At times his dedication to making a deal with the Americans led to heated clashes between the fixer, Gotlieb, and the negotiators, Simon and me. In retrospect, the tension served a purpose, as his insistence on accommodating the Americans pushed us to find a better solution. Even his miscommunication with Sam Gibbons opened an opportunity we were able to capture to Canada's advantage. After the FTA was ratified, Gotlieb retired from the foreign service and set about making his mark in the private sector. He became chairman of the Canadian branch of the giant American public relations firm Burson-Marsteller and served as director of a number of prestigious Canadian and American corporations. He also became chairman of the Canada Council and publisher of *Saturday Night*.

Finally, of the truly remarkable staff at the Trade Negotiations Office, one stands out. TNO general counsel Konrad von Finckenstein was a tower of strength throughout the FTA saga, connecting the concepts of trade policy to the levers of legal authority. He continued to bring rigorous competence and integrity to his subsequent assignments. Although the titles changed, his role was that of the top legal adviser to the government in trade and industrial matters. When it came time to make some sense of the NAFTA deal, Konrad was again called in to take charge. He also advised the panel on direct-to-home satellite television broadcasting. In 1997, he was promoted to the rank of deputy minister as the director of the Competition Bureau of Canada. Marg and I frequently get together, over dinner or a game of golf, with Konrad and his wife, Ursula Menke, who also spent a year as my partner at Strategico.

For me, as for most of those involved, the Canada-US Free Trade Agreement was an important event. But it was only one milestone in an ongoing career. It was only one bout in the wrestling match with the American elephant that continues to this day.

INDEX

INDEX